TAUGHT
by
GOD

TAUGHT by GOD

Teaching and Spiritual Formation

Karen Marie Yust
E. Byron Anderson

CHALICE
PRESS

ST. LOUIS, MISSOURI

Cover art: Getty Images
Cover and interior design: Elizabeth Wright

Visit Chalice Press on the World Wide Web at
www.chalicepress.com

10 9 8 7 6 5 4 3 2 1   06 07 08 09 10

Library of Congress Cataloging–in–Publication Data

Yust, Karen Marie.
  Taught by God : teaching and spiritual formation / Karen Marie Yust and E. Byron Anderson.
    p. cm.
  Includes bibliographical references and index.
  ISBN-13: 978-0-8272-3649-3 (pbk. : alk. paper)
  ISBN-10: 0-8272-3649-2 (pbk. : alk. paper)
  1. Christian education. 2. Christian teachers. 3. Teaching—Religious aspects—Christianity. 4. Education—Philosophy. 5. Spiritual formation. I. Anderson, E. Byron. II. Title.
  BV1471.3.Y87 2006
  268—dc22
                                                          2006006284

Printed in the United States of America

Contents

Something Old, Something New

A Contemporary Dilemma

One of the prevailing assumptions of the twenty-first century is that something new is inherently better than something old. Products of all kinds—soup, cleaning supplies, exercise equipment, baby care items—sport labels proclaiming that they are "new" concepts or at least "improved" versions of their former selves. We are encouraged to let go of the past, with its worn out materials and already finished perspectives, and turn our attention to what is current, newly available, and poised to carry us into the future unencumbered by the debris of the past.

Such a perspective creates a dilemma for Christian teachers. We are, like our cultural peers, privy to the same marketing messages and the longings for new and improved lives they promote. We want to move into the future as much as the next person. Yet we have a long-standing practice of looking to the past for guidance in the present day. We identify the crucifixion and resurrection of Jesus as the pivotal event of our faith tradition. We call a collection of ancient writings "sacred" and have studied them for centuries as texts that reveal God's will for our lives. We are a people with a past reaching all the way back to the creation of the earth, a people shaped by a history of divine covenants, a people enjoined to partake of bread and cup in remembrance of the one we call Christ.

We live, then, in the intersection of a cultural and religious tension. We are people of the present day, eager to embrace the many discoveries and possibilities that a new century holds. We are also part of a religious community of saints that stretches backward through thousands of years and across many cultures and continents. Negotiating these two realities is a daily challenge of discipleship and faithfulness. We teach the faith in the midst of this challenge to persons who are caught in the same tension. Somehow, we must find ways to communicate "the old, old story" to hearts, minds, and ears trained to hear only what is new.

We might rely on nostalgia for certain eras, much as marketers are exploiting the baby boomer fascination with the 1950s, '60s, and '70s to push "retro" furniture styles and radio stations; but this approach has its pitfalls. Its energy comes from its comfortable familiarity and its promotion of an escapist mentality, in which today's problems can be glossed over while we imagine ourselves once again young and idealistic. Or we might try the approach Hollywood is using with old black-and-white films, dressing up the gospel in more colorful digital forms (for example, Veggie Tales and *The Passion of the Christ*), so that it attains mass appeal based on special effects. Here we need to count the cost of engaging persons' senses and emotions without activating their critical thinking skills as well. Our work as teachers must extend beyond nostalgia and presenting a flashy product our students might buy into and sell to others.

This book suggests a way to negotiate the old-new tension in which Christian teachers find themselves in the twenty-first century. It deliberately draws on the teachers and teaching models that animate Christian history in conversation with the issues and concerns of contemporary teachers and learners who seek to follow Christ. Together we explore how various strands of Christian mystical tradition might provide guidance for teachers in the cultivation of our own spiritual lives and the lives of our students. We dig in the fertile historical soil of the church's past to examine rich spiritual metaphors and practices that might root Christian lives and sustain teaching ministries in our time. We survey the fields of American spirituality and note the ways in which this new growth is and is not grafted onto our Christian past. Each chapter illuminates spiritual teachers of the Christian tradition who provide frameworks and strategic practices for contemporary teachers who seek to create education settings in which others might flourish spiritually.

Clark Williamson wrote, "Not knowing our tradition leaves us confused; not passing it on creatively and critically transformed identifies us with the past and leaves us closed off from the present."[1] This book is about discovering the wealth of ideas and experiences Christian teachers can draw on as we creatively and critically shape faithful and effective teaching ministries for the present and the future. It's a task that requires substantially more than simply replicating what was done in the past or devising a new curriculum and method. The contemporary ministry of teaching demands careful and prayerful study of the past alongside critical and contemplative cultural participation, so that something old is also something new in every adult Bible study, children's church school class, youth group meeting, intergenerational worship service, women's circle, men's breakfast, or other educational events.

The Shape of the Text

The book is ordered around four aspects of Christian educational ministries: the identity of the teacher, contexts in which we teach, models for teaching, and evaluation of teaching. The foci of these sections overlap, for roles are defined in relation to contexts, models shape role expectations, and evaluation of models and roles occurs most effectively in context. The reader might wish to imagine the artificial construction of Parts I, II, III, and IV as an invitation to look at the world of teaching through multiple sides of a prism. The view is refracted differently with each effort, drawing the eye toward a variety of subtle nuances and inviting varied interpretations of the subject we see. Some of those differences are significant insights, making our use of the prism seem inspired as a tool for greater understanding. Other differences are misleading, a trick of light that distorts our perception. These interpretations must be checked by the discoveries made through the other lenses we use, so that the final picture is coherent and meaningful.

Part I: Identity of the Teacher seeks to help Christian educators define the character of teachers and learners by reflecting on the communal nature of educational ministries and the traditional elements of a life lived prayerfully. Chapter 1 draws on Martin Luther's concept of the Christian as *theodidacta* (person taught by God) and the stories and writings of the desert fathers and mothers to locate the authority of the Christian teacher in a life attentive to God. Chapter 2 surveys traditional elements of a life of prayer. It suggests that Søren Kierkegaard's *Purity of Heart Is to Will One Thing* and the model of discernment proposed by Francis de Sales in his *Introduction to the Devout Life* can provide a framework for understanding teaching as an outward manifestation of the inner life of prayer. Chapter 3 emphasizes the communal nature of teaching and learning in Christian tradition. It calls those of us who teach to a life of holy listening and encourages us to create a learning context in which we invite students into shared reflection on the ways in which God is making Godself known. It draws on the visions of Julian of Norwich to explore the importance of cultivating "religious imagination" in both teachers and students.

Part II: Contexts of Teaching provides a critical description of cultural understandings of spirituality that constitute the context against which teachers and learners seek to fashion an explicitly Christian way of life together. The chapters in this section also explore the variety of contexts in which teaching for spiritual formation can take place in addition to conventional church school class settings. Chapter 4 draws on the sociological work of Robert Wuthnow and Kurt Hadaway to name the North American context in which we teach and the implications of this context for persons' engagement in and resistance to learning about Christian spiritual practices. In conversation with several contemporary Christian theologians, this chapter explores the extent to which popular views of spirituality are and are not rooted in Christian tradition. Chapter 5 contends that teaching contexts and forms can extend far beyond conventional church school classes and midweek Bible studies. It explores modes of teaching deeply embedded in Christian tradition and pertinent strategies for teaching contemporary learners. These modes include John Cassian's "conferences" with two or three seekers, the development of spiritual correspondence between Jane de Chantal and Francis de Sales, and the writing of an account of Saint Antony's life by Athanasius.

Part III: Models for Teaching introduces teachers to a variety of resources from Christian tradition that can serve as models for educational ministries committed to spiritual formation. Chapter 6 surveys various traditional metaphors for a life of faith and suggests several foundational questions teachers and students must ask about these metaphors in order to creatively and faithfully transform them for contemporary understanding. It explores in depth John Bunyan's metaphor of "journey" in *The Pilgrim's Progress*, Thomas à Kempis's focus on the "imitation of Christ," John Climacus's emphasis on "ascent," and the warrior metaphor of *The Martyrdom of Saints Perpetua and Felicitas* in order to name the positive and problematic aspects of these metaphors as rhetorics for contemporary Christian teaching. Chapter 7 analyzes the teaching function of a spiritual rule in individual faith formation and within communities of learning. The Rule of Saint Benedict is a model for study, with commentary on its historical role and contemporary potential. Exploration of The Rule of the Society of Saint John the Evangelist provides an example of one religious (Episcopal) community's recent creation of a rule attentive to the concerns of the twenty-first century as well as the historic commitments of Christian tradition. Chapter 8 adopts Catherine of Siena's depiction of the Christian life as a bridge by which one lives one's way back to God as a framework for exploring how teachers and students negotiate the tensions between personal, communal, and institutional goals and commitments in discipleship and theological education. Chapter 9 examines various historic and contemporary definitions of knowledge and, using Diadochos of Photiki as a guide, explores the relationship between transformational learning theory and the cultivation of Christian spiritual knowledge. This chapter seeks to demonstrate a dialogical relationship between spiritual knowledge and the mystery of God.

Part IV: Evaluation of Teaching suggests ways in which we as teachers can assess whether our work is faithful in creating a context where persons are formed in faith and the realm of God is celebrated.

Chapter 10 argues that good teaching requires ongoing critical evaluation of the education process. It proposes the use of Ignatius of Loyola's method of the examination of conscience as a means of reflecting on our teaching and the self as teacher. It encourages teachers to attend to a process of constructively naming and confessing sin, seeking God's forgiveness, and participating in the redemptive work of God through actively inviting God's transformation of our teaching. Chapter 11 uses the writings of Henri Nouwen and Simone Weil to explore three temptations that distract us from our calling and the spiritual practices that might animate our evaluative methods and help us resist these common traps.

Encouragement for the Journey

Developing a faithful teaching ministry can be difficult, wearisome, and even discouraging work when market-driven ideals of contemporary North American culture and a perception of the irrelevance of traditional Christian practices leave us longing for easier answers. Simply reading a book will not turn us into teachers who can charm reluctant students with a spoonful of sugar-coated theology and a romp on a mission trip through the ethical dilemmas of the human park. Within these pages, however, are spiritual companions who each have faced some version of the popular culture versus Christian tradition dilemma and discovered ways of responding faithfully in the midst of the tension. Their presence means we are not alone in the struggle. It also means that this problem is not new. In one form or another, Christian teachers have had to confront the question of how the past is related to the present since the church first began to form itself in the wake of Jesus' death and resurrection. Our legacy extends even further back in history, for we are heirs of the Jewish engagement with the same problem. We work alongside persons of other religious traditions who seek a faithful response to the same question in their own settings. By embracing the opportunity to be part of a much larger conversation than the one occurring in our own head or congregation, we gain the support and advice of a much wider spectrum of teachers and learners.

Because of the overlapping issues and concerns inherent in the four aspects of this discussion, the sections and chapters of the book are best read in order. Pausing to read directly from the original spiritual texts quoted and referenced in each chapter will deepen the sense of conversational connection and likely generate insights beyond those discovered by the authors in their own exploration of these texts. Our discussion of classical spiritual texts is necessarily abbreviated more than those who are well acquainted with or find themselves drawn to these inspiring teachers will be satisfied with. This problem is easily rectified through further reading.

PART I

Identity of the Teacher

CHAPTER 1

The Spiritual Leader as Christian Teacher

Who is a spiritual teacher and by what authority does she teach? Two quotations from vastly different sources can help frame this question for us. The first is a saying of Amma Syncletica, one of the desert mothers of early Christian monasticism:

> It is dangerous for anyone to teach who has not first been trained in the "practical" life. For if someone who owns a ruined house receives guests there, he does them harm because of the dilapidation of his dwelling. It is the same in the case of someone who has not first built an interior dwelling; he causes loss to those who come. By words one may convert them to salvation, but by evil behavior, one injures them.[1]

This saying suggests that it is not only foolish but also dangerous to think we can begin to teach about the Christian spiritual life without having first been formed in it by learning to live it. Amma Syncletica also implies that the training required is not knowledge about spirituality or the Christian life we might acquire from reading books such as this one. Rather, the training required is the knowledge, the practical wisdom, acquired by the disciplined living of the Christian life. The "practical life" to which Syncletica refers is the ascetic life, a disciplined life of prayer and attentiveness to God, discussed in the writings of the desert mothers and fathers and manifested in the ways in which they lived such lives.

This definition, however, is not what we have come to expect in contemporary distinctions between active and contemplative spiritualities. We have come to associate "practical" and "active" with action in the world, the outward movement we make in love of and service to our neighbor, such as Parker Palmer describes under the categories of work, creativity, and caring.[2] We have also come to think of the contemplative life as the interior, God-oriented part of our lives. But in the context of the early desert mothers and fathers as well as in the monastic practices and theologies that developed after them, such a distinction is incorrect. Syncletica and those who followed her would argue that the practical life is the life defined by the regular practices of prayer and fasting, psalmody and silence that later theologians, including Martin Luther and John Wesley came to call the "means of grace." The practical life is a means to the contemplative life, the means by which we discipline the attention of our hearts and minds toward God. Thus, it is not the ascetic life that is *sought* by the desert mothers and fathers, but a means of life that is *used* in service of a greater end, a life fully attentive to God. This also means that active and contemplative forms of the Christian life or, more accurately, active and contemplative Christian practices, rather than functioning in opposition to one another, are mutually supportive and necessary modes of living in our quest to know God.

The second quote is part of a vastly different conversation with non-Christian spiritualities:

> Few areas in the field of contemporary spirituality create as much challenge, confusion, and provocation as the role of the spiritual teacher. As a result of charismatic charlatans roaming the spiritual circuit, making their way into conventional households through the nation's most popular magazines and television shows, terms such as "guru" and "spiritual teacher" have become part of our colloquial English vocabulary.[3]

This comment reminds us that the problem of false teachers and the dangers they present is not confined to the early Christian community. Even as we see our neighbors, family members, and friends become disenchanted with traditional religious narratives in what some have called the secularization of North American culture, they still possess a hunger for some orienting life narrative. The plurality of religious traditions present in North American life and the opportunity these provide for encounters with new teachings that have the appearance, if not the reality, of wisdom make us vulnerable to any charismatic teacher who offers to sell us what we seek. The question here is not only who should teach but also by what authority one can teach. When confronted by these questions, we do well to attend to the words of another of the desert mothers, Theodora:

> A teacher ought to be a stranger to the desire for domination, vain-glory, and pride; one should not be able to fool him [or

her] by flattery, nor blind him by gifts, nor conquer him by the stomach, nor dominate him by anger; but he should be patient, gentle and humble as far as possible; he must be tested and without partisanship, full of concern, and a lover of souls.[4]

Theodora's words echo the admonitions in the Letter of James concerning the problems created by the untamed tongue and arrogance of a teacher (Jas. 3:6–18). Syncletica's words echo the warning that begins the same chapter: "Not many of you should become teachers, my brothers and sisters, for you know that we who teach will be judged with greater strictness" (v. 1). So then, who should teach?

One Taught by God

The history of the Christian spiritual life suggests that those who truly teach the spiritual life have been themselves taught by God. The phrase *taught by God* occurs in Christian writings across several centuries. At times, it differentiates "book" and "experiential" learning. More often, it provides a means to describe the source of wisdom found among Christian teachers who clearly did not have the benefit of a theological education (although such attestations are often deceptive) but who, through the "practical" life, have learned the ways of God. At other times, it challenges the institutional authority of the church. For example, the fourth-century North African bishop Athanasius says that Antony, though unlearned in letters, was a shrewd and intelligent man and extremely wise. "When he sat alone on the mountain, if it ever happened that he was puzzled, seeking some solution for himself, this was revealed to him by Providence as he prayed. He was the blessed one becoming, as it is written, taught by God."[5] Ignatius of Loyola, living in sixteenth century Spain, offers a similar description of his own formation in his autobiography:

> God treated him at this time just as a schoolmaster treats a child whom he is teaching. Whether this was because of his lack of education and of brains, or because he had no one to teach him, or because of the strong desire God himself had given him to serve him, he believed with doubt and has always believed that God treated him in this way.[6]

Finally, Martin Luther, at the conclusion of his argument in "The Freedom of a Christian" about the appropriate place of ceremonies and works in the Christian life, calls Christians "to escape from the slavery of works and come to a knowledge of the freedom of faith. Therefore there is need of the prayer that the Lord may give us and make us *theodidacti*, that is, those taught by God."[7] Here Luther is using the call to become taught by God in a rather polemical way to stand against what he perceives to be the ritual and doctrinal errors of the Roman Catholic Church.

We might appropriately worry that the claim that one is best taught by God could make persons and communities vulnerable to the whims of any charismatic figure who, like the biblical prophets, claims a revelation from God. This claim could create more problems than it solves. To decide whether this concept is helpful and perhaps even necessary to our identity as teachers despite its dangers, we need to explore what it means to be *theodidacti*, those taught by God.

Part of the difficulty in understanding *theodidaktoi* is that it is a unique word in ancient and biblical literature.[8] Yet the phrase *taught by God* appears in or is implied by several scripture passages, including some verses of the Psalms, Isaiah 54, Jeremiah 31, Matthew 23, 1 Thessalonians 4, and John 6. A brief exploration of these verses will help us better understand this phrase.

Each of the passages from Psalms suggests God's role as the giver, and therefore teacher, of the law. The psalmist writes, "O God, from my youth you have taught me, and I still proclaim your wondrous deeds" (Ps. 71:17). And, "I do not turn away from your ordinances, for you have taught me" (119:102). Again, "My lips will pour forth praise, because you teach me your statutes" (v. 171). These verses suggest several related conclusions: First, because God is the teacher, it is possible for the psalmist to be faithful. The law revives the soul, makes the simple wise, rejoices the heart, and enlightens the eyes (19:7–8). Second, because God has given the law, contemplation of God's law provides a means of contemplating God and, therefore, of loving God. Those who delight in the law and meditate on it day and night "are like trees planted by streams of water, which yield their fruit in its season" (1:3).

The role of God as giver of the law and as teacher is also part of the eschatological visions of Isaiah and Jeremiah. Isaiah prophesies, "All your children shall be taught by the Lord, and great shall be the prosperity of your children" (Isa. 54:13). As John Oswalt suggests in his commentary on this passage, "the greatest wealth that Isaiah can imagine for Israel is that her children could become disciples of (those who are taught by) the Lord...this is seen as the essence of a relationship with God. It is not a metaphysical union with God that is sought but the learning of [God's] ways and a replication of [God's] character."[9] Similarly, John McKenzie argues that "the lasting city of [God's] good pleasure is...the community of the redeemed, of all those who are 'instructed by [God]' and are 'established in righteousness.'"[10] Jeremiah's vision is similar to that of Isaiah. For Jeremiah, people no longer need to teach one another, because the knowledge of God will be written in their hearts:

> I will put my law within them, and I will write it on their hearts;
> and I will be their God, and they shall be my people. No longer

shall they teach one another, or say to each other, "Know the Lord," for they shall all know me, from the least of them to the greatest, says the Lord; for I will forgive their iniquity, and remember their sin no more. (Jer. 31:33–34)

Both these visions suggest that being taught by God brings new or restored intimacy with God as God's forgiven children. They also suggest that being taught by God is an internal, rather than external, event; God's law is now written on the heart. Yet these prophetic visions also remind us that what is known by or in the heart only becomes evident when manifested in just and compassionate relationships with one's neighbors (see especially Isa. 58:6–10).

The references in the New Testament to being "taught by God" and specifically to forms of the word *theodidaktoi* are few. The gospel of Matthew, given the tradition of reading the Matthean Jesus as the new Moses and the gospel as the new books of the law, has only one reference, and even this is indirect: "You are not to be called rabbi, for you have one teacher, and you are all students. And call no one your father on earth, for you have one Father—the one in heaven. Nor are you to be called instructors, for you have one instructor, the Messiah [Greek: Christ]" (Mt. 23:8–10). Duncan Derrett has argued that this passage serves as a kind of midrash on the passages from Isaiah and Jeremiah cited earlier. It reflects not only a "desire for direct communication with God" but also a desire to be independent of human teachers of the law. "Torah will be possessed by all, and 'knowledge of God,' which implies a true and spontaneous discipline, will be absolutely common and equal."[11] A word of caution is in order here: "spontaneous discipline" does not mean either unformed or uninformed, nor does it mean action only "when we feel like it." Rather, it means that Torah and knowledge of God have been so fully internalized that we can respond faithfully by heart. While Derrett makes his case for this reading, the passage in itself, like James 3, adds another caution about our desire to be teachers. It more directly opens an extended critique of the scribes and Pharisees that culminates, at the end of Matthew 25, with a vision of the final judgment and a spiritual knowledge made evident in one's care for the poor. For Matthew, then, to be taught by God leads away from religious practice (what some might call "works of piety") and toward our participation in the practice of God amidst the suffering of the world (as "works of mercy").

The two passages in the New Testament where *taught by God* appears most explicitly are in 1 Thessalonians 4:9 and John 6:45. Although the passage from John has received more attention from biblical scholars, it is in 1 Thessalonians that Paul seems to have coined the word *theodidaktoi*, "God-taught." The passage reads, "Now concerning love of the brothers and sisters, you do not need to have anyone write to you, for you yourselves have been taught by God [literally "God-taught"] to love one another." Some commentators suggest that Paul coins the word as a means of criticizing Epicurean claims to being "self-taught"; others suggest it is a means to contrast with human teaching. Still others say it provides a means to emphasize the divine source of love.[12] In some ways, the Matthew passage serves as an extended commentary on this sentence. God, who is both law and grace, judgment and love, is the one who teaches us to love and enables us to fulfill the commandments to love. Derrett seems to catch the sense of this in his comment that "by Paul's time the concept of being 'taught by God' was intimately wrapped up with the love of the brethren [*sic*], which implies solidarity and abatement of relative status-consciousness."[13]

The attention given to John 6:45 has been due in part to the puzzle John introduces when he states "It is written in the prophets" and to the fact that this is the first time in the gospel that John has Jesus cite the Old Testament, in this case Isaiah 54:13.[14] The verse reads, "It is written in the prophets, 'And they shall all be taught by God.' Everyone who has heard and learned from the Father comes to me." In context, the passage invites two related directions of thought. First, as in Matthew 23, John is setting up a deliberate polemic against rabbinic Judaism. "Whereas Judaism regarded the Torah as a direct way of hearing God, John puts in its place Jesus, the only true revealer of God."[15] "No longer is Israel the object and the Law the source of God's instruction. It is aimed at all believers without limitation of race or nation, and it comes through Jesus."[16] (We can emphasize from these comments that Jesus has a unique authority as revealer of God; nevertheless, Christian teachers today should not be support such polemicism and supersessionism in relation to Judaism.) Second, if in Judaism "learning the Torah was being instructed by God…and a perfect, inwardly active divine instruction was looked forward to as one of the blessings of the eschatological time"[17] as we see anticipated in Isaiah, then "by applying this text to his own ministry, Jesus is claiming that the eschatological blessings of the last day are already being experienced in his ministry…[and] those hearing Jesus are themselves being taught by God."[18]

Where does this discussion of the "one taught by God" lead us as we think about the spiritual leader as Christian teacher? First, as we see in Luther's argument about the "freedom of the Christian" and his call to be as those "taught by God," the tension between those taught by God and the authority of religious tradition was not unique to the tensions between rabbinic Judaism and the emerging Christian community. The tensions expressed by Luther within the Christian community remain with us today; such tensions are perhaps heightened by the individualism of the modern age. Second, as we saw in the stories about Antony and Ignatius, the evidence of such "God-teaching" is not found in the social or economic success of the teacher; rather, the evidence of God-teaching is found in the character of lives living out the love of God, evidence made visible across the history of the church and continuing to offer glimpses of God's inbreaking and indwelling in our world. Those who claim to be taught by God or those others say have been taught by God make evident such teaching in their faithfulness and obedience to the way of God, by the ways in which God's teaching is written in their hearts, by the ways in which they have internalized God's love and forgiveness, and especially by the ways in which the knowledge they have acquired leads to the love of their neighbors. Third, as the history of Israel and the church make clear, one cannot be taught by God unless one is willing to be attentive to God or to those who speak on behalf of God.

By What Authority?

Our discussion of the *theodidaktoi* already gives some indication of the source of the authority of the spiritual teacher. While such authority often may be noncredentialed, it is never a self-bestowed authority nor an authority one can presume by age and life experience. It is a given and recognized authority. The authority of the spiritual teacher, like that of the prophet, is given by God and is recognized as authentic by the way in which the teacher lives.[19] As Charles Foster writes, "the role of the teacher is also an earned one. In the final analysis, only those who have been taught can point to someone and declare him or her to be a teacher."[20]

The desert fathers provide several examples. In the sayings of Abba Poemen, whose teachings occupy a substantial portion of the sayings of the desert fathers and mothers, we read the following: "Abba Joseph said, 'While we were sitting with Abba Poemen he mentioned Agathon as 'abba', and we said to him, 'He is very young, why do you call him 'abba'? Abba Poemen said, 'Because his speech makes him worthy to be called 'abba'."[21] A second example, perhaps more about teaching than about the teacher but which notes the inseparability of the two, is found in the writing of Gregory of Sinai:

> For just as water, while essentially the same, changes and acquires a distinctive quality according to the composition of the soil under it, so that it tastes bitter, or sweet, or brackish, or acidic, so oral teaching, coloured as it is by the moral state of the teacher, varies accordingly in the way it operates and in the benefits it confers.[22]

In the first example, the wisdom of youth is made evident in speech. In the second example, the quality of what is taught takes on the "taste" of the moral character of the teacher. We may be what we eat, but we teach what we are. We should not put at risk those we teach by inviting them to inhabit a dilapidated house.

In *The Courage to Teach* Parker Palmer explores the idea that we "teach what we are" in his discussion of the "teacher within." Palmer writes, "the call to teach does not come from external encounters alone—no outward teacher or teaching will have much effect until my soul assents. Any authentic call ultimately comes from the voice of the *teacher within*, the voice that invites me to honor the nature of my true self."[23] He observes:

> Education is the attempt to 'lead out' from within the self a core of wisdom that has the power to resist falsehood and live in the light of truth, not by external norms but by reasoned and reflective self-determination. The inward teacher is the living core of our lives that is addressed and evoked by any education worthy of the name.[24]

On the one hand, Palmer rightly points us to the teacher within as the one who speaks the true self, who grants the "power to resist falsehood and live in the light of truth," and who functions as the "living core of our lives." On the other hand, and quite problematically, he suggests that this inward teacher, though neither superego nor conscience, is no more than the identity and integrity of the self: "The voice of the inward teacher reminds me of *my* truth as I negotiate the force field of *my* life" [emphasis added].[25]

Palmer's focus on the authority of the self and of the self's truth becomes most explicit when he speaks of the authority of the teacher:

> External tools of power…are no substitute for authority, the authority that come from the teacher's inner life. The clue is in the word itself, which has *author* at its core. Authority is granted to people who are perceived as *authoring* their own words, their own actions, their own lives, rather than playing a scripted role at great remove from their own hearts… Authority comes as I reclaim my identity and integrity, remembering my selfhood and my sense of vocation.[26]

This reliance on no source for truth other than the self is problematic for Christian teachers. The authority of the Christian spiritual teacher cannot be self-authored for if we teach only our selves and invite students to seek their own selves as authors, have we not turned away from summons to be taught by God? Neither the prophets nor the desert mothers and fathers were authenticated by the perception that they were the authors of their own words; rather, they were authenticated by the perception that their words were God's Word, that the inward teacher who spoke to and through them was God, and that the power and truth manifested through them was from God.

A hymn stanza by Charles Wesley reflects this different perspective:

Author of life divine,
Who hast a table spread,
Furnished with mystic wine
And everlasting bread:
Preserve the life thyself hast given,
And feed and train us up for heaven.[27]

Wesley reminds us that as Christian people we do not author ourselves but are "written," fed and trained up for heaven, by God. The difference between the self-authored teacher and the one taught by God is like the difference between an idol and an icon: "An idol freezes one's gaze on itself; an icon guides one's gaze in its intention toward infinite relatedness."[28] The goal of the Christian spiritual teacher is not to be an idol but to be iconic—to direct attention not to the self of the teacher or the student but by means of the practical life, as we see lived out in the desert mothers and fathers, "to re-direct every aspect of body, mind, and soul to God."[29]

What was it in these teachers that permitted the perception that their words were God's words and that they had been taught by God? Such perception lay not only in the ways in which the teacher's words or actions directed the student to God, but also in the coherence between the teacher's words and life as these had been shaped by the "practical life." As Douglas Burton-Christie notes of the desert mothers and fathers, "the integration of life with words was seen as a special responsibility of the teacher…Only by cultivating a pure heart could one express oneself with integrity and authority."[30] Their authority derived from the purity of their lives, from the visible, more so than audible, sense that those who spoke a word had in some sense become or attained the word spoken.[31] This is a humbling standard for those "inclined to equate intellectual knowledge of the written word with practical knowledge of it."[32] As Abba Silvanus said, "Unhappy is the one whose reputation exceeds his work."[33]

A more contemporary teacher, Charles Foster, describes the teacher's necessary integration of head and heart this way: Many teachers,

relying primarily on the words of formers teachers, some book or printed resource guide…seek to enliven and illuminate some past thought or event. Their teaching may hint at the possibilities of its power for our lives, but they have yet to be possessed by it themselves. They are still trying to grasp its implications in a rudimentary fashion. They do not incarnate its depth or breadth.[34]

The authority of the Christian spiritual teacher, therefore, lies not primarily, and certainly not only, in what the teacher knows about God, but in the way the teacher knows God, the way in which the teacher has been grasped by and learned to embody the love of God, the way in which the teacher has given the fullness of her or his attention to God, enabling the teacher to be taught by God. This, finally, is what it means to be a disciple: to take up a way of life, to follow in a way of life, such that we might learn the wisdom that way offers through the living of it.[35] The practical life, as the desert mothers and fathers call it, is nothing more than understanding that "practice makes perfect." As Maximus the Confessor (ca. 613–662) wrote, "Through the diligent practice of the virtues, the natural intelligence is raised towards the intellect. Through contemplation the intellect leads towards wisdom the man who aspires to spiritual knowledge."[36]

The chapters that follow lead us into the stories of some of those whose lives bore witness to the fact that they had been taught by God. The particular practices and distinctive emphases their lives display are as varied as the persons themselves. Yet each has been claimed in some way as an authoritative spiritual teacher of the church. They sought to ensure that, before they dared receive guests, the condition of their own houses would cause no harm to another. For this reason we titled this chapter "The Spiritual Leader as Christian Teacher" rather than vice versa. One does not move from teacher to spiritual leader, but from the lived spiritual life (being taught by God) to teaching. As Abba Poemen said, "Instructing one's neighbour is for the person who is whole and without passions; for what is the use of building the house of another, while destroying one's own?"[37] Or, perhaps more familiar words on which to end a discussion of the authority of those taught by God: "Unless the LORD builds the house, those who build it labor in vain. Unless the LORD guards the city, the guard keeps watch in vain" (Ps. 127:1).

CHAPTER 2

Teaching from a Life of Prayer

As part of their seminary education and formation, many pastors are required to complete a process of clinical pastoral education. This process, generally done in the context of hospital chaplaincy and therefore in direct confrontation with matters of human life and death, leads persons on a journey of self-discovery. This process invites reflection on questions about who we are in the face of suffering and death. It also invites reflection on how we give an account of the hope in us as Christian people when the sick and suffering want to know why they are suffering.

Our preparation as teachers in and with the church does not often lead us into such direct confrontation with the pain of human life, although more personal work in counseling or spiritual direction may bring us to confront the pain within ourselves. Nevertheless, we are invited in various contexts and with persons of varying ages to give an account of the hope that is in us. If we think of our teaching as one of the means by which we give an account of our faith, then we must ask ourselves: Can we teach about Christian hope if we do not know that hope? Can we teach the Christian scriptures if we have not come to know them as "words of life"? Can we teach Christians to pray if we ourselves do not know a life of prayer? Can we teach what we do not know? Can we teach from who we are not?

The letter of James warns, "Not many of you should become teachers...for you know that we who teach will be judged with greater strictness" (Jas. 3:1). Sara Little begins her book on Christian education, *To Set One's Heart*, with a reflection on James's warning:

Teachers, by teaching, accept the responsibility of seeking to know and increasingly to appropriate the truth they seek to teach, as well as the responsibility of trying to develop those structures and processes which in themselves witness to the truth, and enable those who learn to receive, to build knowledge, to respond to others in faithfulness, and to be transformed by the meaning they find.[1]

We might conclude from Little's statement that knowledge, rather than a fixed object, is something we continuously seek and appropriate. Knowledge is an ongoing process of reaching out and taking in as we participate in structures of truth. Parker Palmer begins his book *The Courage to Teach* in a similar fashion. In his first pages, Palmer argues teaching "emerges from one's inwardness" and projects "the condition of my soul onto my students, my subject, and our way of being together." In other words, "we teach who we are."[2] Although he seems to reverse the movement Little describes from seeking and appropriating to appropriating and projecting he shares with Little a conviction that our work of teaching is intimately tied to personal identity and faith.

If what we teach emerges from who we are, from the ways in which we have set our hearts, then we must teach from a life of prayer. Such a life does not require that we become monks, but it does require some form of discipline or pattern of regular prayer practice. To help us imagine how we might incorporate such a discipline in our lives, we look at two works on the Christian spiritual life addressed specifically to persons living "in the world": St. Francis de Sales's *Introduction to the Devout Life* and Søren Kierkegaard's *Purity of Heart Is to Will One Thing.* De Sales and Kierkegaard, though separated by two centuries as well as by ecclesial affiliation (one Roman Catholic, the other a Danish Lutheran), share a number of concerns, among them a concern for singleness of mind and heart in devotion and faith. Like the writer of James, they believe God provides wisdom to those who ask in faith. They also believe those who are double-minded are unstable and cannot "expect to receive anything from the Lord" (Jas. 1:5, 8). We need to discover how we can prepare ourselves through prayer to become single-hearted as well as single-minded people of faith and then to teach from this place.

Francis de Sales and *Introduction to the Devout Life*

Francis de Sales (1567–1622) lived during the early years of the Catholic Counter-reformation. De Sales gained the attention of the bishop of Geneva, Claude de Granier, as well as of the cardinals in Rome, after undertaking a mission on behalf of Pope Clement VIII to attempt the conversion of Theodore Beza, John Calvin's colleague and successor in Geneva. In 1599, at de Granier's suggestion, de Sales was named coadjutor for the diocese of Geneva. In 1602 de Sales was himself named bishop of Geneva. De Sales spent the years of his episcopacy in the nearby town of Annecy in exile, as had de Granier, because Geneva remained under the influence of the Calvinists and the leadership of Beza. He became known throughout the region for his influence as a writer, preacher, and spiritual director. His missionary and preaching skills were such that he was able to bring many citizens of the area back to Catholicism.[3]

In addition to living and working within a context of tension between the Protestant and Catholic reformations, de Sales also lived and worked in another theological context of extremes: Jansenism and Quietism. The Jansenists were so convinced of their guilt and of predestination that they could not perceive the mercy of God. The Quietists, on the other hand, emphasized God's mercy and the ability of a person to achieve a state of sinless holiness. For the Quietists, God so completely possessed a person "that it is God who performs any given action."[4]

In contrast to these extremes, de Sales asserted the importance of the universal salvific will of God and the importance of the human will in seeking the life of holiness. De Sales also asserted the universality of the call to holiness and of the attainability of that holiness "by all who were willing to put their heart to it."[5] Devotion is not to be confused with daily devotions (e.g., a few minutes with God in Bible study and prayer), as might be easy to do today. Rather, devotion is "a way of practicing the love of God and the love of neighbor."[6] In her summary of de Sales's teaching, Elizabeth Stopp notes that "holiness, that is 'devotion,' is for all; love holds absolute primacy and is the way; Jesus Christ, meek and humble of heart, is the model and the way."[7] *Devotion* or the *devout life* refers not to a particular set of spiritual practices but to holiness of heart and life; devotion is "the spiritual alertness which makes us respond whole heartedly and promptly to what love asks of us."[8] Devotion, or holiness, is an interior and "perfect conformity to the will of God expressed in actions motivated by charity."[9] The life of prayer as it manifests itself in de Sales's work is a combination of receiving from God and acting toward God. It is the cultivation of habits of attention or, perhaps more accurately, habits of mindfulness of God's presence with us and God's love for us. The life of prayer is a manner of being to which all Christian people are called and requires the engagement of heart, mind, and imagination in seeking and practicing the love of God.

De Sales's *Introduction to the Devout Life* first appeared in 1609 (the first English edition appeared in 1613). What is now considered the definitive edition was published in 1619. The work was so popular that by 1656 it had appeared in over fifty languages. It has remained in print and continued to be translated ever since.[10] De Sales wrote it as quite literally "an *intro-ducere*, leading into a life of devotion by the successive stages of a journey."[11] Through this introduction, De Sales seeks "to arouse in [the] reader a complete love of God and absolute confidence in him [*sic*]."[12] De Sales wrote "to instruct those who…are obliged to live an ordinary life as to outward appearances… [God] commands Christians…to bring forth the fruits of devotion; each according to his position and vocation…adapted to the strength, activities, and duties of each particular person."[13] For this reason de Sales's book can help us answer the question of what a life of prayer looks like for those who are not called to the monastic life. De Sales wrote first and foremost to and for laypersons seeking and intentionally living the Christian life. Although he initially wrote to provide counsel to one person, he now directs his counsel to many. He therefore addresses his writing to *Philothea*, "a soul living, or in love with, God" and "a name that can refer to all who aspire to devotion."[14] Because this name describes each of us, the book also addresses us.

Introduction to the Devout Life is written in five parts, with each part attentive to particular practices of self-examination and prayer and also providing the means by which we might undertake a life of devotion and single-mindedness. In the first part, de Sales invites us to explore how we can change "simple desire into a solid resolution" to embrace the devout life. The second and third parts describe the means by which we join ourselves to God through the sacraments and prayer and the virtues we must practice in order to progress in the devout life. The fourth part addresses various temptations we must avoid. The final part considers what we must do to renew the soul and sustain it in devotion through rest and retreat.[15]

De Sales begins the first part with a description of and summons to devotion. He describes a progression in devotion starting with an initial awareness of the presence of God's love and ending with our active and consistent response to that love: "Inasmuch as divine love adorns the soul it is called *grace*,…inasmuch as it strengthens us to do good, it is called *charity*. When it…makes us do good…carefully, frequently, and promptly, it is called *devotion*… Wherever we may be, we can and should aspire to a perfect life."[16] We move toward this perfection of life through a process of purification. We purge ourselves of sin, of our affection for sin, of our affection for "useless and dangerous things," and of our "evil inclinations."[17]

One of the tools de Sales provides for this process is a series of ten imaginative meditations through which we separate ourselves from our affection for sin. In each, we discover a model for a type of prayer that invites sustained consideration of God's love and mercy for us and for the world. The ten meditations lead us (if we do them rather than simply read them) from considerations of our creation out of nothingness by God; through considerations of sin, death, judgment, hell, paradise; and finally through our choosing of devotion and heaven. In each, de Sales guides us into prayer, instructs us how to prepare for each meditation, what to consider, and what affections and resolutions the meditation should lead us to. For example, in the third meditation on God's goodness and gifts to us (God's "benefactions"), de Sales invites us to begin our meditation by placing ourselves in God's presence and asking for God's assistance. As he writes later, we prepare for meditation by placing ourselves in God's presence with the assurance that God is present with us and within us and that God is gazing upon us, even when we do not feel or see that presence.[18] Having begun, we are to consider the corporal benefits God has given us (body, health, comfort), the gifts of mind (knowledge, freedom, dignity), and the gifts of the Spirit (inspiration, admonition, forgiveness, the sacraments). De Sales would have us "marvel at God's goodness" and at our own ingratitude, resolve to be grateful and loyal, and "use diligently all the Church's means to save [ourselves] and to love God."[19] Yet the point is not to "dwell so long on these general reflections…as to change them into special and particular resolutions for [our] own correction and improvement."[20] The inward process leads to outward change.

The second part of the *Introduction* provides instruction in the practice and use of meditation, prayer, and the sacraments. Here de Sales encourages us to create a regular rhythm of prayer throughout the day. This rhythm includes significant time for meditation each morning (he recommends an hour), morning and evening prayer, examination of conscience each evening, and brief "exclamatory" prayers throughout the day. He also encourages us to practice a kind of spiritual retreat throughout the day, retiring "at various times into the solitude of your own heart even while outwardly engaged in discussions or transactions with others."[21] Such withdrawal in the midst of a conversation would be disconcerting, but the purpose of such withdrawal, as well as of the structure of meditation and prayer, is to learn to dwell in our hearts in the presence of God. (As some commentators have noted, the rhythm de Sales describes, while not a monastic rhythm, does depend on a person having a certain amount of time available to oneself each day. In de Sales's own day, such persons were persons of the leisure, not the working, class.[22])

The method of meditation introduced in Part 1 is developed and further explained in Part 2 in order to provide a framework by which to approach prayer and sacrament. In the context of the eucharist, our meditation becomes more explicitly focused on Christ. Meditation on the sacrament leads us into an imaginative centering of our attention "on the life and passion of our Lord," so that, as we observe Christ's "words, actions and affections we may learn by his grace to speak, act, and will like him."[23] De Sales encourages us in frequent prayer and communion because, he argues, we cannot learn to do something without doing it, nor can we learn to do something well without practice. He writes, "Receive the Blessed Sacrament often so as to learn how to receive it well, for we hardly do an action well which we do not practice often."[24] We might well add that we cannot learn to *be* something without being it or practicing it. Similarly, the morning exercise prepares us for the day ahead, waters our work with God's blessing, and opens the windows of our souls "to the Sun of Justice." In our evening exercise, we place ourselves again before Christ and close the windows of our souls "against the shadows of hell."[25]

In the third part of the *Introduction*, de Sales turns our attention to the practice of the virtues, which include patience, outward and interior humility, modesty, obedience, meekness toward one's neighbors and oneself, chastity, poverty, true friendship, and exterior mortification. Much as in his description of the daily rhythm of prayer, de Sales seems to have turned us toward a monastic ideal for the devout life in naming these as the essential virtues. In many ways this is true; departing from the ideal of monastic practice was difficult. Nevertheless, de Sales is attentive to the nonmonastic character of our lives. We recall his expectation that the devout life is possible for any person in any circumstance of life. "In practicing the virtues we should prefer the one most conformable to our duties rather than the one more agreeable to our tastes... Each person must practice in a special manner the virtues needed by the kind of life [one] is called to."[26] The purpose in all of these is to instruct the heart so that all may see "not only holy devotion but also great wisdom and prudence [in a person's] outward conduct and bearing."[27] Perhaps as another reminder of who and where we are, de Sales writes, "Great opportunities to serve God rarely present themselves but little ones are frequent...'Do all things in the name of God,' and you will do all things well."[28]

Readers may find some of his comments concerning desire and marriage inappropriately supporting situations of passivity and abuse. For example:

> a person obligated to a certain duty or vocation should [not] distract himself by longing for any other kind of life but one in keeping with his duties or by engaging in exercises incompatible with his present state...let everyone use the world according to his vocation, but in such manner that he does not fix his affections on it and remains as free and ready to serve God as if he did not use it.[29]

The first statement is, I think, more concerned with not desiring what appear to be greener pastures belonging to others. The second is concerned with the practice of a certain level of detachment from our present situation in life. When read in the context of de Sales's larger discussion, we find both comments grow out of the concern for true devotion as manifested in singleness of heart. We cannot be wholly fixed on God if we are distracted by or focused on other desires. Perhaps this becomes more evident when we read the fourth part, the counsels against temptations. Although De Sales provides specific direction concerning various temptations, he makes one point through all of his counsel: "keep our heart steady, unshakeably equable"; "remain unchanging and ever looking, striving, and aspiring toward God"; be absolutely resolved "never to forsake God and never to abandon his merciful love."[30]

In the final part of the *Introduction*, de Sales reminds us that the progress we have made toward the devout life cannot be sustained unless we attend to its ongoing maintenance. Like a clock requiring winding morning and evening we need to be rewound for God's service morning and evening. Like a clock, we also need annual cleaning and repair, in which we take apart, examine, and repair "every affection and passion" of our life with God.[31] By carefully examining each part of our relationship, we can assess its condition. "The lute player touches all the strings to find which are out of tune and tunes them either by tightening of loosening them. So also if we examine the passions…we put them in tune by means of [God's] grace and the counsel of our spiritual father [our spiritual director]."[32] Under de Sales guidance, we return to the considerations of our lives with which we began the journey, exploring the character of our life with God and Christ, our attitudes toward sin, the commandments, spiritual exercises, our selves, our souls, and our neighbors. He invites us to close our considerations with meditations on the love Christ has for us, especially as expressed in his suffering on the cross, and on the everlasting love God has for us, a love that began when God began to be God, a love therefore without beginning or end.

From the very beginning, de Sales assumes we are seeking a way to say yes to the invitation to and desire for the devout life. Although meditations along the way suggest more traditional models of discernment in which we come to a particular decision, a yes or a no, his concern is with our continuing yes to the love and grace of God. Our willingness to pray and our willingness to receive his direction are among the first manifestations of that yes. Through the *Introduction* de Sales directs each lover of God, each *Philothea*, into the depths of that yes. He helps us see how anyone can easily fall away from the devout life when it does not receive sustained attention. He also helps us see that our yes in love and prayer will require us to say no to all that is inconsistent with that life. Throughout the *Introduction*, he assumes a rather traditional framework in which we undertake the devout life: a significant time of meditation on the mystery of God's love for us, participation in forms of morning and evening prayer, examination of conscience at the end of each day, participation in eucharist and confession, regular (annual) times of spiritual retreat and rest, and a kind of practicing our awareness of God's presence and love throughout the day through brief and occasional acts of prayer and thanksgiving. Yet he believes this life is available to all of us, regardless of the particular condition or character of our lives. What may be at stake for us is not so much that we would attempt to teach that which we do not know, but that without the care and practice of the devout life our teaching would resemble a clock that, for lack of winding or repair, cannot give us the true time, or an untuned lute that, no matter where we place our fingers, cannot play a well-tuned melody.

Purity of Heart Is to Will One Thing

By the time he was thirty, Søren Kierkegaard (1813–1855) had written and published many of his major philosophical-theological works and anticipated laying down his pen to take up a rural pastorate. Yet by 1847 he had completed a new cycle of works, the *Upbuilding Discourses on Various Spirits,* and within the next two years completed *Sickness unto Death,* which many consider his magnum opus. The work popularly known as *Purity of Heart Is to Will One Thing* was published as the first of the three "occasional discourses" included in *Upbuilding Discourses,* where it was entitled "On the Occasion of a Confession."[33]

The context in which Kierkegaard lived and wrote was significantly different from that experienced by de Sales. The primary ecclesial and theological conflicts Kierkegaard experienced were not between Catholics and Protestants nor were they conflicts between the pessimistic predestinarianism of the Jansenists and the holiness sought by the Quietists. Rather, Kierkegaard's work emerged in a context of conflict between reason and piety, secularism and religion, Enlightenment and Pietism. Enlightenment thought argued against the natural depravity of humanity, against seeking the end of life in a "beatific life after death," and against religion and religious practices as forms of oppressive superstition and ignorance. The human person, Enlightenment thought argued, could perfect the "good life on earth…guided solely by reason and experience."[34] His work also emerged in a context in which the church was increasingly indistinguishable from society at large. In Kierkegaard's eyes the church was betraying Christianity by parading itself as a world power rather than preaching the cross of Christ. It had become comfortable, "blind to its compromise with bourgeois life" and reduced to a form of "low-pressure Christianity."[35] Nowhere was this tension more evident to Kierkegaard than in his response to the eulogy of Bishop Jacob Mynster, given by Kierkegaard's former teacher, Hans Martensen. Martensen "referred to Mynster as 'a witness to the truth.'" Although Mynster had ministered to Kierkegaard's family, Kierkegaard wondered how a person who lived a life of prominence and luxury could be a witness to Christ when that witness "meant imitating Christ… undergoing suffering, humiliation, and isolation for Christ."[36]

Kierkegaard did not believe faith or the Christian life was easy. He believed Christianity ought to challenge people to search their hearts and come to know themselves as they really are before God. What we would discover in that search is that "most of us try all our lives to talk ourselves out of our moral and religious knowledge, because we do not want to be led to the sacrifices this knowledge commands."[37] Like de Sales, Kierkegaard leads us into a process of self-discovery that, as Jeremy Walker notes, is "indissoluble from choice and action" and which leads to genuine, total commitment to "the Good."[38] Also like de Sales, Kierkegaard has written in a way that directly addresses the person who seeks a life of single-minded devotion to God. His talk becomes, if we read aloud, our talk to ourselves before God and therefore not only a preparation for confession but also a form of confession. Through this work, Kierkegaard teaches us "how to recognize many errors, disappointments, deceptions, and self-deceptions…to track down double-mindedness into its hidden ways, and to ferret out its secret [and to] unconditionally demand the reader's own decisive activity."[39] In contrast to de Sales, who gives the individual a series of meditations at various stages along the way toward the devout life, Kierkegaard provides a single extended meditation addressed to that "solitary 'individual' who reads willingly and slowly, who reads over and over again, and who reads aloud—for his own sake, [receiving the book] as if it had arisen within his own heart."[40]

In outline *Purity of Heart* appears simpler and more straightforward than *Introduction to the Devout Life*, but it is perhaps more thorough in the depth of personal assessment it calls forth from the reader. The opening sections (parts 1–2) name for us our failure to will one thing; the ways in which sin has separated us from the one thing through "delay, blockage, interruption, delusion, and corruption"; and the necessity of repentance prompted by the "friendship" of remorse.[41] Parts 3–7 explore the various barriers standing in the way of our willing one thing: pursuit of variety, desire for reward, fear of punishment and shame, self-centered willfulness, and the belief that we need not completely will one thing— that we can offer less than full commitment to the good. In parts 8 through 11, Kierkegaard explores "the price of willing one thing" including commitment, loyalty, the readiness and willingness to suffer, and exposure of our clever evasions of the good. As Kierkegaard considers the price of willing one thing and the contrast between the temporal and eternal, he draws our attention to the place of Christ as the one who so willed one thing, the Eternal, that he was "repudiated by the temporal order."[42] The final sections (parts 12–15) explore what we must do and how we are to live if we are to single-mindedly seek the good. These sections, assuming we truly yearn for and will the good, ask us "what kind of life do you live, do you will only one thing, and what is this one thing?"[43] It does not matter, Kierkegaard argues, whether our occupation is "great or mean, whether you are a king or only a laborer…whether you earn a great deal of money or are building up great prestige for yourself." Rather, is our occupation such that we can live "conscious of our eternal responsibility before God?"[44] In the end, it is not a question of how much we have been entrusted with, but of our "attitude of mind," our "attitude toward others," and our "faith and faithfulness."[45]

In many ways, the one question Kierkegaard asks concerns our attitude of mind. Do we will one thing? If not, we live a double-minded existence. Just as the writer of the Letter of James portrays worldliness as a consequence of double-mindedness (Jas. 4:1–10), Kierkegaard insists that anyone who wills anything other than the Good does not truly will the one thing and, therefore, does not truly will the Good.[46] The whole of his discourse is to help us root out the various forms of double-mindedness within us. It is there when we seek to judge others rather than ourselves; it is there when we seek the Good because of some anticipated reward, fear of punishment, a sense of shame, or a sense of serving one's reputation or glory; it is there when we believe we can serve the Good in some limited fashion.[47] In all, if we truly seek to will one thing, we seek to "unconditionally serve the Good in action."[48]

What does this mean for the subject of this chapter, teaching from a life of prayer? Unlike what we find in de Sales's *Introduction to the Devout Life*, we are hard-pressed to find guidance for the life of prayer in Kierkegaard's *Purity of Heart*. As an extended exercise in confession and self-examination, *Purity of Heart* leads to one simple yet difficult point: The means and the end of Christian life are the same—to use only those means that are genuinely good and to seek that which is the genuine Good. We are to will one thing, the Eternal, the Good.

As Kierkegaard's later works make evident, the Christian life has little to do with "intellectual assent to dogma, regular churchgoing, ecclesiastical reform, or middle-class morality but in following Christ's pattern of selfless love and service in everyday life."[49] Rather, the Christian life and the life of prayer, although Kierkegaard does not explicitly name it this way, is the life of the individual. The individual conscience stands before God, not the conscience of a crowd. The individual speaks about oneself, rather than about others or others speaking about the individual, in the presence of God. The individual, conscious of one's eternal responsibility before God, must account for the way in which one lives one's life.[50] And the self that stands before God is the same self that stands before a group of students to teach. We cannot teach others to be single-minded in their pursuit of God and the Good if we are ourselves not single-minded in our seeking. Nor can we teach as if others can know God for us or as if another can confess our sins for us. The point is neither that we must become giants in prayer nor that our lives must demonstrate that we have attained perfection in holiness. It is not that we perfectly and consistently hit the mark, but, as Kierkegaard suggests, that our aim is consistent: "the aim is the more reliable indication of the marksman's goal than the spot the shot strikes."[51]

Similarly, it is not a question of how much we have been entrusted with, but of how faithful we have been with that which we have been given.[52]

Conclusion

These two works do not represent the fullness of Christian traditions and practices of prayer. De Sales perhaps comes closest to describing what we might consider traditional practices; Kierkegaard remains at some distance. And yet both call us as teachers to a form of attentiveness that requires singleness of heart and will in prayer and self-examination. Both structure a process through which we must first and continually appropriate the truth we seek to teach. Both insist that attention to the inward life leads to transformation of the outward life. And both are convinced that the life and work they describe are available to any person, regardless of economic circumstance, social position, or education. What neither tells us is what our lives and the lives of our students will look or be like if we undertake this work; we only know at the end that all our lives will be different than they are today if we teach as disciplined persons of prayer and invite our students into a similar practice of single-minded attentiveness to God.

CHAPTER 3

Life Together as Teacher and Learner

The year was 1935 in Hitler's Germany. A young Lutheran pastor and scholar, responding to an appeal from his denominational superiors, left his self-imposed exile in London to organize and lead a clandestine seminary for twenty-five pastors-in-training in the Confessing Church. The account of their attempt to live as an intentional Christian community of learning and ministry is the subject of their leader's 1938 publication, *Life Together*. The ideas and insights Dietrich Bonhoeffer shared in that small volume were a witness then and remain a testimony now to the formative potential of a model of teaching and learning that is deliberately communal in nature.

Much of the rhetoric associated with education in the United States has eschewed communal language, emphasizing instead the nurture of individual potential for the sake of personal achievement and success. Parker Palmer, in a critique of conventional education systems, contends that "conventional pedagogy is not only non-communal but anticommunal" because of its expectation of competition among students and its tendency to dismiss most types of cooperative efforts as cheating.[1] He labels the common practice of gathering students into classroom-based groups "a mere pedagogical convenience" for the sake of delivering information more efficiently, rather than the creation of true communities of learning.[2] He likens our conventional attempts to teach and learn in such settings to the story of Adam and Eve in the garden of Eden, where the lures of personal knowledge and power distract us from seeking together "a knowledge that calls for our own conversion."[3]

Conversion lay at the heart of Bonhoeffer's vision for the Finkenwalde seminary. He wrote that "the goal of all Christian community" is for persons to "meet one another as bringers of the message of salvation."[4] The Word of God is both author and subject of Christian communal life; in such a community, we are and learn to become by the grace of God the body of Christ. Bonhoeffer warns against the dangers of dreaming up ideals of Christian community that do not recognize first and foremost the central role of divine grace in shaping our life together. He urges us to approach others with our desire for community out of gratitude for all God has done and will continue to do in our lives: "Because God has already laid the only foundation of our fellowship, because God has bound us together in one body with other Christians in Jesus Christ, long before we entered into common life with them, we enter into that common life not as demanders but as thankful recipients."[5] Communities of learning, then, draw their life and truth from our grateful response to God's gracious and creative presence among God's people.

Palmer draws from the desert fathers a related conclusion. He tells a story about Abba Felix, who names the brokenness of the monastic community as the reason for God's silence in their world. The Abba, who had been the mouthpiece of God for the other brothers, was no longer receiving from God words for the community because the members of the community were no longer seeking to live out the good news they had already heard. The brothers beg the Abba to tell them something, anything, that will satisfy their need to believe that God is still revealing Godself to them. But the Abba observes that the relationship between teaching and learning had been broken by the inactivity of the learners, and so a word from him will not satisfy the brothers' true need to know God. Palmer reflects, "Abba Felix tells us that if truth is to be taught, then teaching and learning must take the shape of truth itself—a community of faithful relationships. Education in truth must bring teacher and students and subject into troth with each other, into the very image of the truth it hopes to convey."[6] If either teachers or students refuse to be in genuine relationship with one another or, indeed, with the subject of their study, then true education cannot occur.

Palmer does not tell the story of Abba Felix in order to establish or reinforce a hierarchical relationship of teacher over student, even though he could argue that the Abba is more learned and experienced with regard to spiritual matters. Instead, Palmer uses the story of Abba Felix to redefine the theological concept of obedience in a way that encourages mutuality in the life teachers and students have together. He begins by examining the etymology of the term and its significance for our understanding of the concept in relation to spiritual formation: "The word 'obedience' does not mean slavish, uncritical adherence; it comes from the Latin root *audire*, which means 'to listen.' Obedience requires the discerning ear, the ear that listens to the reality of the situation, a listening that allows the hearer to respond to that reality, whatever it may be."[7] The Abba's students failed to be obedient because they were not listening to the Abba's words in a way that generated the fruit of the Spirit in their lives in response to the Spirit's articulations via the Abba's mouth. The Abba, on the other hand, modeled obedience by listening intently to the true needs of his students and responding with teaching that refused to give the students what they had requested (yet one more repetition of a truth they do not really want to hear) and instead provided a way for them to reestablish the necessary habit of careful listening. The story of Abba Felix invites both teachers and students to participate in an educational community designed to encourage faithfully listening to where the reality of God's desires for God's people meets the realities of our needs in any particular time and place.

Holy Listening

In the parlance of some spiritual direction literature, the practice of "holy listening" is a way of being with others in which we are fully present and attentive to the ones who have invited us to accompany them on their spiritual journey. Margaret Guenther suggests the role of a spiritual teacher/director is to be "deeply attentive to the person sitting across the holy space, open and permeable to all that is said and unsaid, revealed and hidden [so that] by example and by judicious interpretation, she helps the directee toward equal openness and attentiveness."[8] This directing is not an easy task; Guenther observes that both students and teachers are more inclined to listen for what they want or expect to hear rather than remain open to what God will reveal to the attentive. Jesus calls the crowd's attention to this human proclivity when he reminds them of their lukewarm response to John the Baptist's prophetic words and enjoins, "Let anyone with ears listen!" (Mt. 11:15)[9] The apostle Paul, preaching to the Romans from a text taken from the prophet Isaiah, also underscores this perennial problem: "For this people's heart has grown dull, and their ears are hard of hearing, and they have shut their eyes; so that they might not look with their eyes, and listen with their ears, and understand with their heart and turn—and I would heal them" (Acts 28:27).[10] Even among those who might count themselves attentive to God—those, even, who would be teachers—the temptation to stop our ears when God is speaking is great. Jesus sometimes despaired of his own disciples, those he intended to send out as teachers to the nations, ever hearing the genuine good news he was proclaiming. "Do you have ears, and fail to hear?" he asked them after the miracle of feeding the four thousand leaves them still worrying about where their next meal is coming from (Mk. 8:1–21). Listening attentively to God's word is difficult work; and for the teacher whose task is to prepare the space for the truth to receive such a careful hearing, obstacles can stop the ears of both teacher and student and complicate the task.

Listening for an Ordinary Word

One potential obstacle is an insistence that God's word make itself heard in a dramatic way. Guenther writes:

> In this we resemble Naaman the leper, a powerful general who traveled from Syria to seek healing from the prophet Elisha. Elisha did not meet him in person, but sent a messenger to tell him to wash himself in the River Jordan. Outraged at the matter-of-fact simplicity of the proposed treatment, Naaman exclaimed: "Behold, I thought that for me he would surely come out, and stand, and call on the name of the Lord his God, and would wave his hand over the spot, and cure the leprosy!"[11]

More is going on in this story than a high-ranking official demanding to be treated with a respect he imagines is due him because of his station in life. Naaman also brings his cultural assumption that power must manifest itself in particular ways or it is not genuine power. He cannot imagine a form of divine power that doesn't assert itself in the manner to which he is accustomed, and so he cannot hear in Elisha's message a word from God for him. Fortunately, his servants are not hindered by the same assumption, and they step in to encourage Naaman to hear the message given him in a different light: "Father, if the prophet had commanded you to do something difficult, would you not have done it? How much more, when all he said to you was, 'Wash, and be clean'?" (2 Kings 5:13). Their willingness to point out another way of interpreting what he had heard created a space in which Naaman could enact the word of God and discover the wholeness that comes from careful listening. As spiritual teachers, we must embody the role modeled by Naaman's servants and encourage students to set aside their cultural assumptions about how God works in favor of exploring what God is actually doing in their lives.

Creating Time and Space

A second obstacle is our unwillingness to take the time and create the space required to listen carefully to one another. Henri Nouwen observes that it is difficult to practice this kind of hospitality with others, for the other is a stranger, someone different from and possibly even unknown to us, and such otherness can generate fear and defensiveness. Confronted with persons who do not share our perspective or experience God in exactly the same way we do, we may feel compelled to convert them to our way of thinking or anxiously await their judgment on the authenticity of our spirituality. As teachers, we may fear that other, more persuasive, voices may subvert our planned agenda or that persons will pose questions and offer insights that confuse us or reveal our ignorance of spiritual matters. Nouwen's reflections suggest that we must acknowledge this "back-stage hostility" before we can begin to offer true hospitality to our students.[12] He urges us to imagine hospitable space as an environment in which persons can encounter and be changed by God rather than subtly expected to become an adherent of the teacher's way of life.

We must not only contend with our own fears and anxieties; we must also prepare ourselves for our students' suspicion that we might be trying to make them over in our image rather than inviting them to explore their own likeness in the *imago dei*. Nouwen warns that the work of a teacher committed to hospitality

> is like the task of a patrolman trying to create some space in the middle of a mob of panic-driven people for an ambulance to reach the center of the accident. Indeed, more often than not rivalry and competition, desire for power and immediate results, impatience and frustration, and, most of all, plain fear make their forceful demands and tend to fill every possible empty corner [of the space we have carved out].[13]

These spiritual stumbling blocks and trip wires can clutter a learning space with so much debris that teachers and students may spend more time picking their way through the rubble than engaging in thoughtful and attentive conversation with one another and God.

A particularly large boulder in this problematic landscape is our and our students' preoccupation with maintaining the personal worldviews we have cultivated for ourselves. When someone else talks about experiences or asks questions that do not reflect our own way of being and concerns, we may politely nod and superficially affirm their right to say what they are saying, but we don't permit their words to challenge our own well-guarded and familiar perspective:

> Preoccupations are our fearful ways of keeping things the same, and it often seems that we prefer a bad certainty to a good uncertainty. Our preoccupations help us to maintain the personal world we have created over the years and block the way to revolutionary change. Our fears, uncertainties and hostilities make us fill our inner world with ideas, opinions, judgments and values to which we cling as to a precious property. Instead of facing the challenge of new worlds opening themselves for us, and struggling in the open field, we hide behind the walls of our concerns holding on to the familiar life items we have collected in the past.[14]

Palmer calls this a "dangerous subjectivism" in which we are tempted to settle "for a truth that consists of little more than our private perceptions and needs."[15] Our fears restrict us to what little truth we can put together from our limited, individual spiritual experiences and our uncritical acceptance of our feelings of comfort and discomfort as satisfactory judges of what is right and good for us. Julian of Norwich, a fourteenth century Christian mystic, captures well the spiritual dilemma such subjectivism creates:

> This is the reason why we have no ease of heart or soul, for we are seeking our rest in trivial things which cannot satisfy, and not seeking to know God, almighty, all-wise, all-good. [God] is true rest. It is [God's] will that we should know [God], and [God's] pleasure that we should rest in [God]. Nothing less will satisfy us.[16]

When we as teachers set aside our own preoccupations and fears, we can better invite our students to seek their rest in God rather than in the unsatisfactory trivialities offered them by the gods of consumerism, professional achievement, and social status. We can cultivate a kind of careful and critical listening to one another that encourages students to talk about their unholy desires, their paralyzing fears, and their ineffectual but cherished defenses. Such sharing requires us to model vulnerability in our own reflections and to establish guidelines for the group that safeguard the confidentiality and respect for others necessary to support risk taking in the quest for truth.

Fostering Religious Imagination

A third obstacle is our failure of imagination. In *Sensing Beauty*, John Eusden and John Westerhoff write:

> All learning depends on the ability to image, to picture both accurately and imaginatively. We can deceive ourselves if we do not image accurately the way things appear, but we also need to be able to perceive what is not visible—to vision, to see, to picture with the imagination. All learning and growth depend on the combination of these abilities.
>
> To vision the good, the true, and the beautiful; to image reality as it is now and as it might be; to perceive the difference— these capabilities are needed for any human community. To make images of reality so it cannot be missed and to make images of a vision desired can help to make possible the closing of the gap between them.[17]

Perhaps this is why the scriptural admonishments that those who have ears ought to hear are almost always accompanied by similar injunctions to open our eyes and see. The King James translation of Proverbs 29:18 observes, "Where there is no vision, the people perish"; and the footnote in the Scofield version is quick to point out that the choice of the word *vision* here "indicates a revelation from God, such as the visions that the prophets saw."[18] The *New Revised Standard Version* substitutes *prophecy* for the word *vision* in the earlier translation, in part to clarify the same issue noted in C. I. Scofield's notes. The vision we need to have is a prophetic one that sees reality as it is and imagines how God wants it to be. Furthermore, the NRSV replaces "perish" with the more literal phrase "cast off restraint," not because a loss of vision isn't deadly, but because to have no vision—no sense of God's way of seeing the world—with which to align our lives deprives us of a referent structure by which our activities come to have existential meaning and purpose. Without visionary restraints to order our lives, we are as good as dead spiritually.

Religious educator Maria Harris points us toward the work of Paul Ricoeur for further understanding of the role of religious imagination in spiritual formation. She quotes from his discussion of human salvation in *History and Truth* his observation that "the imagination is par excellence, the instituting and constituting of what is humanly possible; in imagining possibilities, human beings act as prophets of their own existence."[19] Ricoeur is pointing to the ability of religious imagination to alter our perceptions of what the purposes and structures of our lives are, to challenge our assumptions about what is real in God's sight and what is illusory despite its popular acceptance as inherent truth. Religious imagination opens up new possibilities for how we think about situations and respond to them.

Beginning from this starting point and drawing on the reflections of Philip Wheelwright regarding artistic imagination, Harris suggests that religious imagination has "contemplative, ascetic, creative, and sacramental" characteristics.[20] The contemplative aspect involves attentive listening to and being in the presence of God so that God might reveal Godself and God's vision to us. The ascetic dimension creates the necessary detachment from the human propensity to want to make others over in our image, allowing us to participate in holy listening with others. Imagination in its creative aspect stirs the heart and mind with new images and provocative ideas that challenge the hegemony of our current understandings and practices. It is thus also sacramental, for it is able to mediate the holy in ways that transform the body of Christ.

Teaching that fosters the religious imagination is rich in symbols, images, rituals, poetic language, music, dance, and all other forms of artistic expression that encourage creative interpretation of beliefs and experiences. It also welcomes silence and stillness as friends who lead us into relationship with the God of mystery. It offers freedom from personal and communal bondage through communal practices of detachment from cultural expectations and destructive social norms. It creates a numinous space in which revelation can and does occur. We teach with the hope of creating the conditions necessary for "revelatory moments," and such revelations are the basis for our communion as the saints of God.[21]

Julian of Norwich

A classical example of the kind of visionary imagination we need to cultivate as a community of faith can be found in Julian of Norwich's *Revelations of Divine Love*. Living in England in the latter half of the fourteenth century, Julian, at the self-professed age of thirty and one half years, received a series of sixteen visions that she and others believed were a response to her fervent prayers for greater understanding of and participation in the passionate love of Christ. She was deathly ill at the time of the "showings" and perceived the illness itself as a response to a petition for God's purging of her sins so that she might grow closer to her Savior. Following her recovery, Julian wrote an account of her visions, which she then expanded twenty years later to include her ensuing meditations on the sixteen revelations and their meaning for Christian belief and life. This later account is especially useful as a contemporary tutor regarding the power and necessity of religious imagination for teaching and learning.

Julian describes her visions as manifesting themselves in multiple ways. She wrote, "All this blessed teaching of our Lord was shown in three ways: by physical sight, by words formed in my intellect, and by spiritual sight."[22] Her descriptions of the visual images of Christ that appeared before her eyes are like the prophet Isaiah's account of his vision before the throne of God, and her rendering of God's words to her reflect the same mix of conversation and proclamation recorded in Isaiah 6. In addition, these things she saw with her eyes and heard with her ears were accompanied by theological insights and practical "ahas" also given by God to her "spiritual sight," allowing her to see, hear, and know more than the images and words might plainly convey. These insights and practical implications came to her as extensions of and elaborations on the word of God already revealed to Julian and the church through the scriptures and the community of faith. Her visions are set within and illuminate the life of the Christian community; they are recognizable as God-given visions because of their ability to speak to the needs of the church in her day. Julian did not interpret her visions as a call to throw out the basic doctrines of the church or sever ties with institutional Christianity. She wrote, "And in this blessed revelation I saw nothing counter to what had been already revealed."[23] Nor did Julian share her visions in order to call attention to herself or to enhance her reputation as a spiritual teacher.

> So I beg you all for God's sake, and advise you for your own, to stop thinking about the poor wretch who was shown these things, and with all your strength, wisdom, and humility look at God, that in [God's] loving courtesy and eternal goodness [God] may be willing to show it to all and sundry, to our own great comfort.[24]

Her desire is to know and make known the amazing and mysterious love of God in Christ for the edification of all.

Julian understood that God employed her imagination in giving the visions. She wrote of being "led in imagination" to see an image of humanity comforted[25] and of seeing heaven "in my imagination" as a house overseen by God, the divine host.[26] She also perceived that God was making certain images available to her by bringing them to mind[27] or using experiences that "lifted my mind to heaven,"[28] where images of heavenly things could be seen. Her final vision occurred as a dream, the stirring of her imagination by God in her sleep.[29] Throughout the *Revelations*, the creative aspect of human imagination is portrayed as a useful tool for divine revelation, and Julian seeks to experience God and understand the teachings of the church by offering her imagination to God for whatever God might chose to reveal through it.

Sometimes Julian worried that her visions were not dramatic enough to be actual revelations, succumbing to the same obstacle of grandiose expectations that can cause us to stumble. Of the second showing, in which she saw Christ's battered face, she wrote, "This second revelation seemed so ordinary and commonplace that I was much perplexed when I saw it. I was worried, afraid, and anxious, wondering for some time whether it were in fact a revelation."[30] Only after wrestling with this concern for a time and waiting for "greater insight" from God did she receive the spiritual wisdom necessary to make sense of what she had seen in a spiritually formative way. She discovered that the image of Christ's face revealed to her more clearly the ways in which human sinfulness causes human suffering and obscures the beauty and goodness of God's love and creativity.

Julian also struggled with the problem of preoccupation identified by Nouwen. In her writings about the seventh vision, she describes alternating between "a supreme and spiritual pleasure" and "a sense of loneliness and depression, and the futility of life."[31] She believed that God gave her both experiences so that she might understand and embrace God's presence in both emotional spaces, rather than lose touch with God in times of fear, suffering, and doubt. While she identified her preoccupation as a divinely-inspired teaching moment, she includes in her commentary an admonishment of those who would retreat into the preoccupations that torment them: "It is not God's will therefore that we should grieve and sorrow over our present sufferings, but rather that we should leave them at once, and keep ourselves in his everlasting joy."[32] The risk of losing ourselves in our fears and doubts is even greater if we do not recognize our preoccupations as sufferings to be lamented, but embrace them in the form of Palmer's "dangerous subjectivism" as an alternative form of salvation. The power inherent in the vivid images Julian shares with us from her divinely-inspired imagination is the ability of her visions to establish a framework within which our own imaginations loose themselves from the bonds of subjectivism and meet God.

A Creative Life Together

Pastor and seminary professor Eugene Peterson once told an interviewer, "We must see the imagination as an aspect of ministry. What we're really talking about is creativity. We're participating in something that God is doing. [God] is creating new life."[33] When we come together as teachers and learners, we also come together as persons called by God to participate in the ongoing creation of God's realm on earth. When we gather to bring the salvation story alive again for each other, we continue God's work of incarnating the good news in human form. The teacher, on behalf of her- or himself and a group of students, cannot accomplish alone either of these activities, which are really elements of one another. The teacher's task is to guide students in the formation of a community of teaching and learning that practices holy listening, welcomes the "strangeness" in each participant that separates us from one another, and cultivates the religious imagination in all its aspects. Put simply, teachers invite students to join them in developing ears that hear and eyes that see God's transformational activity in the world and chose to respond to this activity by offering their God-given talents and abilities in this work. Personal and cultural resistance to this shared responsibility to hear, see, and respond to God can be intense; and the desire on a single teacher's part to create a creative learning environment is only the beginning of the process. Developing a transformative life together as teachers and learners is a lifelong process of becoming by the grace of God the one body in Christ that God has already made us to be.

PART II

Contexts of Teaching

CHAPTER 4

The Contemporary Search for Spirituality

Christians have long pointed to culture as a significant factor in shaping the way persons experience, interpret, and engage the holy. Some, like the desert fathers and mothers discussed in chapter 1, found the political, socioeconomic, and civil religious systems of their fourth-century world distracted their attention from God in such a way that they felt compelled to leave behind the world as they experienced it and seek God's face in less culturally "noisy" places. They created alternative monastic cultures where they could engage in the work of prayer and contemplation. These new cultures were not without their own distractive elements; the desert ascetics discovered that many of the concerns of the society they had abandoned still held considerable sway over their internal thoughts and orientations. As Douglas Burton-Christie writes, separating from their cultures of origin and reorienting their hearts and minds on God required a "long process of purification"[1] in which the renunciation of worldly possessions and ideals could take greater and greater hold. Christie notes that the desert fathers and mothers "recognized that attachment to things could compromise the freedom from care which the solitary life promised them; that possessions could inflame desires to the point where they became all-consuming."[2] They left behind all they had in a bid to break free from that which they considered spiritually deadening and find spiritual life.

Seventeenth century English Puritans also feared the corrupting influences of their cultural context. John Bunyan's classic spiritual allegory from that time, *The Pilgrim's Progress*, endeavors to show the dangers of adopting a "worldly-wise" approach to life by introducing to readers lamentable characters by the names of Mr. Worldly-Wiseman, Mr. Legality, Civility, Formalist, and Hypocrisy.[3] Bunyan's hero, Christian, leaves neighbors and family to "seek an inheritance, incorruptible, undefiled" by "all the world."[4] Like Saint Augustine before him, Bunyan had a vision of a God-ruled city that stood in marked contrast to the social systems and beliefs of his time. His message was that one's culture is not to be trusted as one's guide when eternal life is at stake.

Some early twentieth century Christians envisioned a potentially positive role for culture to play in forming persons in faith even as they remained aware of problematic cultural influences. Walter Rauschenbusch, a theologian identified with the founding of the American social gospel movement, celebrated conjugal and parental love relationships as inspirational personal and social experiences that could teach Christians much about the love of God. He counted democratic forms of government as means and signs of the establishment of God's realm on earth because they created "social solidarity" among God's people.[5] He also contended that "super-personal forces of evil" in the guise of institutional corruption in the church, state, and business world threatened to undermine "the purity of family life" he believed so necessary to Christian nurture.[6]

H. Richard Niebuhr, writing just thirty years after Rauschenbusch, took up the question of culture's relationship to Christian faith quite directly in a series of lectures published in book form as *Christ and Culture*. He defined culture as "that total process of human activity and that total result of such activity…[commonly called] civilization…[which] comprises language, habits, ideas, beliefs, customs, social organization, inherited artifacts, technical processes, and values."[7] He then suggested that Christian thinkers across time have identified five types of relationships between Christ, the embodiment of human spiritual perfection, and culture. Two types establish the ends of the spectrum by, in one case, describing Christ and culture as two realities in opposition with one another and, in the other, as two realities in agreement. The three remaining types fall between the two poles, characterizing Christ and the Christian life as superior to culture, in ongoing paradoxical tension with culture, or as a force transforming culture.[8] At the conclusion of his discussion, he noted that all talk about God and the spiritual life is conducted by humans who make decisions from "relative points of view and relative evaluations" shaped by their cultural location.[9] Hence, he believed that Christians are called to make faithful decisions "in view of the fact that the world of culture—[humanity's] achievement—exists within the world of grace—God's Kingdom."[10]

These historic testimonies to the unavoidable interactions between culture and spirituality suggest that we too need to consider the role culture plays in our lives and the lives of those we teach. How do the various aspects of human life that Niebuhr attributed to culture affect contemporary persons' engagement in and resistance to learning about Christian life? What assumptions about the nature and purposes of spirituality do these aspects   cultivate? What resistances to cultural assumptions and practices might need to be cultivated in our time? What cultural forces lend themselves to the nurture of robust spiritual lives and deserve our support? Studying the effects of culture on persons' spiritual formation creates new openings for teachers to connect meaningfully with the issues and concerns that contemporary learners bring to their spiritual explorations. Evaluating those effects in light of Christian tradition assists teachers in challenging learners to join with all the saints through Christian history in recognizably faithful practices of discipleship.

Sociological Research

In the mid-1990s, religious sociologist Robert Wuthnow embarked on research designed to describe and analyze American concepts and practices of spirituality since World War II. The project involved interviews with two hundred people, multiple surveys of public opinions about spirituality, and reviews of previous studies and published commentaries by other scholars. Wuthnow concluded that shifting cultural paradigms in the United States have radically altered persons' perceptions of spirituality. He argues in *After Heaven: Spirituality in America Since the 1950s* that "a traditional spirituality of inhabiting sacred places has given way to a new spirituality of seeking [in which persons] increasingly negotiate among competing glimpses of the sacred, seeking partial knowledge and practical wisdom."[11] The traditional spirituality to which he refers has been strongly associated in the United States with Christian houses of worship, and the decline of this "dwelling spirituality" (to use Wuthnow's classification) is presumed to be one reason for the decline in church affiliation and attendance among mainstream Protestants.[12]

Among the cultural changes Wuthnow documents are shifts in work/life patterns and beliefs, altered perceptions of institutions and authority, and evolving social issues that affect relationships and values. He notes that persons no longer expect to spend the bulk of their time living and working in a single job in the same community; instead, commuting, interstate transfers, and career changes are part of a typical worker's experience. He suggests that the rise of professionalism and new economic patterns of consumption generated by sophisticated marketing campaigns have also produced "a shift from spiritual production to spiritual consumption," in which Americans expect religious "experts" to produce spiritual goods for consumption by the masses.[13] He chronicles our movement from institutionally-prescribed rules and behavior to lifestyles constructed through media messages and social negotiation among relatively valued moral options. Individual and social identity, he says, are no longer ascribed by authoritative communities or achieved through attaining significant institutional positions. Instead, persons negotiate their social status using a wide range of moral frameworks and social practices, and a person's identity may be constructed differently in various settings.[14] An adolescent may have one type of status within the family, another in the school setting, and a third on the neighborhood corner, with each identity being constructed and performed according to the particular social norms and habits valued in those settings. An adult may excuse or even engage in behavior at work or at a party that he or she would condemn in familial relationships because of the assumption that separate moral codes can be associated with different social settings. Settings may still provide some degree of control over what can be negotiated in each space because of lingering elements of prescriptive social authority within them, but overarching social mores no longer connect and dominate all social arenas.

Wuthnow describes various stages within these change trajectories that roughly correspond with certain decades in twentieth century American history. He associates the 1950s with a period of church-based institutional power that extended to homes, schools, businesses, and governmental bodies. Spirituality was equated with church membership; persons were expected to conform their beliefs and practices to the expectations of a congregation that was "comfortable, familiar, domestic, offering an image of God that was basically congruent with the domestic tranquility of the ideal home."[15] In this era declarations of Christian faith ("in God we trust," "one nation under God") were added to American currency and to the pledge of allegiance.[16] Christian identity relied primarily on one's uncritical acceptance of the faith offered by the neighborhood church and the church's acknowledgement of one as a morally upright citizen in the community.

The social experimentation and unrest of the 1960s disrupted the orderly spirituality of the church. Wuthnow observes:

> The sixties questioned middle-class, white-bread definitions of who God was and of where God could be found, making it more uncertain how to be in touch with the sacred. In this process, more Americans drew inspiration from the struggles of the poor, from the rich spiritual traditions of African Americans, from other world religions, from rock music and contemporary art, and from changing understandings of gender and sexuality. If the result was more complex, it was at least more true to the broad variety of human experience.[17]

Wuthnow contends that the 1960s and early 1970s emphasis on "freedom of choice" emerged as a response to a growing awareness of multiple and diverse communities of belief and practice and an extension of the length of time young adults spent exploring life options before settling down to begin a family.[18] The concept of "spirituality" was fractured from "religion," and many people began to equate genuine spirituality with insights and actions leading to social change rather than with church membership. Practices of contemplation and meditation remained meaningful for some as ways of tending to their "spirit" while they engaged in social activism. Young people encouraged one another to dabble in a variety of spiritual traditions in search of practices to promote inner and social peace.

Much like a pendulum swinging from one extreme to another, the late 1970s and 1980s saw the emergence of a strictly disciplined form of Christian spirituality as a corrective response to the seemingly unbridled freedom of the preceding era. The Moral Majority attempted to control human behavior through legislating conservative religious codes of conduct. In such an approach, "moral and spiritual discipline was promoted in the name of the social order itself, almost as if clear rules for individual behavior could substitute for the sacred dwellings in which Americans were presumed to have lived in the past."[19] Wuthnow points out, however, that American interpretations of spiritual discipline varied, creating multiple ways in which persons permitted themselves to shape and be shaped by their culture and beliefs. Some persons adopted a "discipline of detachment," in which they tried to learn to give up control of their environment and "be content with circumstances as they are."[20] Congregations and some self-help groups promoted a related form of spiritual discipline, in which cultivating a positive and cheerful attitude was the overarching and daily goal. Still others focused on receiving "divine guidance" through their spiritual practices; although, Wuthnow observes, "People talked about receiving divine guidance, but what they meant, when pressed to explain, was that they felt better about what they were already doing."[21] Discipline was also defined as living out a commonsense belief in the goodness of humans and their ability to fashion a good life for themselves. Wuthnow identifies Ronald Reagan as the epitome of this kind of spiritually disciplined person. The 1980s, then, promoted spiritual practices that would alleviate people's guilt about wanting things for themselves and reassure them that they deserved and were capable of achieving a good and happy life as the culture was depicting it.[22]

Wuthnow associates two trends with the spirituality of the late 1980s and 1990s. Illustrated by the popularity of the television show *Touched by an Angel* the first was a widespread interest in miracles and ephemeral beings. As society became increasingly focused on individual experience and growth, people began seeking emotional and specific encounters with a sacred realm that had seemed lost among the secularity of their environment. These encounters acted as emotional comfort and as confirmation of a person's inherent goodness rather than as harbingers of God's terrifying and awe-inspiring power.[23] They are "proof" of an unexplainable reality beyond the everyday, but their very inexplicable nature means they require little time or attention beyond grateful acceptance of them as a useful part of a self-affirming worldview. They fit well with the second trend of the last decade of the twentieth century: a spirituality consisting of nothing more than one's personal and individual experience of that which is presumed to be sacred. This form of spirituality understands the person as a seeker on a journey to discover the self as a being with sacred power and significance. Wuthnow reflects: "The potential for spiritual insight is everywhere; it must, however, be sought. Indeed, the process of seeking, the journey, now becomes more important than the destination."[24] The spiritual journey becomes its own religion apart from God and faithfulness to God. Wuthnow cites M. Scott Peck's perspective that "everyone has religion because religion is simply one's understanding of life."[25]

Religious sociologists have reflected on the various ways in which persons who came of age in these distinctive social eras have become cohorts who represent the spirituality of that time. A contemporary faith community is not only a reflection of current social norms; it also contains within it the strata of historical views on spirituality embodied by the generations who participate in it. Nancy Eiesland and Stephen Warner suggest that congregational leaders need to conduct an "ecological analysis" of their faith community and its neighborhood if they want to understand how this phenomenon and other aspects of the church's social environment affect people's beliefs and practices.[26] In particular, they point to the diverse ways in which individuals use their particular histories, expectations, and cultural contexts to attach spiritual meaning to their activities. Mapping the connections persons construct to help them negotiate the various implicit and explicit factors in their day-to-day meaning-making offers one way of identifying the spiritual strata present in a group. A retired couple who came of age in the 1950s is much more likely to construct connections that represent the "dwelling" orientation toward spirituality described by Wuthnow than is a young adult who attended college in the 1990s and has moved and pursued multiple casual relationships while seeking career advancement and intimacy. The latter may participate in a congregation primarily for its young adult group or because the services of worship generate a good feeling about life; the former may attend services faithfully each week because they cannot imagine another option for those who would consider themselves good moral citizens. The forty-something caught in the "sandwich generation" of simultaneously raising young children and caring for elderly parents may seek in congregational life a reinforcing structure for the late 1970s and 1980s spiritual discovery of discipline as the key to successful living. In each case, their perspectives on spirituality shape their encounter with the contemporary church and were shaped by the social contexts of their earlier years as well as the social norms and practices of the early twenty-first century.

Theological Reflection

Anglican theologian Rowan Williams offers a theological analysis of shifting Western understandings of spirituality that is based on changes in the cultural context. He contends that contemporary societies have taken to creating icons out of famous people who are affirmed as "a classic statement of a particular kind of life" and who become "in some way an image that binds people together, provides a common point of reference and a common touchstone of acceptability."[27] This is lamentable because it focuses our attention on what we find engaging within human society and limits our imagination and our awareness of God's transcendence of human perspectives. Williams argues that Christians need to rediscover the notion of an icon as a passageway that enables some aspect of divine reality to shine forth less fettered by human assumptions and expectations. He suggests that cultures throughout the ages have constructed social icons to help communities glimpse the spiritual realm and choose to order their affairs in relation to those visions. He warns that societies that disconnect their icons from the transcendent risk losing the human soul to its fictitious alter ego: "[t]he controlled self, making its dispositions in a vacuum of supposed consumer freedom and determining the clothing in which it will appear."[28]

Michael Warren, a Roman Catholic professor of religious education, claims that congregations are complicit in this exchange when their activities, and specifically, their services of worship, do more to assist persons in avoiding a God of radical and life-changing power than to create a space where God can transform those assembled. He resists the impulse of both dwelling and seeking spiritualities to equate goodness with participation in a particular ritual or practice. Instead, he argues that genuine Christian spirituality links ritual actions with "implications for how a community lives out its relatedness, its resources, and its obedience to God."[29] He would reject the coziness of a 1950s-formed spirituality because it does not question the prescribed norms of social behavior upon which it is based. He would applaud the 1960s spiritual orientation toward linking contemplative practices with social activism, but not that era's detachment of religion from spirituality. The notions of spiritual discipline that mark spiritualities formed in the late 1970s and 1980s would be disqualified because of their emphasis on individual happiness and success rather than the coming of God's realm for all. One need not even speculate as to his assessment of the spirituality of the late 1980s and 1990s; contemporary society's trivialization and dismissal of the transcendent and of our human need for daily transformation by God provoke his current role as a prophet calling God's people back to a relationship with the Holy One.

Warren challenges us to see that the assumptions shaping our everyday lives have consequences for the way we pray and act and, hence, for our spirituality. Drawing on the work of French sociologist Pierre Bourdieu, he argues that secular economic, political, and social structures have tremendous power to generate the kinds of spiritual orientations in people these structures need for perpetuation. It is therefore not sufficient for the church to think of spirituality only in terms of whether or not people pray or gather with a community to worship. Christian spirituality is also about the "attitude and commitment found in the behavioral patterns of daily life" and how well these embodied orientations testify to the Christian gospel.[30] Warren contends that the "life practice" of most North Americans testifies to narcissistic beliefs in individualism, consumerism, and relativism, easily identified by a simple inventory of one's wallet and date book.[31] Quoting John Kavanaugh, he writes, "The great paradox of finding one's identity in wealth is ultimately the paradox of all idolatries: entrusting ourselves to our products, our silver and golden gods, *we become fashioned—re-created—in their image and likeness.*"[32] For a people created originally in the image of God, such refashioning is an affront to the Creator and a fall from grace for God's people.

Miroslav Volf approaches the theological significance of the interplay among socially-constructed beliefs and practices and Christian claims in a similar fashion. He writes:

> right practices well practiced *are likely to* open persons for insights into beliefs to which they would otherwise be closed. Inversely, wrong practices can "suppress the truth" (Romans 1:18)—that is, have an adverse impact on which beliefs are deemed true and how beliefs that are deemed true are understood.[33]

Thus, the person who has been re-created in the image of the consummate consumer may reject the idea of *imago dei* as hopelessly irrelevant to a twenty-first century way of life because the marketing images that guide his or her purchases have already imbedded themselves deep within the human psyche and other possibilities simply can't compete. The preference for "new and improved" ideas and images crowds out consideration of older concepts. The consumer may even conclude that to accept an identity as one made in the image of God is to fall from the higher advertiser-conferred status as minor deity and lord of one's personal realm. The gospel is considered and found wanting in relation to the beliefs produced alongside the goods purchased and consumed.

Consider the cultural shift to support concepts of spiritual discipline during the late 1970s and 1980s. Discipline has been an aspect of spiritual formation throughout the life of the church, but the meanings assigned to the concept in the recent past took their power from the culture of upward mobility associated with climbing the corporate ladder, the "let go and let God" rhetoric of twelve step programs, and postmodern doubts about Truth with a capital *T*. These orientations may resist and even replace historic spiritual metaphors of ascent (discussed in chapter 6) and accountable adherence to a spiritual rule conceived by a community of faith (chapter 7). The power of practices associated with a form of spiritual discipline designed to affirm and comfort the individual in her or his pursuit of the good life may impede consideration of other spiritual goals, for example, communion with God and justice for all God's people.

Palmer draws our attention in particular to the clash between historic concepts of spiritual freedom and obedience and the interpretations of those ideas in contemporary society. He points to the scriptural understanding of freedom as a state acquired only through obedience to God, in which one gains one's life by laying it down. He notes that the liberal ideal of education, which still holds some sway in institutions of higher education, resonates with this understanding in its desire to liberate persons through disciplined study from the limitations imposed on them by ignorance. Popular interpretations of these ideas, however, sever the relationship between the two.

> But today, we conceive of freedom and obedience as contra-dictory states. We regard freedom as the autonomy of the self-seeking self, the self cut loose from traditional and communal bonds, and we think of obedience as the act of slaves, not free persons."[34]

Palmer is quick to observe that those who have traditionally been coerced into obedience—women, persons of color, developing nations—are right to be suspicious of the relationship between the two when obedience has not been freely chosen. Nevertheless, he insists that the search for spiritual truth is a communal activity with commitments to life for all, not just for those who succeed in achieving personal wealth or social status.

Pedagogical Implications

These theological critiques of contemporary spiritualities suggest that those who teach need to create learning contexts that emphasize the communal, visionary, transformative, and practical aspects of Christian spirituality. This will not likely be an easy task, given the degree to which current social norms emphasize individuality, immediate gratification, human progress, and the separation of body and soul. Fortunately, Wuthnow offers us the idea of a "practice-oriented spirituality" into which we can invite persons who are willing to explore an alternative to their current understanding and practice of the spiritual life.

Wuthnow developed the concept of "practice-oriented spirituality" in response to interviews he had with persons who simultaneously found value and limitations in the "dwelling" and "seeker" spiritualities of their friends and families. These persons were uncomfortable relying on a particular religious community as their spiritual anchor or refuge, in part because of concerns about geographic mobility and in part because they did not share the dwelling orientation toward religious practice as a refuge from the world. However, they were strongly attracted to the communal emphasis characteristic of dwelling spirituality and to its historic function as a norm against which to measure one's beliefs and practices. They retained some of the skepticism of institutional religion common among their peers and believed in the mingling of the spiritual and the mundane that characterizes most seeker spiritualities. They rejected notions of absolute truth, but they also questioned the usefulness of an uncritical relativism for spiritual well-being. Wuthnow asserts that their form of spirituality is "a more orderly, disciplined, and focused approach to the sacred" than its seeker-oriented kin, observing:

> The people we talked to who were trying to practice their spirituality from day to day were not immune from having to choose what to do and where to focus their attention, but they tended to settle into a routine that permitted them to cultivate a deep spirituality rather than being influenced by their moods, circumstances, or exposure to constantly changing ideas.[35]

Practice-oriented spirituality is, then, a commitment to a particular and intentional way of life over a sustained period of time with the expectation of being spiritually anchored by one's practices rather than being dependent on specific locations or social frameworks to provide or define one's spirituality.

The practicality of this form of spirituality is apparent in the day-to-day engagement in a spiritual routine that keeps the minds and bodies of its practitioners focused on God and God's hopes for the world. The formation of daily habits of spiritual practice draws persons more deeply into the mind and heart of God, creating greater resistance to the spiritual trends and fads of any particular era. The shape of this routine is taken from the historic witness of the communities of Christian disciples who have gone before us; it reflects a thoughtful contemporary appropriation of classical spiritual disciplines. The practitioner never practices the faith alone; he or she is always part of a community of people scattered across time and space and yet engaged in similar routines. Practice-oriented spirituality is also transformative and visionary, both because of the way it reshapes the self-understanding of persons and because of the way it draws persons into relationships of care and compassion with others. Wuthnow explains:

> By engaging in spiritual practices, the practitioner retreats reflectively from the world in order to recognize how it is broken and in need of healing; then, in recognition that the world is also worthy of healing because of its sacral dimensions, the practitioner commits energy to the process of healing.[36]

The spiritual life thus becomes a movement between inward reflection and outward service, calling forth a new vision of the self as a child of God and the world as God's creation.

When we invite persons into a practice-oriented spirituality, we invite them to imagine themselves as members of a broad and diverse community of Christians to whom they are accountable for the continued witness of the gospel in our time. This sense of accountability can be nurtured through participation in a faith community that asks of its members, What are you doing each day to cultivate love of God and neighbor? We need to provide spaces where Christians share with one another details about the spiritual routines they are trying to establish, challenge each other to explore unfamiliar practices that might prove fruitful, encourage one another when old habits are hard to break and new ones difficult to establish, and pray for one another.

Palmer enumerates several tensions teachers must manage if such spaces are to be effectively created and sustained. One is the tension between openness and boundaries, a second is that between silence and speech, and a third between thinking and feeling. In order for a space to encourage openness, teachers must dispel the myth of their or any other group member's all-encompassing expertise and welcome difficult and probing questions while resisting the impulse to resolve each question in the time allotted. He notes what many pastors and Christian educators who have tried to recruit church school teachers already know: many people are afraid to teach because they don't want others to know how ignorant of spiritual and theological matters they are.[37] Those of us who do teach may mask this same insecurity with an over-abundance of descriptions and explanations designed to convey our knowledge and quash any questions we might not be able to answer. Palmer invites us to remember "that the anxiety created by our ignorance calls not for instant answers but for an adventure into the unknown," an adventure we share with others within the safe and confidential bounds of a covenanted group.[38] Rules of hospitable interaction designed to demonstrate concern for each person's spiritual struggles and insights help to keep the adventure a transformative rather than destructive experience for all participants.

The tension between silence and speech also needs our attention as teachers, but not in the usual way of planning lessons designed to keep a session moving so no awkward silences slow down or impede the learning process. Palmer urges us "to abandon the notion that 'nothing is happening' when it is silent, to see how much new clarity a silence often brings."[39] Even when we speak, he suggests that questions are often more effective than instructive words, in that questions encourage persons to listen for the responses God stirs within them and the additional questions those responses generate for their consideration.[40] Good teaching, then, leaves plenty of room for silence amidst the spoken words that provide useful information, personal experiences, and structures of accountability to the group's purposes.

The third tension, which is between thinking and feeling, can be a tricky one to manage. Given the propensity of several of the cultural contexts described by Wuthnow to encourage spiritualities concerned with self-help and self-development, participants in small learning communities may mistakenly try to engage in group therapy rather than spiritual exploration with one another. Taking one another's emotional temperatures can expand to the point that little time is left for group spiritual discernment of God's work in one another's lives, let alone for intellectual and experiential exploration of the varieties of spiritual practices that may shape and inform a life of faith. As teachers, we must guard against the equation of spiritual experience with emotional experience, while recognizing that learning takes place more fully when mind and emotions are both engaged in the process. Palmer reminds us that persons who participate in any kind of formal learning experience enter into that process with a variety of feelings, including fears, that must be acknowledged if they are to feel safe enough to risk learning something challenging.[41] Encouraging persons to share what they feel when they explore a practice as well as what they think the practice's purposes are and why it might generate resistance or approval in them generates both emotional and critical reflection. Providing information about the historical roots and theological rationales for practices and discussing the degree of authority these claims might have for contemporary persons' lives, while offering opportunities to experiment with the same practices and reflect on those experiences, challenges both mind and emotions to remain involved in spiritual exploration. Spiritual communities require teachers who care about what people think and how they feel, recognizing that thoughts and emotions inform one another in the same way that cultural contexts shape spiritual perspectives.

Neither we nor those we teach participate in spiritual life as disembodied or disconnected persons. All of who we are as physical beings and all that our cultural context has made us to be comes into play when we relate to the Creator as created beings. We come to spiritual formation already formed in part by God and in part by the social norms and practices of our coming-of-age years and our current life commitments. While God can be present in the latter forces, too often North American culture has misshaped us spiritually, creating a need for us to teach and be taught alternative possibilities for living faithfully as God's people. Creating intentional Christian relationships that embrace a practice-oriented spirituality is a mode of teaching that promises to offer such alternatives.

CHAPTER 5

Modes of Teaching the Spiritual Life

Teaching contexts and forms can extend beyond conventional church school classes and midweek Bible studies. In the history of Christian spiritual formation, the church school is quite recent. As Brett Webb-Mitchell suggests, "the church in its entirety is a school of Christian discipleship, a place and a people created and called by God, infused with the Holy Spirit, where we are to learn Christ, to follow Christ, and to be more like Christ in our daily lives."[1] He describes the ways in which Christian education has become focused on the individual rather than the community. He also describes the ways in which the church has turned the Bible "into an object of our investigation rather than a subject intended to engage us."[2] Webb-Mitchell's comments help make us aware of how the context in which we teach shapes our expectations about what teaching looks like. In a classroom, we tend to be focused on individual learners and information to be learned. But Webb-Mitchell encourages us to think about how the whole of church life is a classroom, teaching, instructing, and forming us as a community. He also encourages us to think about the work of Christian education less as learning information and more as "learning Christ," a learning that emphasizes who we are and what we do rather than what we know.

In this chapter, we explore several modes of teaching that, while possible in a conventional classroom setting, push against this setting and the typical forms that result from it. Although several of these modes seem to replicate hierarchical teacher/student relationships, these modes are more concerned with patterns of relationship through which we are helped to become more like Christ, knowing Christ in our bodies and hearts as well as in our minds. This is not to suggest that book learning is wrong (or else we would not bother writing and you would not bother reading), but that one kind of learning comes through particular forms of living and enables scripture or theological texts to open themselves to us. All of these modes depend on particular personal relationships that begin with a person who is seeking to fully, even perfectly, live the Christian life and who approaches a wise elder either in person or in writing. The persons in the relationships may be friends or companions, fellow members of a particular community or virtual strangers, but they are not equals. One is clearly the teacher, the other the student.

Webb-Mitchell explores the teacher/student relationship through the images of a master craftsperson and apprentice. The craft in which the apprentice is being shaped is that of "performing the gospel in Christly gestures."[3] Although these very names suggest a continuing hierarchy of knowledge and power, he reminds us that the goal is not to keep the apprentice in the mode of apprenticeship but for the apprentice to be so well-formed in Christly gesture as to be able to move into the role of a craftsperson teaching a new generation of apprentices.[4] Furthermore, in contrast to the popular American television version of this relationship, at no point in the apprenticeship of Christly gesture will the master say, "You're fired!" The hierarchy of knowledge and power present in this relationship is tempered by the power of grace. A time will come in the learning process when the apprentice will have the skills that equal or even surpass the teacher; a time may even come when the roles reverse, or when the apprentice leaves the "workshop" of one craftsperson for that of another to further hone the craft. Webb-Mitchell summarizes the process:

> For the apprentice, there is a beginning to the learning of the craft; in the intensification of learning there is a deepening of skill to better discern what is good versus what is of poor quality; and there is a period of passage, of leaving one's master to either come under the guidance of a new master or to become a master craftsperson who is ready to take on an apprentice.[5]

The three modes of teaching and learning we explore in this chapter all depend in some way on a master/apprentice relationship. These modes include the spiritual conference as exemplified in the work of the fourth century monk John Cassian, the spiritual correspondence of Jane de Chantal and Francis de Sales, and the spiritual biography of Antony as narrated by Athanasius.

The Spiritual Conference—John Cassian

John Cassian (ca. 360–435) remains an elusive but influential figure in the history of the church. His two primary works, the *Institutes* and the *Conferences*, were frequently published, abridged, prescribed for reading (for example, in the *Rule of Benedict*), and referred to. Alongside the sayings of the desert mothers and fathers, Cassian's work represents the fullest exploration of the purpose and practice of the Christian monastic in the first millennium of the church. As Columba Stewart notes, the themes of "purity of heart" and the "reign of heaven" underlie the whole of Cassian's theology.[6] The *Institutes* set out the rules of monasticism and explore the "origins, causes, and cures of the principle faults" or sins. In this sense, they address and structure the life of the "outer person" and are oriented toward purity of heart. The *Conferences* develop themes presented in the *Institutes* but are "directed at the 'inner person' striving for perfection.[7] In this sense, they are intended to move us from purity of heart to contemplative knowledge of God. Through both, Cassian gives "an overview of the monastic life, explaining where to begin, what to do, what to expect along the way, and where it all leads."[8]

Our primary concern here is with the *Conferences*. When we hear this term, some of us might immediately think of events away from home, involving long days, short nights, and being talked at for hours on end. In some ways, the structure Cassian presents is not far from this. But at its root, *conference* carries overlapping meanings. It is the action of bringing some things or some persons together, as in a collection. It is also the action of conferring with others, taking counsel on some important subject.[9] The *Conferences* of John Cassian are both of these things. As a written document, they bring together the stories and teachings of the monastic fathers. They also tell the story of a small group of persons gathering for counsel. Cassian represents the *Conferences* as a series of conversations among three people—himself, his friend Germanus, and the elder or teacher. In most of the conversations, both Cassian and Germanus remain in the background; they present an initial question to the elder, occasionally but rarely intrude with questions seeking clarification, and sometimes conclude with a comment about continuing after a meal or a night's rest. The elders at whose feet Cassian and Germanus sit "were to be accepted without question as repositories of authority and the keepers of tradition."[10] This could be, and often is, problematic, but Cassian is clear that the authority of these teachers did not lie in what they said; their words were valid only because their deeds were observably so.[11] As Boniface Ramsey notes in his introduction to Cassian's fourteenth conference with Abba Nesteros on spiritual knowledge, there is a difference "between a rhetorical skill that passes for spiritual knowledge and holiness that provides true spiritual insight."[12] The authority of the elders presented by Cassian is an authority located in body and gesture, in the witness of their lives as well as in their words. The words only make explicit what is already present in practice.

The *Conferences* as Cassian presents them are not, except in appearance, verbatim transcripts; they are constructed with specific pedagogical purposes, presenting ideals of the Christian life and then exploring the problems and various practical considerations that might make the ideal unattainable.[13] In reading them, we discover they sound more like lectures than conversations. The *Conferences* are, in most cases, "elaborated versions of past conversations—occasionally, and perhaps often elaborated beyond immediate recognition."[14] As Stewart notes, "deeply rooted in the Christian and monastic traditions [Cassian] knew from experience and from wide reading, he shaped his monastic theology according to the needs he perceived in his own time and place."[15]

Cassian's fourteenth conference, referred to earlier, provides both an example of a conference and an overview of his theological pedagogy. Cassian and Germanus come to the holy Abba Nesteros indicating that they had "committed some parts of Holy Scripture to memory and desired to understand them" (14.1.1). This desire for understanding provides Nesteros with the invitation to speak about the kinds of knowledge. After noting that each art and discipline has its own order and method of instruction, Nesteros proceeds to describe the two-fold order and method of spiritual knowledge: practical knowledge (*praktike*), which results in "correction of behavior" and "cleansing from vice" and theoretical or spiritual knowledge (*theoretike*), which is "the contemplation of divine things and…the understanding of most sacred meanings" (14.1.2). Practical knowledge is required for and precedes spiritual knowledge; spiritual knowledge is not required for and comes only to those who have practical knowledge.

Practical knowledge is itself two-fold: knowledge of "the nature of all the vices and the method of remedying them" and "discerning the sequence of the virtues and forming our mind by their perfection" (14.3.1). Nesteros notes that we cannot learn these things by guesswork but must be taught by God "who alone knows the ability and intelligence of what he has made" (14.3.2). And regardless of our profession or pursuit, we must strive "to attain to perfection in the work [we] have undertaken" (14.5.1). Once again we are challenged to be *theodidacti,* permitting practical knowledge to lead us to purity of heart.

Spiritual knowledge is three-fold. Here Nesteros addresses the four modes of interpretation that will come to fuller exposition in the medieval church: the literal/historical, the allegorical, the tropological, and the anagogical. The latter three constitute the three-fold nature of spiritual knowledge (14.8.1). Allegory reveals the spiritual concealed by the historical, tropology provides moral instruction, and anagogy, like prophecy, directs us to "the invisible and to what lies in the future" (14.8.5–6). Using the example of the city of Jerusalem, Nesteros helps us see that allegorically, the city refers to the church; tropologically, it refers to the human soul; and anagogically to the heavenly city (14.8.4). Spiritual knowledge, building on practical knowledge and the purity of heart that develops from it, leads to the vision of the heavenly kingdom.

Along the way, Cassian and Germanus each interrupt with one objection. Cassian despairs of the way he continues to be distracted by all he has learned in his secular studies. Nesteros responds by encouraging him to apply the same diligence he once gave to those studies to "the reading of and meditation upon spiritual writings" (14.12.1; 14.13.1). Germanus objects that some "who are entangled in different vices...boast of their spiritual learning." Nesteros responds by saying true knowledge is not revealed in eloquence and skill in speech or even the appearance of knowledge. "No one can properly arrive at searching into the testimonies of God unless he first enters undefiled upon the way of Christ by his practical way of life" (14.16.3). As Columba Stewart comments about these sections, spiritual knowledge "is not acquired learning but the experience of the monastic life" brought to bear on scripture; and without the practical knowledge cultivated by living the monastic life— that is, without purity of heart—"one cannot advance to spiritual knowledge; without spiritual knowledge, one cannot comprehend the biblical texts that are the monk's constant companion day and night."[16]

Nesteros concludes his conference with a few words about ineffective spiritual teaching. Ineffective teaching, which in Cassian's theology means teaching that leads neither to purity of heart nor to a vision of heaven, is the result of two things: either the teacher has recommended things he or she has not experienced (one cannot teach about purity of heart without being pure of heart), or the student has closed his or her eyes and ears and rejected the "saving and holy teaching of the spiritual man" (14.18.1). In hindsight, most of us who teach can identify times when we have engaged in or encountered such ineffectual practices. Exploring how we or our students fell into such traps may help us recover the singleness of mind and heart required to avoid them in the future.

This exploration of spiritual conferences as a mode of teaching highlights several pedagogical points that aid our development as effective teachers. First, we are reminded that each art or discipline has its own order and method of instruction. In Cassian's case, the two collections, the *Institutes* and the *Conferences*, are a working out of the order and method by which Christians come to spiritual knowledge. In the former, Cassian focuses his attention on developing practical knowledge or purity of heart. In the latter, as in the fourteenth conference, Cassian's focus is on cultivating spiritual knowledge and the heavenly vision. Second, practical knowledge is not limited to those living the monastic life; it is open to all who seek purity of heart through attention to the elimination of vice and the cultivation of virtue. Third, what we often think of as instruction, the learning of information, is only the beginning and, in many cases, the least important component in spiritual knowledge. However, good instruction, coupled with thoughtful questions and responses, can help orient learners' hearts and minds to useful ideas and practices. Fourth, we cannot teach what we do not know. As a contemporary parallel to Cassian and Germanus's pilgrimage through the desert, think of the many Protestants who have turned to monastic women and men, those living the disciplined life and engaged in practical knowledge, for spiritual direction and counsel. Finally, although perhaps most obvious, the holiness and integrity of a teacher cannot overcome the willful blindness and deafness of a student.

Correspondence—Jane de Chantal and Francis de Sales

In chapter two, we introduced the life and work of Francis de Sales. There we noted that his *Introduction to the Devout Life* seems to be addressed to an individual lover of God, *Philothea*, and to her concerns. But we did not discuss the ways in which the *Introduction* grew out of the spiritual direction de Sales's provided, often by letter, to several women, and especially to Jane de Chantal. Here we want to explore teaching by letter, or correspondence, and examine several of the many letters written by or exchanged between de Sales and de Chantal.

Before doing so, however, we want to briefly situate teaching by letter in the wider tradition of the church. Obviously, de Sales was not the first church leader to provide leadership or to teach by letter. We know letters have served the apostolic work of the church from its beginning. As Elisabeth Stopp notes in her introduction to a collection of de Sales's letters, when you cannot reach people in person, you write— letters, pamphlets, books, broadsheets, even e-mail.[17] We see the apostle Paul doing just this. The letters were "an indispensable feature of Paul's apostolic mission,"[18] making it possible for him to be "present" to various church communities even when he was not able to be physically present with them. Although his letters are clearly written to communities rather than to individuals, we see Paul speaking personally but not privately, dealing with real issues in the life of the church, and writing theologically but not in the form of a dogmatic treatise.[19] Paul used his letters "to instruct, encourage, rebuke, nurture, and console his churches" even as he used them to "defend his gospel and apostleship."[20] Clement of Rome and Ignatius take up their pens and continue this tradition in the second century; Athanasius, Augustine, and Jerome do so in the fourth century, as does Gregory the Great at the end of the sixth century.

Although the speed with which e-mail can be exchanged and the ease with which it can be deleted is changing the ways in which we correspond with one another, letters continue to be used in spiritual direction and guidance. Glenn Hinson notes the special character of letters in spiritual direction: Letters "leave a more permanent record," permitting their recipients to "turn to them again and again and share them with others" (sharing made easier today by e-mail). "Letters encourage greater care and conciseness" and in the delay between their exchange (an interval made more problematic by e-mail) allow or even force extended reflection. The time between letters "may tone down a notch or two the universal tendency to expect immediate spiritual maturity."[21] He also notes that "spiritual guidance through correspondence requires special gifts and skills and insight": vulnerability, acceptance, expectancy, and constancy.[22]

De Sales wrote thousands of letters, believing it to be part of his apostolic work as it was for Paul; perhaps a tenth, or about two thousand, remain. De Chantal also wrote some two thousand letters. Out of the approximately four hundred letters she wrote to de Sales, perhaps fifty remain, with most of the rest destroyed by de Chantal after de Sales's death.[23] In the beginning of their nineteen year relationship, the letters were clearly those of a spiritual director and directee, but as de Sales becomes more self-disclosing over time the letters make evident an "intense and mutually supportive friendship" that greatly influenced their spiritual orientations. In many ways, what we see reflected in their letters is the emergence of the ideal Salesian relationship, "a union of hearts...forged out of a mutual desire for the fullness of love found in God" through which "the living presence of Jesus comes to be enfleshed in the world."[24] It is unfortunate that, for the most part, we have only one side (de Sales's) of the conversation.

De Chantal first encountered de Sales in 1604 when he was preaching a series of Lenten sermons in Dijon. At the time of their meeting, she was a young widow struggling with an emerging sense of (religious) vocation even as she was responsible for a young family and a baronial estate. In many ways, de Chantal's life was shaped by the kind of suffering foretold of Mary when Simeon told her a sword would pierce her soul (Lk. 2:35). De Chantal outlived three of her four children, one dying as a child and two as young adults. Hers was a life shaped by loss and grief. What began as a series of letters providing spiritual direction led, by 1610, to de Chantal and de Sales cofounding the Visitation of Holy Mary (the Visitandines), a community for women "who were not sufficiently young, robust or free of family ties to enter one of the austere reformed women's communities" but who nevertheless felt a call to be "'daughters of prayer' and cultivate a deep interior intimacy with God."[25] It was in and through these communities that Salesian spirituality most clearly came into practice.[26] Although she did not write anything like de Sales's *Introduction to the Devout Life*, her role in the development of Salesian spirituality through the founding of these communities and her correspondence with de Sales extended de Chantal's spiritual influence far beyond a simple relationship between a spiritual director and directee.

Elizabeth Stopp describes de Sales's letters as "dictated by the questions and frame of mind of his correspondent [keeping] strictly to the points at issue" yet showing de Sales speaking and writing "from personal experience as well as from his wide learning."[27] Unlike Cassian's *Conferences*, they were not systematic, "but wholly personal, [applying] no ready-made set of principles, no rigid set of rules to the living personality which confronted him." Every letter "was addressed to an individual man or woman in a particular set of circumstances and of a particular temperament which he understood with penetrating insight."[28] Furthermore, de Sales and de Chantal emphasize a life of devotion that, while still emphasizing detachment from all that is not God, is manifested in and enhancing of everyday human experience.[29] Unlike Cassian, whose monastic tradition led him to emphasize Jesus' call to come away to a quiet place in the desert or garden, the Salesian tradition seems to say that you need not go anywhere; wherever you are, no matter how busy you are, no matter what your work or situation in life, you can find God in that place. "Insofar as one recognized the call of God, the will of God, in where one was and what one was, any situation could be embraced wholeheartedly."[30] Although the ecclesial context in which the Visitation of Holy Mary was formed quickly required it to adopt the cloistered life of traditional women's monastic communities of the time, the primary vocation of de Chantal and those who joined her continued to focus on being "daughters of prayer" wherever and in whatever circumstance they found themselves.

De Chantal's letters were no less particular to the individual person, temperament, and circumstance than were de Sales's letters. While she did not have the wide intellectual formation de Sales had, her letters show her making use of her own experience, especially in her roles as wife and mother, embracing as a whole her own life as well as the lives of her directees and the communities under her supervision. "One went to God in the contexts of the events in which one found oneself."[31] De Chantal had "the mature integrity to value and trust her own experience, to acknowledge the value and importance of relationships and the sacred quality of an attachment that nurtures, provides, sustains and protects in cooperation with a God who does likewise."[32]

Given the volume of correspondence written by both de Chantal and de Sales, the length of many of de Sales's letters, and de Chantal's destruction of most of her letters to de Sales, it is difficult to chose any one letter, or series of letters, as representative of this model of teaching. Nevertheless, let us begin by looking at excerpts from one letter of each that is not addressed to the other.

The first excerpt is from a short letter written by de Sales in July 1607 to Marie Brûlart, wife the president of the Burgundian parliament, who, like de Chantal, had sought direction from de Sales after hearing his series of Lenten sermons in 1604:

I cannot refrain from writing you at every opportunity that
comes my way. Please believe me—do not be over eager; be very
careful to serve God with great gentleness, for this is the right
way of setting about his service. Do not want to do everything,
but only something, and no doubt you will do much. Practice
the mortifications which come your way most often for that is
how to begin; then we shall go on to others. You should often
kiss the crosses which Our Lord has himself put into your arms;
do not stop to find out whether they are made of precious and
fragrant wood: they are crosses all the more when they are made
of vile, worthless, foul-smelling wood. It is strange how this
always comes back into my mind and how this is the only song
I seem to know. I am sure, my dear sister, that this is the hymn
of the Lamb; it is rather sad, but harmonious and beautiful: My
Father, may it be done not as I will, but as you will.[33]

In the second half of this letter, de Sales continues his theme of
embracing that which comes our way rather than seeking out more
extravagant forms of sacrifice or discipline. He offers by comparison the
image of Mary Magdalene seeking the Jesus of glory in the garden and
her lack of recognition of him when he appears to her in the garb of the
gardener:

You would like him to offer you different and more distinguished
mortifications. But the ones that look best are not in fact the
best...before you see him in his glory he wants to plant many
flowers in your garden; they may be small and humble, but they
are the kind that please him; that is why he comes to you clothed
in this way.[34]

Several things should be notice in this brief letter. First, de Sales is
responding to the questions and concerns raised by Madame Brûlart.
His desire to write to her is a desire based on her need for direction
rather than his need to offer it; yet, de Sales clearly has some sense of
personal investment in this relationship. Second, his concern is not with
seeking or achieving the kind of "heroic" measures of spiritual discipline
we might expect of the desert fathers and mothers. Rather, he invites
her to give her attention to the ordinary, to embrace the small measures
of discipline or virtue right in front of her, and to learn to see even these
small things as given to her by God. Third, he reminds her that the task
at hand is not to seek her own will, but God's will. Finally, he not only
draws her into the gospel story but uses this to shift the image of those
mortifications closest at hand from that of "vile, worthless, foul-smelling
wood" to that of "small and humble flowers" planted in her garden.

The second excerpt is from a letter de Chantal wrote in response to
a request from a Visitandine woman she had not met, perhaps around

1640. Many of de Chantal's letters address problems in the formation and management of the growing number of Visitandine foundations under her care. However, as this excerpt shows, this did not prevent her from responding personally and pastorally to all that came her way:

> Although I have never met you, I know you and love you very much. Your letter showed me very clearly the state of your soul and the sources of its pain and perplexity, which is your overeagerness to attain the true happiness you desire, and your lack of patience and docility to the will of Him who alone can grant it to you. Therefore, if you really want to acquire the spirit of your vocation, you will have to correct this overeagerness. Do everything you are taught in a spirit of gentleness and fidelity in order to reach the goal toward which you are being guided, cutting short all thought of attaining it except in God's good time. It seems to me that you are not satisfied with doing those acts required for your perfection, but that you want to feel and know that you are doing them. You must put an end to that and be content with telling God, without any feeling, "Lord, with all my heart I desire to practice such and such virtue just to please You." Then, set to work, although without feeling, and lovingly resolve to serve God in this way, desiring nothing more. If you do this, you will soon find yourself in that state of tranquility and peace which is so necessary for souls who wish to live virtuously, according to the spirit, and not according to their own inclinations and judgments.[35]

We might well ask if we can possibly love someone we have never met. But de Chantal is responding to a woman in one of her foundations who has written with an open (and eager) heart; this makes the woman one of de Chantal's own. De Chantal responds in kind, with love and gentleness as well as with concrete direction and admonition. The concerns of this letter echo the letter from de Sales to Brûlart, addressing themes of simplicity, nonheroic spirituality, gentleness, and patience. As with de Sales's letter, de Chantal's letter expresses a concern for detachment from self-will, especially as that will is expressed in feelings attached to or sought in particular spiritual disciplines. But de Chantal also strikes a contemporary note. In a cultural context in which we have given free reign to our attachments to and idolizations of personal experience and feeling, de Chantal reminds us that we are called to do many things, many of which we may not feel like doing. Although there is a kind of parental "I don't care what you feel, just do it," de Chantal keeps this admonition in a Salesian context that emphasizes detachment from all things for the sake of attachment to God and to God alone.

As a final example, let us turn to the one complete set of exchanges between de Sales and de Chantal that has been preserved, the letters written while de Chantal was on her annual retreat in May 1616.[36] At the heart of this exchange is the tension de Chantal was experiencing around the question of detachment, especially the tension she was discovering between the Salesian understanding of detachment for the sake of complete reliance on God alone and the total dependence she and de Sales had on one another. As de Sales noted in a letter written a month before the retreat, God has made them "one heart, single in its spirit and life."[37]

De Chantal set as her task for the retreat to "renew [her] vows and [her] general reliance and abandonment of [her]self into God's hands" and to consider what would move her "most to make this perfect and conditional surrender so that [she] can truly say 'I live, now not I, but Jesus Christ lives in me.'" Her first letter to de Sales was a request to extend her retreat because news of his illness had kept her distracted and she was of "a greater inclination to quiet [her] spirit in God a bit more."[38] As Wright notes, "the very person who had fueled and increased her love of God was now the only barrier between her and the total surrender that she sought to achieve."[39] In response, de Sales encourages her to continue the work of her retreat, "denuding yourself and abandoning yourself to Our Lord and to me." At the same time, he guides her toward the more radical detachment that she sought:

> Furthermore, my very dear Mother, you must not take any kind of nurse but you must leave the one who nonetheless still remains [i.e., de Sales himself] and become like a poor pitiful creature completely naked before the throne of mercy, without ever asking for any act of feeling whatsoever for this creature. At the same time, you must become indifferent to everything that it pleases God to give you, without considering if it is I who serve as your nurse. Otherwise, if you took a nurse to your own liking you would not be going out of yourself but you would still have your own way which is, however, what you wish to avoid at all costs.[40]

In her next letter, de Chantal notes the good his letter does her. She then observes:

> I feel that my spirit is utterly free and with I don't know what kind of infinite and profound consolation to see itself in God's hands like this…it seems to me that I ought not to think, desire or affirm anything anymore except whatever Our Lord makes me think, love and will at the same time that the superior part [of my soul] prescribes it.[41]

This brings an extended, intimate, and, as Wright notes, vivid response from de Sales in which he rejoices at her nakedness before God. He continues: "So in our affections we must remain completely naked forever, my very dear Mother, even though, in effect, we reclothe ourselves. For we must have our affection so simply and absolutely united to God that nothing can attach itself to us."[42] He encourages her to sing "the canticle of our nakedness, 'Naked I was born in my Mother's womb,' [and naked I will return. The Lord gives and the Lord takes away. Blessed be the name of the Lord]."[43]

In her final letter in this series, de Chantal sounds a shift in her relationship with de Sales: "it seems to me that I no longer have any part of [your dear Spirit] now that I find myself so denuded and stripped of all that was most precious to me."[44] She recalls an earlier conversation with de Sales at which time she did not think she had anything left to leave. Now she understands differently: "How easy it is to leave what is outside ourselves. But to leave one's skin, one's flesh, one's bones and penetrate into the deepest part of the marrow, which is, it seems to me, what we have done, is a great, difficult and impossible thing to do save for the grace of God."[45] De Sales responds with one more letter to close this part of their conversation, affirming what has happened between her and God and, therefore, between the two of them:

> This evening affirm that you have renounced all the virtues, desiring them only in the measure that God gives them to you and not wanting to be concerned to acquire them except to the extent that his goodness will use you in this way according to his will…
>
> Do not think anymore about the friendship nor the unity that God has created between us, nor of your children, your body, your soul, nor anything whatsoever. For you have given everything to God. 'Clothe yourself in Our Crucified Saviour,' love him in his suffering, offer up prayers to him. Do not do what you must do because you are inclined toward it any longer but purely because it is God's will.[46]

In this series of letters, we see the development of a new paradox: no longer does the one who has led de Chantal to her love of God stand in the way of the fulfillment of that love; rather, the detachment that comes through this exchange leads to a new and different kind of intimacy, a paradoxical "detached intimacy." De Chantal's experience is a kind of conversion—a realignment of her affections, a restructuring of her virtues, and growth in the lucidity and power of her partnership with God's work in the world.[47] In her experience of complete dependence on God alone, de Chantal discovered a new strength that sustained her through the busyness of her work with her communities as well as the loss she experienced in the deaths of her children.

In this exchange of letters we also see a clear example of the changing relationship between master and apprentice (teacher and student) described at the opening of this chapter. They bear witness to the process of an apprentice distinguishing herself from the master, or perhaps of the child differentiating herself from the parent. Although de Chantal is aware that she has had to put her own hand to the work, de Sales is a willing and active partner in the process. As her work in founding and sustaining the Visitandine communities progresses, it becomes increasingly clear that these communal workshops of Salesian spirituality are not her inheritance from de Sales, but something they have created together, shaped and refined in light of the differing gifts each brought to their spiritual correspondence and partnership.

Life Narrative and Hagiography: *The Life of St. Antony*

If the work of Christian education is less about learning information and more about "learning Christ," a learning that emphasizes who we are and what we do rather than what we know, then such learning is perhaps most clearly encouraged in the many stories of the lives of saints. As L. Gregory Jones notes, "people's lives are significant means whereby people glimpse examples of how we ought to live."[48] The growing importance of mentors and the work of mentoring—whether with new pastors, new teachers, confirmands, or new Christians—are evidence of this. But this is not a new process in the life of the church. Throughout its history, it has recognized "the importance of narrating saintly lives in order to provide mediations of the imitation of Christ."[49] In the final section of this chapter, we turn our attention to this teaching mode as present in Athanasius's narrative *Life of Antony*.

To begin our exploration, we need to consider two interpretive and intersecting frameworks through which to approach a text about a saint: hagiography (*hagio* means *holy*, so a "writing about the holy ones") and theology. Jones suggests the importance of this intersection when he argues, "Christian beliefs are not so many 'propositions' to be catalogued…but are living convictions which give shape to actual lives and actual communities…the only relevant critical examination of Christian beliefs may be one which begins by attending to lived lives."[50] This is not to downplay the importance of theological reflection but to highlight the ways in which our lives function as theological "texts" freely available for reading to anyone who chooses to look at us.

The lives of various early Christians have been recounted and celebrated in heroic tales, apocryphal acts, and martyrologies (such as the early third century martyrdom of Perpetua and Felicity discussed in the next chapter). But Robert Wilken argues that writings focused specifically on the lives, rather than the deaths, of the saints (for example, Pontus's mid-third-century *Passion and Life of Cyprian*) did not begin until late in the third century.[51] Athanasius's fourth-century *Life of Antony*, written at the request of a group of monks shortly after the saint's death in 356, becomes something of a template for the lives of saints that follow in the succeeding centuries.

Unlike a martyrology, which focuses on persistence in the midst of persecution and faithfulness in the face of death, a life narrative focuses more on imitating the life, rather than death, of Christ. Gerard Loughlin suggests that, in many ways like the gospel narratives of the life of Christ, these life narratives are set before us "as a text to consume in order that we might grow in the strength and hope of Christ. We are not so much enjoined to get inside the text, as to let the text get inside us, so that we are nourished by its word and enabled to perform its story."[52] The lives of the saints are important because these saints have themselves been gathered into and consumed by the story of Christ, "which they seek to extend and elaborate, repeating his life in their own."[53] Their power comes less from what they mean and more from what they show us, giving them, as Edith Wyschogrod argues, a kind of imperative force, which to understand requires that we allow ourselves to be swept up in this force. "The comprehension of a saint's life...is a practice through which the addressee is gathered into the narrative so as to extend and elaborate it with his/her own life."[54] For Wyschogrod, the saints' lives do not present us with a theory of living but with "flesh and blood existents."[55] We measure the success of these narratives not "in aesthetic or cognitive terms but rather in regard to whether the addressees [the listener or reader] experience the saint's spiritual rebirth as an existential command" to follow the path of this disciple.[56] Finally, Wyschogrod notes, these hagiographies present us with a paradox. On the one hand, they present an extreme context in which to search for and live in imitation of Christ. On the other hand, these narratives demonstrate just how impossible it is for humans to live perfectly the divine life, "to bring the divine life into plenary presence.[57] At the intersection of these two is the saint's life, revealing what is humanly possible in the midst of this impossibility.

The theological framework of the saints' lives is not always as explicit as we find in the *Life of Antony*. The storylike character of the narrative may lead us so into the narrative that we miss the theological argument being played out in the account of the saint's life. What Athanasius presents to us is not only the story of a life to be imitated but also, through that life, a theological argument about the nature of God and humanity. Athanasius, representing the orthodoxy of Nicene Christianity as bishop of Alexandria from 328–373, is concerned with challenges to Christian belief and doctrine, in particular the challenges of Arianism to the divinity of Christ and the support Arians sought for their position from the Egyptian monks. Briefly, the Arians argued that Christ differed essentially from God and was a fallible and suffering creature. Christ's identity as "son of God" is such only by God's grace and Christ's obedience. Christ was chosen and named *son* on account of the works he performed, works which we, as creatures like him, can replicate. Salvation, to the extent possible for us, is the result of our obedience and success in imitating Christ.

For Athanasius, in contrast, the renewal of God's image in us was accomplished by Christ's dwelling in humanity; Christ came and taught us at our own level and revealed God through direct contact with us. God's descent in Christ raises us up. Our salvation is fully realized and guaranteed only because Christ is not a creature but is one in substance with the Father. Salvation is always God's work in us, with our cooperation.[58] Antony provides an example of this; his abilities to overcome evil, to confuse the worldly, and to offer healing to others were possible only because Christ is working through Antony. The power and grace sent by Christ are the source of all that Antony accomplishes. As an instrument of God's saving activity, joined to the saving work of Christ, Antony contributes to the salvation of the world by entering the desert to engage the devils in battle.[59] Athanasius presents the believer and the Lord as coworkers in the way of virtue, before whom the demons are rendered powerless.

These theological concerns suggest that Athanasius's *Life of Antony* is not only a spiritual text but also (as, at least implicitly, are all spiritual texts) a theological argument in a narrative mode. Given this, it is difficult to summarize what Antony teaches us. We are best instructed by Antony by engaging his story. Only in this way, as Athanasius suggests at the beginning of his narrative, can we "learn how [Antony] began his discipline, who he was before this, and what sort of death he experienced, and if the things concerning him are true—so that you mighty lead yourselves in imitation of him" and acquire a "sufficient picture for ascetic practice."[60]

Antony was born to wealthy Christian parents.[61] He was a serious child who accompanied his parents to worship and paid close attention to the scripture readings, carefully taking "to heart what was profitable in them." Although living in relative affluence, he did not seek luxury or pleasure but found satisfaction in the things set before him. Sometime around the age of eighteen, his parents died, leaving him responsible for the home and a sister. As he pondered how the disciples had forsaken everything to follow Christ, he heard Matthew 19:21 being read in church: "If you wish to be perfect, go, sell your possessions, and give the money to the poor, and you will have treasure in heaven." This he did, eventually placing his sister in the care of a convent. As Athanasius reports, he did not go immediately to the desert, because "there were not yet many monasteries in Egypt, and no monk knew at all the great desert." Yet Antony began a process that would take him from a kind of apprenticeship through the imitation of a hermit near his village, to living in the tombs near his village, then into the desert, and finally to the "inner mountain." He was tempted initially by the memory of his former life, possessions, and responsibilities. His success in defeating these temptations, as with all of this temptations, he attributed to the grace of God working within him and the "success of the Savior." The temptations, rather than decreasing, became increasingly internal to the self and continued throughout his life. Throughout all, fortified by his reliance on Christ and the sign of the cross, he prevailed.

Athanasius reports that Antony lived as a hermit in the tombs for some twenty years. Only after this long battle did he emerge, more by the action of his friends than his own desire, to be seen by others. In these encounters, the Lord worked through him to heal, exorcise, console, and reconcile; gifted by the grace of speech he persuaded many to take up the solitary life and became as a father to them. At this point, again at the request of others, he began to teach about the disciplined life. He encouraged them to live as though making a new beginning each day, persisting day by day in the ascetic life, holding to the discipline in the confidence that they "have the Lord for [their] coworker in this."[62]

Eventually wearied by the demands on him and "apprehensive that...either he might become prideful or someone else might think more of him than was warranted," he set out for the "inner mountain" of the desert.[63] Here he continued his prayer and discipline, and here the devil resumed his torment of Antony. But as before, those who had followed his way sought him out for advice. As his reputation continued to spread, his message remained constant: "It is not we who do it, but Christ, who does these things through those who believe in him. You believe too, then, and you will see that what we have is not skill with words but faith through love that works for Christ."[64] When his life drew to a close, Antony once again encouraged those who had shared the disciplined life with him: "Be watchful and do not destroy your lengthy discipline, but as if you were making a beginning now, strive to preserve your enthusiasm...Draw inspiration from Christ always, and trust in him. And live as though dying daily, paying heed to yourselves."[65]

This overly brief accounting of Antony's life cannot do justice to what the narrative of his life teaches. Yet we can make some observations about this narrative. First, we see that it was not *what* Antony taught that drew others to him. It was *how* Antony lived his life and what others saw happening to him as a consequence of that life that commended the ascetic life to others. The *Life of Antony* reminds us that the witness of our lives is a crucial aspect of teaching for spiritual formation.

Second, although theory and theology about this life are significantly present in Athanasius's narrative, both the shape of the narrative as well as the fact that it is the narrative of a life suggests the priority of practice.

This priority is most clear when we see that Antony does not begin to teach others about the ascetic life until he himself has lived it for over twenty years. The discipline he lives, keeping the faith and observing the commandments, yields the fruit and wisdom of his life. And this fruit and wisdom lead Athanasius to commend the reading of this life not only to Christians but also to pagans. Athanasius's narrative insists we are more truly formed as teachers by living the disciplined Christian life over an extended period of time than by attending a few workshops on spirituality.

Third, the details of Antony's life, only hinted at in this summary, provide a picture of the path toward Christian wisdom and holiness. This path, perhaps to our dismay, does not permit a single brief journey to the mountaintop of enlightenment. Rather, the picture we see is of a life that moves progressively from community to solitariness, to solitariness in community, to a final solitariness. This journey is more like life in the "valley of the shadow of darkness" than one on the dizzying heights of Mount Hebron. We also see a life in which each move brought encounters with seemingly more powerful demons; living the ascetic life became harder rather than easier even as Antony's complete reliance on Christ and the power of Christ to work through him seems to increase. This progression from hard to harder may seem counter-intuitive in two ways: The practices neither become easier for the teacher, nor can the teacher make these practices easy for the learner.

Finally, Antony and the shape of Antony's life insist that the tasks of Christian spiritual formation are daily and never-ending. Each day requires that we make a new beginning; each day requires a renewed commitment to the discipline we have undertaken; each day requires our utter reliance on the grace and power of Jesus Christ. Even the practical wisdom that comes to be manifest in Antony is not a wisdom possessed through the "wisdom of Greek reasonings, but in the power supplied to us by God through Jesus Christ."[66] No one, not even the teacher, graduates from the school of Christian life.

Conclusion

In this chapter, we explored three modes of teaching: the conference between students and teacher, the exchange of letters between two persons who grow in authority in their own communities yet who also grow toward an equality of authority in their relationship with one another, and the life of the saint presented for our imitation. Each in their different ways have demonstrated a concern for patterns of relationship through which we are helped and can help others to become more like Christ, learning and knowing Christ in our bodies and hearts as well as in our minds through particular forms of living. Each has also invited us into an apprenticeship that intends to shape us as performers of the gospel "in Christly gestures" and to make of us "craftspersons" of the Christian life. Finally, although each of these modes of teaching—conference, letter, and life—are present before us in the form of texts to be read and studied, and although each calls forth rigorous theological reflection, each also calls us into patterns of practice. The resistance we experience in moving from text to practice makes this life a difficult apprenticeship; neither teacher nor student can escape the need for "putting our own hands to the work" in the daily living of the Christian life as we seek to cultivate spiritual wisdom.

PART III

Models for Teaching

CHAPTER 6

Images of the Christian Spiritual Life

Christian communities across the ages have adopted a number of different images in their descriptions of spiritual life: It is the holy banquet we anticipate when we gather at the Lord's table. It is a place or series of places in which we live—the desert, the mountain, and the heavenly city. It is the means by which we come to live in these places—journey, pilgrimage, exile, or ascent. It is an interior experience or knowledge—the dark night, the illuminative way, purification. It is a sense of union, communion, or marriage with the Holy.[1] Each of us likely has some image dominating our understanding or experience of the Christian spiritual life, although we may not always hold that image consciously before us. What does the Christian spiritual life look like to you? What one image dominates your understanding or experience?

In this chapter, we explore just a few of these images, with attention to the ways in which they may both help and hinder our understanding of the Christian spiritual life. In particular, we want to look at two kinds of images: those that help us imagine ourselves as sojourners in the world and those that speak of our internal transformation. Under the heading of the Christian journey, we explore the images of pilgrimage and ascent, with particular attention to John Bunyan's *Pilgrim's Progress* and John Climacus's *The Ladder of Divine Ascent*. Under the heading of internal transformation, we explore the images of imitation and warfare, with particular attention to Thomas à Kempis's *The Imitation of Christ* and *The Passion of Perpetua and Felicity*. We might also call these latter images aspects of a broader image of "putting on Christ."

The Christian Journey

Two biblical stories, one of Abraham and Sarah and the other of the exodus from Egypt, provide a starting point for our reflection on the

Christian journey. Abraham and Sarah's story begins with God's words "Go from your country and your kindred and your father's house to the land that I will show you" (Gen. 12:1). The story that unfolds is a story of frequent travel: up to the land of Canaan, back to Egypt in a time of famine, and back to Canaan. They do not cease their travels until they come to their final resting place in a cave in the field of Ephron (Gen. 25:9–10). They travel with God's blessing and support, they are frequently tested, and they doubt God's promises. Yet throughout the story of their travels, the biblical writers remind us that God's everlasting covenant is with them.

The story of the exodus also reflects the movement from homeland to Egypt and back. The forty-year sojourn in the Sinai desert begins with God's word to Moses: "I have given heed to you and to what has been done to you in Egypt. I declare that I will bring you up out of the misery of Egypt, to…a land flowing with milk and honey" (Ex. 3:16–17). We know how this story unfolds. As with Abraham and Sarah, Israel travels with God's promise and blessing. Israel is tempted and tested, and Israel tests God's promise.

These stories may not appear encouraging as models of the Christian spiritual life. Our hope is that when we set out on this journey with God we will travel a direct, uninterrupted, and safe path; and then our hopes are disappointed when we encounter challenges from others not on this path, when we are confronted by the barrenness of the desert through which we travel, or when the journey seems to be taking a long time. Like children on a cross-country vacation trip, we long to know: Are we there yet?[2] John Bunyan and John Climacus can help us explore the desires behind this question as well as suggest landmarks to show us where we are along the way.

The Pilgrim's Progress

John Bunyan (1628–1688) was born in poverty, worked as an itinerant mender of pots and boasted of "not having had a classical education, because the lack of it made him more dependent on scripture and experience."[3] In 1655 he became a member of the Particular Baptists, a separatist group that emphasized not only believer baptism by immersion but also a strong view of the Calvinist doctrine of limited atonement (a belief that suggests Christ did not die for all persons, but only for the elect). Within a year of his affiliation, he was invited to preach several times. Bunyan was so effective in his preaching that he was soon called and appointed to a ministry of the Word. Much of his writing, although not specifically sermonic, grew out of his preaching.[4]

The Particular Baptists, as with other dissenting groups in seventeenth century England, experienced some growth during the period of the English commonwealth (1640–1660). Then, as other dissenting groups, it experienced significant persecution after the restoration of Charles V to the English throne in 1660. Bunyan wrote the first part of *The Pilgrim's Progress* while imprisoned for religious dissent from 1660–1672, describing the Christian's pilgrimage from the City of Destruction to the Celestial City in order to "escape from the wrath to come." It is, Bunyan writes, "the journey of the saints on the way to glory."[5] *Pilgrim's Progress* was first published in 1678 and has become a classic of the English Puritan tradition.

Bunyan begins his story with an author's apology, that is, a defense of this mode of writing about the Christian gospel:

This book will make a traveller of thee,
If by its counsel thou wilt ruled be,
It will direct thee to the Holy Land,
If thou wilt its directions understand:
Yea, it will make the slothful active be,
The blind also delightful things to see…
This book is writ in such a dialect
As may the minds of listless men affect:
It seems a novelty, and yet contains
Nothing but sound and honest gospel-strains.[6]

As Bunyan notes, the form may seem novel, but through it he communicates clearly his understanding of the Christian life and the difficulties persons of his day and of ours experience in trying to live faithful lives.

Christian begins the journey. *The Pilgrim's Progress* begins with the man soon to be named "Christian" walking through the "wilderness of the world, a great burden on his back." Christian opens "the book" and begins to cry "What shall I do?" Evangelist, who appears at several points throughout the story to help Christian when he strays from the narrow path, answers Christian's question with "Fly from the wrath to come." Evangelist points him first toward the Wicket Gate, which Christian cannot yet see, and then to a shining light which he can see and which leads him to the gate and the city beyond it. Christian pleads for his wife and children to join him, but they are unwilling and call him back. Crying "Life, life, eternal life," he runs from his family, not looking back.[7] He weeps (eventually) for their loss; but in part 2, published six years after the first part, we discover that after Christian's death they follow his example and undertake their own pilgrimage to the Celestial City.

Along the way, Christian encounters a number of false pilgrims. Descriptions of them and explorations of their character could take a book of its own. Fortunately, the very names Bunyan gives them reveals their falseness or shortcomings: Obstinate, Pliable, Worldly-Wiseman, Simple, Sloth, Presumption, Formalist, Hypocrisy, Timorous, Mistrust, Discontent, Shame, Talkative, Hategood, By-Ends, Ignorance, Little-Faith,

and Atheist. Christian also encounters two giants, Despair and Diffi-
dence, who take him captive. In contrast to these false pilgrims, several
symbolically named persons come to Christian's assistance throughout
his journey: Evangelist, Help, Interpreter, Faithful, Hopeful, Knowledge,
Experience, Watchful, and Sincere.

Prior to Christian's arrival at the Wicket Gate, he and his temporary
travel companion Pliable fall into the Slough of Despond, a marshy bog
that threatens to swallow Christian. Bunyan describes the Slough: "still
as the sinner is awakened about his lost condition, there ariseth in his
soul many fears, and doubts, and discouraging apprehensions, which
all of them get together, and settle in this place; and this is the reason of
the badness of this ground."[8] Pliable, unburdened by consciousness of
his sinfulness, is able to eventually climb out of the Slough. Christian,
however, so weighed down by the burden of his sins, is unable to get
out of the Slough on his own. He finally does with the assistance of
Help. Once back on the path, Christian encounters Worldly-Wiseman,
who points Christian toward the village of Morality and to a man and
his son, Legality and Civility, who live there, suggesting they will be
able to relieve Christian of his burden. As types representing the Law,
they do not and cannot remove his burden; rather, Christian becomes
paralyzed, requiring Evangelist's assistance and exhortation. Evangelist
notes that Worldly-Wiseman is attempting to turn Christian from the
way, to "render the Cross odious" to him, and is pointing the way to
death rather than life. Evangelist counsels Christian to strive to enter at
the narrow gate (the Wicket Gate) and to prefer the Cross over all other
treasures.

Through the Wicket Gate and to the Cross. At the gate Christian
encounters Good Will and recounts the first part of his journey, with
Good Will interpreting who and what Christian has encountered. (Note
that the gate is not the beginning of Christian's journey; it is arrived at
only after setting out on the journey.) Once through the gate, Christian
comes to the House of the Interpreter, who teaches him about those things
that are profitable to his salvation. After leaving the Interpreter, Christian
comes up a small hill, upon which "stood a Cross, and a little below in
the bottom, a sepulchre."[9] Here Christian's burden drops from his
shoulders and falls into the sepulchre, never to be seen again. The cross
is the sign and instrument of salvation. Three Shining Ones appear; one
pronounces forgiveness, the second reclothes him, and the third places
the seal of the Spirit on his forehead and gives him a sealed scroll to read
on the way. Christian sings:

Thus far did I come loaden with my sin,
Not could aught ease the grief that I was in,

Till I come hither. What a place is this!…
Blessed Cross! Blessed Sepulchre! Blessed rather be
The man that there was put to shame for me.[10]

As he continues his journey, he climbs a hill, coming to the House Beautiful, a house "built by the Lord of the Hill…for the relief and security of pilgrims," (a sign of the church) where he encounters Discretion, Prudence, Piety, and Charity.[11] After a night of rest, they clothe him in the armor of Christ (Eph. 6), which he soon needs.

Entering the valley of humiliation, Christian encounters Apollyon, who claims to be prince and god of the country and, therefore, claims Christian as his servant. Apollyon is a figure of the apocalyptic beast and an enemy of the true Prince (Christ). Christian engages in battle with Apollyon, is wounded but not killed, and finally triumphs.

Christian and Faithful. After Christian's encounter with Apollyon, he enters the valley of the shadow of death. The way is difficult and fearful, but as he walks Christian hears the voice of another saying "Though I walk through the valley of the shadow of death, I will fear no evil."[12] This gives Christian both hope and strength. Soon seeing the source of this voice ahead of him, he runs to overtake and pass the person. In passing, Christian smiles "vaingloriously" and, "not taking good heed to his feet," stumbles in his eagerness and self-satisfaction, falls, and cannot rise again.[13] The person, Faithful, helps Christian to his feet. Faithful recounts his journey, noting the ways in which he avoided or escaped the detours Christian encountered. As they travel together, they meet Talkative, who provides both Christian and Faithful occasion to teach. Christian describes to Talkative the distinction between saying and doing, summarized as "The soul of religion is the practic [practical] part."[14] Faithful contrasts two kinds of knowledge, that which "resteth in the bare speculation of things" and that which "is accompanied with the grace of faith and love, which puts a man upon doing even the will of God from the heart."[15] Faithful then summarizes for Talkative (and the reader) the signs of God's grace: conviction of sin, faith in Christ, "a life answerable to that confession,…a life of holiness,…to promote holiness in the world…by a practical subjection in faith and love to the power of the Word."[16]

Christian and Faithful soon come to the city of Vanity, known for its continuous fair. Vanity is the city of the world, the city of "getting and spending." Walking through the fair, Christian and Faithful are taken notice of for their different clothing and way of speaking, as well as for their disinterest in the merchandise for sale at the fair. The townspeople examine and then imprison the two, where they are examined again, tortured, and caged (perhaps Bunyan's remembrance of his own prison experience). Faithful, true to his name, refuses to worship the gods of mammon represented by the fair and is martyred. Christian somehow escapes, almost immediately meeting Hopeful.

The By-Path and the Doubting Castle. Hopeful was converted by Faithful's and Christian's witness at the fair in Vanity. Traveling together, they are eventually tempted by an apparently easier way, the By-Path Meadow. Here they encounter Vain-confidence who, after nightfall, falls into a deep pit along the By-Path. Christian and Faithful hear him fall, hear Vain-confidence's groaning and, as a storm rises, begin to despair of turning from the path. Traveling in the storm they come upon the Doubting Castle.

Two giants, a husband and wife, own the Doubting Castle. Their names are Doubt and Despair. Many have been held captive by and succumbed to their power. Hopeful, true to his name like Faithful, comforts Christian in their captivity; but they continue to despair. They are almost overcome by their doubts and are tempted to commit suicide. Yet, on Saturday night, praying from midnight to the break of day Christian remembers that he has the key called promise that opens any lock in the Doubting Castle, and they escape. The story of the Doubting Castle provides an image both of the transition from the tomb to the resurrection, from Holy Saturday to Easter, as well as a reminder of the story of Paul and Silas praying in prison (Acts 16:25–26).

A vision of the Celestial City. After their escape, Christian and Hopeful meet four shepherds (Knowledge, Experience, Watchful, and Sincere) who show them the hill of Error, the mountain of Caution, the By-Way to Hell, and a telescopic glimpse of the Celestial City. Having come this far, they reach a place called the Enchanted Ground, about which they had been warned. As sleep on this ground is fatal, they should remain watchful and sober. Nevertheless, Hopeful becomes drowsy; only Christian's watchfulness saves Hopeful from the fatal sleep. Christian notes at this point the importance of not traveling the path alone. Hopeful at last recounts the story of his conversion, a pattern that has been repeated in the lives of many others since. Hopeful tells of his awakening to sin, notes the various means by which he was made conscious of his sinfulness, of his endeavor to mend his life, his recognition of his inability to save himself, his need to obtain the righteousness of Christ, the sufficiency of God's grace, and, in accepting God's grace, the "joy and desire to live a holy life"[17] At long last, the travelers come within reach of the city only to discover a river that must be crossed; as there is no way around it, nor is there a bridge across it, they must go through it. Although long freed from his burden, the thought of his sins weighs Christian down, and he begins to sink. Hopeful bears him up with a reminder of Christ's promises, evoking in Christian a vision of Christ. Christ says to Christian, "When thou passest through the waters, I will be with thee, and through the rivers, they shall not overflow thee" (Isa. 43:2, KJV). They are greeted on the shore, again by Shining Ones, leave their "mortal garments behind" at the river, are led to the gate and welcomed into the city with the words "Blessed are they that are called to the marriage supper of the Lamb."[18]

Several themes in *The Pilgrim's Progress* warrant attention when we consider its image of the Christian life as pilgrimage in relation to teaching. First, the geography of the pilgrimage is not important. Rather, the experiences and persons encountered along the way enable our continued spiritual transformation. As Monica Furlong suggests, the primary concerns for the pilgrim are the temptations of conformity and abdication of responsibility. These continue to be temptations for teachers and students today. Furlong writes:

> The real temptations of the journeying Christian…are that of conforming to 'this world,' losing one's integrity by trying to please others, and soothing one's conscience by legalistic arguments…[and] that of abdicating choice, of letting oneself be led by others into beliefs or conduct of which there was no inner understanding, and to which there was no genuine consent.[19]

Second, although Christian seems to set out on his own, he is guided and accompanied along the way, especially by Evangelist, Faithful, and Hopeful, but also by many others. A community of faith supports and directs the journey. No Christian teacher undertakes the work as a private contractor; he or she comes to the work as a member of and supported by the community of faith. And as Gordon Wakefield suggests, when old friends are taken from us (Faithful), new ones are given (Hopeful), a sign of the "inexhaustible communion of saints."[20] Third, at no point on the journey can Christian presume to be safe from temptation, distraction, or poor judgment. Even within sight of his destination, his faith is tested as he crosses the river. The Christian teacher today can expect no less.

In addition to Bunyan's characterization of the process of conversion, summarized so well by Hopeful, there are several theological themes that Bunyan continues to develop. First, nothing we do or are, obedient or not, contributes to the process of our salvation. As Bunyan notes, "by laws and ordinances you will not be saved."[21] Our salvation depends "entirely on the utterly free and gratuitous love of God…conveyed to us through Jesus' intercession as priest at God's right hand."[22] Our obedient response in faith does not lead to salvation but responds to what God in Christ has already done for us. Similarly, our work as Christian teachers is but our faithful response to God's gifts to us. Second, the Christian seeking truth must be prepared to reject a hostile society as well as the hypocrisy and self-deceit one encounters in the church.[23]

Such deceit is often not the result of any specific intent to deceive. It is, rather, the result either of temporary faith, such that a person appears to be a believer, or of a lack of self-knowledge, whereby a person believes oneself to be better than is truly the case.[24] Therefore, Christian persons, teachers and students alike, need to continue to grow in self-knowledge and in wisdom to discern the true from the false pilgrim, the faithful from the hypocrite. A third theme concerns the genuineness of one's belief: one's belief and conduct "must match to the last detail."[25] As the conversation among Christian, Faithful, and Talkative suggests, saying and doing must be consistent. Our lives often speak louder than our words. Finally, although we could explore many other themes with Bunyan's pilgrim, we should note that Christian's journey is a pilgrimage toward the heavenly city, toward the city of God. It is neither a random search for meaning nor a process of self-discovery. It is a journey of faith and transformation, and a good teacher keeps these goals and the ultimate destination in mind.

The Pilgrim's Progress is an engaging story. The process of transformation and the resistances encountered along the way, as personified in the various false pilgrims, still resonate with our experiences today. Yet we must also assess carefully the arguments Bunyan presents. For example, must we, like Bunyan, believe in a doctrine of limited atonement in which God does not will the salvation of all persons? Must we believe our trials are heaven-sent as means of discipline or punishment by God? While such beliefs were common in Bunyan's day and remain so in ours, the trials faced by the Christian pilgrim and the suffering experienced by false pilgrims are largely of their (or our) own making. Trial and suffering occurs when they (or we) fail to heed the words of the Evangelist or stray from the path to the Celestial City. Although Christian believed he had to choose between family and salvation, we should question the appropriateness of a Christian abandoning home and family. God called Abraham and Sarah to leave their homeland together; and the exodus was a pilgrimage undertaken by family and faith community members, skeptics and believers together.

The Ladder of Divine Ascent

Another image of the Christian life as journey is that of ascent. Although the story of Jacob's ladder contributes to the way in which this image develops, the biblical stories that appear in the common lectionary for celebration of the Transfiguration, including Moses' ascent of Mount Sinai and Jesus' ascent of Mount Tabor, provide the primary reference points for this image. Moses ascends Mount Sinai to receive the covenant and is transformed by his encounter with God (Ex. 33:17–23; 34:29–35); this transformation prompted early church writers, such as Gregory of Nyssa in his *The Life of Moses*, to use Moses' ascent as an image of the Christian mystical life. Jesus ascends Mount Tabor, where he holds conference with Moses and Elijah and where God proclaims him the Beloved. Jesus too is transformed by and reveals the glory of God (Mt. 17:1–8; Mk. 9:2–8; Lk. 9:28–36). Beyond the lectionary, a number of the Psalms use images of pilgrimage and ascent, especially those related to the festival pilgrimage up to the temple mount and to the entrance into the temple. For example, we read in Psalm 24, an entrance psalm, "Who shall ascend the hill of the Lord? And who shall stand in his holy place?" (v. 3) In Psalm 122, part of the group of pilgrimage songs or songs of ascent (Ps. 120—134), we read "I was glad when they said to me, 'Let us go [up] to the house of the LORD!'" (Ps. 122:1) Whereas Bunyan's pilgrim travels by means of a narrow path from the City of Destruction to the Celestial City, these stories suggest a narrow path up a mountain or, when a mountain is not available, a ladder between heaven and earth.

John Climacus (ca. 579–649), or John of the Ladder, lived in the Sinai desert at the foot of Mount Sinai. He arrived there when he was sixteen, lived for forty years as a hermit, and then was elected abbot of the central monastery at Sinai.[26] In contrast to *The Pilgrim's Progress*, written for laypeople and strongly anti-Catholic, *The Ladder of Divine Ascent* was written primarily for a monastic audience and is often read in Orthodox monasteries each Lent. Nevertheless, it continues to be valued by many Orthodox laypeople for its concern with the spiritual and psychological struggles of daily life and its attention to the cultivation of Christian virtues such as obedience, humility, and discernment. In this sense, it is more concerned with the active life—the disciplines and practices of the Christian life of words and body—than with the contemplative life.[27]

The ladder has thirty steps, one "for each year in the hidden life of Christ before his baptism."[28] Climacus encourages us to eagerly climb the ladder seeking the "unity of faith and the knowledge of God," at the full maturity and stature of Christ who, "baptized in the thirtieth year of His earthly age,…attained the thirtieth step on the spiritual ladder."[29] The ladder is usually portrayed in iconography with Climacus standing near the foot of the ladder, Christ at the top reaching out in welcome to those who have completed their climb, and the open jaws of a dragon or the abyss at its foot to catch those who fall. On one side, demons attempt to trip those who climb, on the other side angels offer encouragement.[30]

Most commentators divide the ladder into three sections, or stages, of the ascent. The first stage is the initial break from the world through renunciation, detachment, and exile (steps 1–3). The second stage involves the practice of the active life through obedience, penitence, remembrance of death, sorrow, struggles against the passions, simplicity, humility, and discernment (steps 4–26). The final stage is the contemplative life as manifested in stillness, prayer, dispassion, and love (steps

27–30). Richard Lawrence suggests that this structure parallels the theological structure of the Nicene and Apostles' creeds. In the first steps, God works as creator to fashion the person as a new being. In the extensive second set of steps, Christ works in the person as the person struggles with the passions and seeks to transform one's human nature. The brief third set of steps reflects the work of the Holy Spirit. Here the person is "so totally dependent on the internal action of the Holy Spirit that it cannot be described in words."[31] It may be tempting to believe this extensive structure is a structure for "works righteousness," the means by which a person effects one's salvation. But Lawrence insists, as do many Orthodox theologians, that the work of transformation occurring in the person through the ascent of the ladder is not our work but the "work of the Three Divine Persons within the soul. The initiative and power are those of the Father, Son, and Holy Spirit. The work of the monk is to accept the offered gifts, to allow himself to be transformed, to let the Triune God lift him up into a sharing of the divine life itself."[32] Whether it is primarily our work or God's work is more a matter of perception. As Kallistos Ware notes, if "on the earlier rungs we are chiefly conscious of our toil and struggle,…on the higher rungs we are more and more aware of the freely granted grace of God."[33]

A number of parallels exist between *The Pilgrim's Progress* and *The Ladder of Divine Ascent* in addition to their shared attention to the Christian life as a journey. First, the structure of the spiritual life is similar. Just as Christian does not begin his journey at the Wicket Gate, so too the primary work of ascent does not begin until after the first few steps in which the person has separated oneself from the ways of the world. Climacus writes, "No one can enter crowned into the heavenly bridechamber without first making three renunciations. He has to turn away from worldly concerns, from men, from family; he must cut selfishness away; and thirdly, he must rebuff the vanity that follows obedience."[34] In regard to this third renunciation, think of Christian's "vain-glorious smile" and his stumble when he seeks to overtake Faithful. We, too, may smile in satisfaction at our spiritual progress and stumble as we wrongly insist we must take the lead to demonstrate our righteousness.

Second, both Bunyan and Climacus emphasize the importance of personal experience. This is especially important to Climacus if one is seeking to teach others about the spiritual life. Climacus argues that talk about such things as humility, the fear of God, or "assurance of the heart" is meaningless to someone who has never experienced them. It is, he writes, "like a man who with words and examples tries to covey the sweetness of honey to people who have never tasted it."[35] This is a theme we have encountered numerous times already; here it underscores our inability to help others navigate their spiritual journeys if we are not experienced navigators ourselves.

Third, both writers call attention to the importance of self-knowledge and discernment. The imperfection of Christian's discernment, as much as his encounter with false pilgrims, leads him into difficulty along the path. For Climacus, the development of discernment is reflected in three forms. For beginners, it is reflected in "self-knowledge." For those midway up the ladder it is reflected in the "spiritual capacity to distinguish unfailingly between what is truly good and what in nature is opposed to the good." Finally, "among the perfect, it is a knowledge resulting from divine illumination." Bunyan probably would not describe it this way, but he would agree with Climacus when Climacus describes discernment as "a solid understanding of the will of God in all times, in all places, in all things."[36] Climacus argues that this ability is not restricted to monks. "Whatever you do, however you live, whether you live under obedience or whether you are independent, in what you do openly or in your spiritual life, let it be your rule and practice to ask if what you do is in accordance with the will of God."[37] This might be a useful injunction to keep before us in our studies, classrooms, and other preparation and teaching spaces.

Finally, both writers describe the goal of the journey not as self-fulfillment but as a coming to see God face-to-face. For Bunyan, this occurs when Christian enters the Celestial City and joins in the songs of its citizens in praise of God. Chapters 19 and 21 of the Revelation of John provide biblical images of this goal. For Climacus, the goal of seeing God face-to-face occurs in contemplative silence. Although Moses is denied this face-to-face encounter on Sinai, his experience in the dark cloud (Ex. 19:9, 24:15, 34:5) does end with the vision of God found in the "still small voice." For Bunyan, the journey ends with Christian coming to dwell in the Celestial City. For Climacus, the journey continues as the place of encounter with God is not a place where we take up permanent residence, but a place to which we come occasionally and by the grace of God. Implicit in both writers is this caution: We cannot presume to have arrived at the goal; we must attend to where we are on the journey, looking to the path or ladder and striving to discern the true way for our personal pilgrimage and for the student sojourners we chance to meet along the way.

Putting on Christ

A second primary image of the Christian spiritual life is that of internal transformation. It should be clear from the preceding discussion that the ways of pilgrimage and ascent are also concerned with this transformation. The distinction we make here, therefore, is that internal transformation is less concerned with where we go and more explicitly concerned with who we become when we "put on" the person of Christ.

Several biblical texts provide a framework for this discussion. One text, Mark 8:34–35, focuses on the way of the cross: "If any want to become my followers, let them deny themselves and take up their cross and follow me. For those who want to save their life will lose it, and those who lose their life for my sake, and for the sake of the gospel, will save it." A second is the hymn of Christ's self-giving in Philippians: "Let the same mind be in you that was in Christ Jesus, who,...emptied himself, taking the form of a slave, being born in human likeness. And being found in human form, he humbled himself and became obedient to the point of death—even death on a cross" (2:5, 7–8). In Thomas à Kempis's *The Imitation of Christ* and *The Passion of Perpetua and Felicity* we consider two ways of imitating Christ, one (Thomas à Kempis) focusing on an imitation of Christ's interior life, the second (Perpetua) on Christ's external life, especially Christ's death on a cross.

The Imitation of Christ

Thomas à Kempis (ca. 1379–1471) was born in Kampen, Netherlands ("à Kempis" means "from Kampen"). He first encountered the Brethren of the Common Life, a community shaped by the *devotio moderna*, or "new devotion," begun by Gerard Groote, while attending school in Deventer from 1392 to 1399. Thomas entered the monastery of St. Agnes, where his brother John was prior, was invested as a monk in 1406, and ordained in 1413. Thomas left the monastery only twice, once while his community lived in a two-year exile, the second when he went to care for his dying brother who had since become the prior of another community. At several times, Thomas was elected subprior of the community and served as its novice master. It was perhaps after his first term as novice master that he wrote the *Imitation of Christ*.[38]

The *devotio moderna* was, in part, a response to the growing scholasticism of Christian theology and a call for a renewal of piety among individuals and communities. Groote's movement was "suspicious of an academic theology that had no bearing upon the concrete realities of life or offered little encouragement to progress in virtue."[39] As Thomas would write: "Endless reading and talk do not satisfy the soul, but a good life puts the mind at rest, and a clean conscience brings great confidence in God...[W]hen the day of judgment comes we shall not be asked what we have read but what we have done, not how well we have spoken but how devoutly we have lived."[40] The movement's concern for the renewal of piety and attention to the inner life of the Christian grew from its belief that the inner life establishes the foundation for the outer life. The life of prayer is the "source of vitality for the life of action...a rightly ordered devotion becomes the true source of outward acts of charity."[41]

The Imitation of Christ is actually a collection of four pieces Thomas wrote between 1424 and 1427. Each piece carries its own title: "Admonitions for the Spiritual Life" (the first chapter of which is entitled "The

Imitation of Christ," which becomes the title for the whole), "Toward the Inner life," "Of Inner Comfort," and "On the Sacrament." One of the primary arguments of the book is that "by shaping the inner life of the individual around meditation on the life and passion of Christ, the imitation of Christ could be achieved in the midst of the most demanding of lives."[42] That is, although Thomas intends the Christian to live the way of the cross, the focus of his work is on the inner life of the Christian and on Christ's interior presence in us. In books 1 and 2, Thomas writes:

> Remember what you set out to do, and place before you the image of the Crucified. When you look into the life of Jesus Christ you may well be ashamed that you have not tried harder to be like him, even though you have followed the ways of God for a long time. A religious person who trains himself intently and devoutly in the holy life and Passion of the Lord will find everything he needs, and he will find it in abundance.[43]

> …rest your thoughts on Christ's passion and dwell freely in his Sacred Wounds. If you go for refuge to Jesus's Wounds and to the precious marks of his Passion with humility and love, you will feel great comfort in troubled times…Prop yourself up with Christ and for Christ if you wish to live with Christ. If just once you could perfectly enter the inner life of Jesus and experience a little of his passionate love, then you would not care at all about what you might gain or lose in life.[44]

Thomas makes explicit his emphasis on the way of the cross at the conclusion of book 2 (chapter 12). To those who think the way of the cross is harsh, Thomas responds that the way of final judgment and fire is far worse. "Everything," he writes, "is founded on the cross, and everything consists in dying on it, and there is no other road to life and to true inner peace than the road of the holy cross and of our daily dying to ourselves."[45]

Book 3, "On Inner Comfort," is the longest of the books. It is shaped as a dialogue between the disciple and Jesus, as if the disciple has so entered into Christ's inner presence on the cross that Jesus is present for conversation. The dialogue continues to emphasize obedience, humility, and self-surrender. This conversation occurs only in the silence of the heart. The book begins not with the disciple speaking but with Jesus saying to the disciple "be silent, and visit the quiet recesses of your own heart. It is there that you will hear God's voice." Later in the book, Jesus again counsels the disciple, "I would willingly speak to you and reveal my inner thoughts if you would carefully await my coming and open the door of your heart to me. Be prudent, watch in prayer, and be humble in all things."[46] Toward the end of book 3, the disciple acknowledges that the Christian life is only the way of the cross: "the life of a good monk—as of any good Christian—is a cross, but it is also his compass to paradise."[47]

In the final book, "On the sacrament," the dialogue between Jesus and the disciple continues. The book begins with Jesus inviting all "who labor and are heavy burdened" to the feast at the Lord's table. The first chapters, although carrying both argument and exhortation, are formed as prayers, as addresses to Christ. These chapters provide the disciple's response to Christ's invitation, a response of wonder at the generosity of this invitation, acknowledgement of the presence of Christ in the sacrament and of the importance of frequent and worthy reception of it. Thomas writes/prays:

> in the Sacrament of the altar you are fully present, my God, in the person of Jesus Christ, and each time that you are worthily and devoutly received we enjoy the abundant fruit of eternal salvation.[48]

> In this Sacrament my weaknesses are cured and my passions are held in check, my temptations are overcome as they become less burdensome, grace is more greatly infused, virtue once started now increases, faith is made firm, hope is strengthened, and love's embers are fanned into flames, spreading ever wider.[49]

Although Thomas is not writing an explicitly sacramental spirituality, reception of the sacrament becomes a significant means by which the disciple both meditates on the Incarnation and passion of Christ and takes in and participates in the life of Christ and the way of the cross.

Throughout *The Imitation of Christ* Thomas emphasizes rather traditional monastic themes: simplicity, humility, obedience, and purity of heart and life. His invitation to inner devotion to the crucified Christ and to intimate friendship with Christ are themes that have continued to speak to nonmonastic persons throughout the centuries since he wrote these words. Thomas also invites us to rigorous self-examination, to attend to our own behaviors and attitudes rather than to those of our neighbors and friends: "You will never be inward and devout unless you stop talking about other people and start watching over yourself."[50] But our use of this image of "putting on Christ" must be sensitive to the life experiences of learners and the cultural messages directed at them. Thomas's emphasis on the way of the cross, especially his devotion to Christ's crucifixion, the necessity of human affliction and suffering, of "patiently enduring great calamities and trials,"[51] can be an especially difficult and inappropriate path for persons who have routinely experienced physical or emotional abuse or who live in oppressive political contexts. Such emphasis on suffering can easily lead to passivity in the midst of abuse and a confused understanding of the loving God who, as Thomas so clearly understood, willingly suffered in our place.

The Martyrdom of Perpetua and Felicity

The story of Perpetua and her friends draws us directly into a context of political oppression and the physical way of the cross.[52] As we find in Jesus' prediction to Peter that he would be bound and taken where he did not choose to go (Jn. 21:18–19) as well as in the story of the stoning of Stephen (Acts 7), the way of martyrdom is part of the biblical story of the way of the cross. What is distinctive about Perpetua's story is that it is, for the most part, "the first hand account, from AD 202, of the conversion, trial, spiritual life and death of a 22 year-old woman."[53] Yet Perpetua's martyrdom is anything but a passive response to her situation. Her martyrdom reflects instead a model of active resistance and engagement with the powers of her world. As Lisa Sullivan notes, Perpetua's story describes "North African against Roman, female against male, daughter against father." She is "an example of a member of a submissive group…appropriating the imagery of the dominant in order to converse on the dominant's terms."[54] Perpetua is the "warrior martyr," the "strong woman of faith." Her story was preserved, retold, and reinterpreted to strengthen the faith and witness of an oppressed religious minority who professed Jesus as Lord and Messiah.

The telling of Perpetua's story begins and ends with the voice of an editor who is presented as an eye-witness to her martyrdom. The editor provides a biblical and theological framework with which the reading/listening community is to understand the story. Following the editorial introduction, Perpetua's story is told in the first person. She recounts her arrest following an edict by Septimius Severus prohibiting conversion to Judaism and Christianity, her brother's and father's attempts to convince her to change her mind, and her small group's experiences of imprisonment and trial. Intertwined within this narrative are the accounts of four visions Perpetua has while in prison. The first provides a prototype for Climacus's image of the ladder: the deacon or catechist of her community, having already offered himself to martyrdom, awaits her at the top to welcome her into heaven; a serpent at the foot of the ladder awaits her downfall; and the sides of the ladder are made up of weapons to afflict and test her in her climb. The second and third visions are of her younger deceased brother—a vision of him suffering from the deforming illness from which he died and then a vision of him restored to health by her prayer. The final vision is a vision of herself as a warrior preparing for and victorious in battle with the devil. The story concludes with the account of a vision by one of her companions, Saturus, and then the editor's account of their martyrdom in the arena.

Although the whole of Perpetua's story is worthy of attention, her fourth vision continues to draw comment. Pomponius the deacon comes to the prison door and leads her up to the arena:

> And there came out against me a certain ill-favoured Egyptian with his helpers, to fight with me...And I was stripped, and I became a man. And my helpers began to rub me with oil as their custom is for a contest; and over against me I saw that Egyptian wallowing in the dust. And there came forth a man of very great stature...bearing a rod like a master of gladiators, and a green branch whereon were golden apples. And he besought silence and said: The Egyptian, if he shall conquer this woman, shall slay her with the sword; and if she shall conquer him, she shall receive this branch...And we came nigh to each other, and began to buffet one another. [The Egyptian] was fain to trip up my feet, but I with my heels smote upon his face. And I rose up into the air and began so to smite him as though I trod not the earth...And I caught his head, and he fell upon his face; and I trod upon his head. And the people began to shout, and my masters began to sing. And I went up to the master of the gladiators and received the branch. And he kissed me and said to me: Daughter, peace be with thee. And I began to go with glory to the gate called the Gate of Life.[55]

What can we make of this vision? First, the fact that she has visions grants her authority in the life of the community. Such visions are signs of God's presence and power with her. Second, martyrs do not volunteer, but are chosen by God.[56] Pomponius coming to the door of the prison to lead her is one sign of this selection. The editor of her story also makes this clear in an acclamation near the end of the account: "O most valiant and blessed martyrs! O truly called and elected unto the glory of Our Lord Jesus Christ!"[57] Third, in Perpetua's context a woman had no power, certainly not a young woman with an unweaned infant. Neither Perpetua nor her comartyr Felicity fit the stereotypic images of devout women as chaste virgins or performers of miracles. Perpetua is transformed into a person of power, in this case, a man. She is anointed with oil as if an athlete preparing for a contest. Yet the anointing with oil would also call baptism to mind in her Christian contemporaries. Those preparing for baptism would have received anointing with oil as a means of strengthening for their contest with the evil one (the oil of exorcism) and as a sign of the power of the Holy Spirit (the oil of chrismation). She is placed in the arena as a gladiator in combat with a giant power (possibly imperial Rome) and promised death or life. Finally, she is victorious. Yet we know from the end of the story that Perpetua and her friends are eventually killed. Kate Cooper suggests their deaths are still victories because the

Christian martyr subverting "humiliation by embracing death with equanimity" makes a powerful social gesture: "for a martyr to best [her] executioners by dying with dignity, [her] message intact...struck at the heart of the social contract."[58]

If, in Thomas's *Imitation of Christ* we are led more to the "mind" of Christ by our contemplation of the Incarnation and crucifixion, in Perpetua we are led to a physical sharing in Christ's death. Through martyrdom, the martyr shares directly in the suffering of Christ, receives a baptism "in blood" as did Christ, and achieves victory in death as did Christ. We can continue to tell these stories as means of claiming the continuing presence of Christ in and with communities, in order to strengthen and enable them to claim power in the midst of their own persecution and suffering.

Conclusion

In all four of these texts, we find a number of common themes and in many cases surprisingly common images: an emphasis on personal experience, the expectation that the Christian life is a life of trial and suffering if not of death, the image of Christian life as a contest or struggle with the powers of temptation and evil, and the experience of the Christian person as a stranger traveling through the world to a better place. Yet all four of these texts also pose problematic images and questions: What are the limitations of self-sacrifice, surrender, and obedience? What temptations and trials experienced in our own day are reflected in the trials described by Bunyan, Climacus, Thomas, and Perpetua? With whom and how do we undertake the battle? Is the Christian as warrior still an appropriate image, given its abused and abusive history? What other images might we create for the Christian in active resistance to "powers and principalities"?

In any given teaching context, a variety of images warrant our close attention. However, choosing to teach in conversation with historic images of the Christian spiritual life demands that we eschew literal interpretations and applications. We might invite learners to approach each image with both a hermeneutic of generosity (open-minded interpretative interest) and a hermeneutic of suspicion (mindfulness of cultural bias). The power of these images lies in their ability to evoke our hidden fears and longings and provoke movement along a spiritual path. An image that is too comfortable for us or our students loses its evocative/provocative edge. An image that disregards genuine personal torment or social oppression destroys our spiritual lives. Either way, these images have the power to help or hinder our understanding and practice of the Christian spiritual life.

CHAPTER 7

The Rule as Teacher

We live in an ambivalent age. On the one hand, Christian congregations that provide clearly marked boundaries in membership with particular expectations about how persons participate in the lives of those congregations seem to be growing. Many mainline congregations, often those who have claimed to be most welcoming and least concerned with the disciplines of the Christian life, are declining. On the other hand, we continue to live with the consequences of individualism and the idealization of personal autonomy. Various corporate officers have bent and broken the rules of finance and commerce; some have been convicted and sent to prison; others have eluded prosecution or other forms of accountability. Leaders in various government offices act as if rules of international law apply only to countries other than our own. Yet many monastic and religious communities around the country are seeing a growth in the number of nonmonastic persons seeking oblate, "cojourner," or friend relationships with their communities, relationships that invite living the community's rule of life to the extent possible in persons' particular life situations.

In this ambivalent age, what does it mean for us to think about a rule of life as a teacher? How does a rule of life teach? How does a spiritual rule function in individual faith formation and in communities of learning? We begin our response exploring an image found in the Rule of Saint Benedict (RB) and echoed in the Rule of the Society of Saint John the Evangelist (RSSJE). That image is a school for the Lord's service.

At the conclusion of the opening section of the Prologue, Benedict writes:

> We intend to establish a school for the Lord's service. In drawing up its regulations, we hope to set down nothing harsh, nothing burdensome. The good of all concerned, however, may prompt

us to a little strictness in order to amend faults and to safeguard love. Do not be daunted immediately by fear and run away from the road that leads to salvation. It is bound to be narrow at the outset. But as we progress in this way of life and in faith, we shall run on the path of God's commandments, our hearts over-flowing with the inexpressible delight of love.[1]

"A School for the Lord's Service"

While both Benedict and the RSSJE use the image of the school to describe the whole of monastic life, it also functions to describe the purpose of the rule itself. The rule schools us in the way of the Christian life, describes the path of the Lord's commandments, and sets us on the road to salvation. For the Society of St. John the Evangelist, "the community is a school of reconciliation, conversion, and healing for sinners, in which we can grow in our capacity to give ourselves to God."[2] The rules of these communities serve less as legal codes to be rigidly applied and more as constituting documents that "articulate the identity of the community, express its ruling values and ideals, and specify its practices." As such, monastic rules enable a community "to sustain its specific identity and focus" even as its leadership changes. Monastic rules also enable "the Church to confirm and validate the vocation of the community and hold it accountable."[3]

We might have difficulty thinking about many of the communities in which we live or participate as "schools for the Lord's service," especially when the church school has fallen on hard times. In much of the North American church, we have tended to limit church schooling to children and the volunteers we recruit to teach them; by extension, the church school also refers to the classrooms scattered throughout our church buildings. We have also increasingly come to treat church more as a place where we are served with comfort and care in times of crisis and need. Church has become for many a social club or place of personal retreat rather than a school to which we come in expectation of transformation. What might it mean to shift our thinking from "church schooling" to "church as school"?

To the extent that we think about what a school is, we think of a school as a particular place, even a building or group of buildings, to which we go for instruction. Our church buildings have throughout history been such places; the development of the Sunday school as first a place for basic literacy education and only secondarily for Christian or religious education suggests a historic blurring between what we today think of as public schools and the church school. In such places we generally think of learning as acquiring a particular skill or body of information. We learn how to do something. In some cases, we think of schools as places in which we are preparing ourselves for some later action or work. We learn "how" in school; we later apply what we learn in our work. In this sense, a school is not only a place of instruction, but also a place of preparation for something yet to come.

Yet a school is also a people gathered for some common purpose or associated with some particular set of practices. In this sense, a school is a community of practice. We might think, for example, of schools of artists. On the one hand, an art school is a place of instruction and practice in particular artistic skills. On the other hand, we may think of modernism or abstract expressionism as a school of art, a group of artists joined together by a common method, form of expression, or understanding of the work of the artist. The church is a school in this sense as well. Whether we gather in a storefront, meeting house, or gothic cathedral, we as the church are a people with a shared work. We are joined together in baptism by a common commitment to the way of Jesus Christ, to love God and our neighbors. We learn and share common practices—baptism, the Lord's Supper, congregational song, prayer in the name of Jesus—and common texts we acknowledge as Holy Scriptures.

A school is also a people gathered together in a relationship of teacher and student, master and disciple. We attribute a certain amount of authority to that teacher, give ourselves over to learn from the teacher, and attempt to be faithful in implementing what we have learned. In our various church traditions, we have persons specifically called as teachers of the faith—Sunday school teachers, catechists, pastors, bishops. As Christian people, however, we also acknowledge that to the extent we consider ourselves disciples of Jesus Christ, Jesus is the one true teacher or master to whom we commit ourselves. It is, in the end, the way of Jesus that we seek to learn and live.

The school Benedict describes in his rule for monasteries is in many ways the same school in which all Christian people are called to enroll. Whether we have been led toward baptism as adults or have lived from our baptism as children, our faith calls us to enroll in the school of Christ, to learn from Christ. In this school, our primary intent is to learn Christ by following in the way of Christ rather than learning about Christ (although this too must happen along the way). Benedict calls his community to "prepare our hearts and our bodies to wage a battle of holy obedience" (RB Prologue 40) to Christ's precepts, to learn the ways of life that permit us to resist the ego influences that would lead us away from Christ's way. Benedict invites us, as he invited his community, to engage in a system of communal practices that lead to "personal integration for spiritual progress in a world which tends to fragment a person."[4]

Esther de Waal brings together the themes of the school as a place and people learning the integrating way of Christ with two comments. First, as a place and people, we enter a school knowing that we do not learn alone "but as part of a company."[5] We do not come as a disciple, but as the company of disciples, in twos or threes as we see in the calling of Jesus' first disciples, in the company of the twelve, in the seventy, and in the multitudes that gather for a feast on the hillside and lakeshore. Second, de Waal writes, "In Benedict's school we shall learn Christ, not in any intellectual or cerebral way but in heart and mind and feeling. If Christ is my true self, living out of whom I discover my fullest humanity, then the Rule is there to lead me into the growth of the Christ-self."[6]

In our exploration of the rule as teacher, then, our starting point is with the rule as a school in which we practice the way of Christ with others who are also seeking to live "the Way." But, as is the case with most schools, even when various schools share common tasks, the particular ways in which those tasks take shape and come to be lived out will vary according to the particular emphases of the school or, in this case, rule of life. Three rules will shape our exploration: the Rule of Benedict, one of the oldest; the Rule of the Society of Saint John the Evangelist, one of the most recent; and the General Rules of the Methodist Societies, which were foundational in the initial organization of the reform movement that became the Methodist church.

The Rule of Benedict

Although we have used the RB to shape the discussion from the beginning of this chapter, we have not yet looked at it in any detail. As we do so, remember that the RB has generated a substantial amount of commentary and discussion over the course of its fifteen-hundred-year history.[7] The intent here is not to provide a detailed commentary but to survey the background, content, and insights of Benedict's rule.

The little we know about Benedict comes from the *Dialogues* of Gregory the Great, written as many as fifty years after Benedict's death, in which Gregory does not intend a biography but a teaching document about the ways in which God works in a person's life, much like we saw in Athanasius's *Life of Antony*.[8] Benedict was born around 480 in Nursia, northeast of Rome, and died from a fever on March 21, 547. As a young man he was "sent to Rome for school and there experienced the religious conversion that led him to renounce the world."[9] The world Benedict attempted to leave behind was a world of increasing chaos. Rome had suffered significant decline in political leadership and power; it was increasingly under attack by the people to its north (especially the Ostrogoths and Lombards) as well as from the east by the Byzantine empire. The church had weathered several major challenges to the orthodox faith and was seeing various fissures emerge between west and east, Latin Roman and Greek Byzantium.

Benedict did not see himself as either a reformer of the church or the founder of a movement. He fled the world seeking to live the Christian life, first with a small group of ascetics, then in solitude at Subiaco, and, after forming a number of communities in Rome, finally at Monte Cassino, eighty miles south of Rome. In each place, with each community, and with the rule, he sought to be "the father of a community, who handed on to his sons the traditional monastic wisdom he had received from others."[10] The rule was written primarily for one community; it did not acquire any kind of normative or exclusive status for monastic life until the ninth century. This wisdom included the writings of Cassian and the church fathers, the sayings of the earlier desert monastics, and other monastic rules such as those of Basil and Augustine, as well as the Rule of the Master, on which Benedict heavily relied.

In its continuity with and reliance on scripture and the writing of the early church fathers, the RB serves as a practical guide for cultivating and living the Christian virtues. Benedict locates the monastic life, as all of Christian life, firmly in the center of scripture (in good Protestant fashion!) and tradition (see RB 73). As a school for the Lord's service the rule provides a practical summary of the gospel and an outline of how to live the gospel life. In its intent that we learn to live the gospel life, it makes clear the soteriological purpose of the disciplined life, to work out our salvation in the midst of a community. As Columba Stewart has noted, "the genius of Benedict was to situate the individual search for God within a communal context that shaped as well as supported the quest. For him community was not simply the place where one seeks God but its vital means."[11]

Overview of the Rule of Benedict

The RB is written in seventy-three chapters. Although this may seem to provide enough detail to regulate all aspects of monastic life, it does not. Rather, it provides the principles for monastic life in a way that makes the rule adaptable over time to many different situations. This, perhaps, is what has allowed it to shape Benedictine life for fifteen centuries.

Stewart suggests that the RB can be divided into four major sections. The first section includes the prologue and chapters 1 through 7. The prologue "invites the individual Christian to follow the Lord's call to monastic life."[12] The task set before us is to "run on the path of God's commandments, our hearts overflowing with the inexpressible delight of love" (RB Prol. 49). Chapters 1 through 3 set out the basic framework of monastic life, describing the kinds of monks, the qualities of the abbot, and the need to seek counsel within the community. Chapters 4 through 7 provide a "primer of monastic spirituality,"[13] detailing the "tools for good works": obedience, restraint of speech, and humility. Where chapter 4 provides a practical description of Christian life, chapter 7, in its detailing of the twelve steps of humility, provides a theological description of the journey one makes through this life.

The second section, chapters 8 through 20, provides instruction for the ordering of communal liturgical prayer. This includes the timing and ordering of the daily offices (set times throughout the day for prayer), the ordering of psalmody in the office, and a brief theology of prayer, noting that it is not "our many words" that draw God's attention but "our purity of heart and tears of compunction" (RB 20:3).

The third section, chapters 21 through 67, addresses the structure and practices of monastic life. This includes such things as the correction and conversion of those who stray from the rule; possession and use of material goods; the regulation of food and sleep; the rhythm of work, prayer, and study; the care of the sick and elderly; the reception of guests; and the reception of new members. As Stewart notes, the RB is not a severe document. "It allowed Benedict's monks adequate sleep, decent nourishment, sufficient material goods, and a manageable round of liturgical and individual prayer."[14]

Benedict deals generously, or perhaps with a "generous strictness," with the foibles of human nature. Benedict is a good psychologist and spiritual guide. He understands, in a rather sophisticated way, the varied, complex character of human life. He is mindful of the differing needs of young and old, the sick and the strong, the simple and the intellectually sophisticated. This sense of care was sounded at the beginning of the rule, where Benedict states his intention "to set down nothing harsh, nothing burdensome" although "the good of all concerned…may prompt us to a little strictness in order to amend faults and to safeguard love" (RB Prol. 46–47).

The final section, chapters 68 through 73, provides a theology of monastic life "with a particular emphasis on love."[15] Here Benedict addresses how monks relate to one another without presumption or pride and in mutual obedience. The end of chapter 72 makes explicit the work of love and charity that is at the heart of monastic life: "To their fellow monks they show the pure love of brothers; to God, loving fear; to their abbot, unfeigned and humble love. Let them prefer nothing whatever to Christ, and may he bring us all together to everlasting life" (RB 72:8–11). What may surprise some first-time readers is Benedict's continued insistence that the real rule for monks is scripture and that monasticism is "simply a form of Christian life itself."[16] In this light, monasticism is not for the exceptional Christian, but it is a means to live the virtuous Christian life in and with the church. Nevertheless, as is true of the other rules we explore in this chapter, the perfection of life and love described in the RB and the formation it provides comes not by reading about it but by living it as best we can in the various places of our lives. The single promise the monk makes of stability, *conversatio* (usually translated as "fidelity to the monastic way of life"), and obedience is such a promise to seek perfect love (see RB 58:17). But as Brian Taylor interprets these actions, it is also a promise nonmonastics can make. For Taylor, stability is "a lifelong commitment to one's vocation, family and friends—being fully accepting of this life as a vehicle of grace." To promise *conversatio* is to promise "openness to growth and change, willingness to look at oneself and to be challenged by God and others." Obedience, perhaps the promise many of us most struggle with as we read this or other rules, is "fidelity to this Rule and to the limits, demands, disciplines, and rhythms of the life we have been given."[17] Benedict closes: "Are you hastening toward your heavenly home? Then with Christ's help, keep this little rule that we have written for beginners. After that, you can set out for loftier summits of the teaching and virtues we mentioned above, and under God's protection you will reach them" (RB 73:8–9).

The content of the RB provides a curriculum for the Christian life; its form models for us the kind of attention to space, structure, and details a good curriculum requires, even in the guidelines for the community's corporate prayer. As is needed in any teaching relationship, Benedict is attentive to the character of human relationships. He provides not only job descriptions for leaders and participants in the learning community but also guidelines for addressing the diverse needs of different learners and helpful disciplines for managing group dynamics. As we prepare to teach in contemporary schools for the Lord's service, the RB can help us shape both the content and the form of the curricula we employ.

The Rule of the Society of Saint John the Evangelist

The Society of St. John the Evangelist was founded in 1866 by Richard Meux Benson (1824–1915), an Anglican priest, with two Oxford companions, Simeon Wilberforce O'Neill and Charles Grafton (an American priest).[18] The community was formed at the parish in Cowley, located on the east side of Oxford, thus their common name the "Cowley Fathers" (although not all in the community were or are ordained priests). The SSJE was the first men's monastic community founded in England after the Protestant reformation. In 1870, three members of the community moved to Boston to establish the community in North America. Martin Smith, in his introduction to the RSSJE, suggests that SSJE, like many Anglican monastic communities, can be characterized as "living an ordered community life based on regular common prayer, while expressing the call to service in many different forms of ministry."[19] For the North American congregation, this service has taken the form of providing hospitality, leading retreats, offering spiritual direction, developing a publishing house, and creating programs that serve the poor and youth living in the city.[20]

Although the SSJE is almost 140 years old, the current rule of the North American congregation dates from 1996. Smith describes the original rule, written by Benson, as "setting very demanding standards of personal and collective austerity, gravity, and spiritual concentration."[21] (This perhaps fits our own stereotypes of what a monastic or spiritual rule is.) The original rule was conservatively updated by the English congregation in the late 1960s but remained silent about many areas of communal life that faced the brothers at the end of the twentieth century, such as employees, friendship, health, rest and recreation, and old age.

Beginning in the late 1980s, the North American congregation began a communal process of conversation and reflection that led to a revised rule articulating the community's vision and the covenant by which it lives. In the revision, the community sought to express its confidence in the tradition they had inherited. But as Smith writes, they were "convinced that authentic continuity would not consist in carrying over excerpts from the old Rule, but in [their] inner appropriation of the tradition and its re-articulation."[22] In a chapter on "the grace of tradition" (chap. 3), the RSSJE claims that faithfulness to tradition is not a "mere perpetuation or copying of ways from the past, but a creative recovery of the past as a source of inspiration and guidance in our faithfulness to God's future."[23] Like its predecessor, it guides the community's worship and prayer, work and rest, discipline, authority, and accountability. The RSSJE ensures that "all of the different elements of a Spirit-filled life in Christ are valued and given their due place in the whole."[24]

Overview of RSSJE

The RSSJE is organized into forty-nine brief chapters, each addressing one question or practice in the monastic life. These chapters might be loosely organized into five primary themes: the mission and purpose of communal life in the SSJE (1–5); the vows of poverty, celibacy, and obedience to which the monastic commits himself (6–14); the disciplines of worship, prayer, and silence (15–30); mission and service (31–34); and the rules governing initiation, formation, and continuing life in the monastery (35–48). A final chapter summarizes the hope of glory in Christ with which the community lives and which animates their life together. This final chapter provides a doxological conclusion to the RSSJE.

Mission and purpose. Following the model of John, the beloved disciple who lay close to the heart of Christ, the SSJE understands itself to be called into being by God to seek the unity of God's children, enacting a ministry of reconciliation in and through Christ. Although all Christians are called to life in community, the SSJE believes it has a particular vocation to be a "sign to the church," a society within the church for the strengthening of the common life of the body of Christ (chap. 9) The community, as is true of most communities, is not a gathering of the like-minded or of those who agree on all things. Rather, the SSJE, like other expressions of Christian community, serves as a means for conversion and the working out of one's salvation (chap. 10).

Monastic Vows. Traditional Christian monastic practice in the Western church has been framed by the three "evangelical counsels" or "counsels of perfection": poverty, chastity, and obedience. They are considered counsels rather than commandments because they are not incumbent on all Christians, only on those seeking perfection.[25] So, in Matthew 19:21, Jesus instructs the young man seeking eternal life, "If you wish to be perfect, go, sell your possessions, and give the money to the poor." In the RSSJE, the vow of poverty (chap. 6–8) becomes a means of self-emptying, of *kenosis*, by which a person is enabled to live simply, to share all things, to separate oneself from all "that opposes God's way of self-spending love," and to join oneself in real solidarity with the poor (chap. 17). The RSSJE is careful to distinguish between voluntary poverty and forced deprivation. Poverty is something the monk takes on rather than has forced upon him or herself.

Similarly, the vow of chastity, usually but not always interpreted as a vow of celibacy, grows in part from a reading of Matthew 19:10–12, where Jesus recognizes a place for voluntary celibacy but acknowledges that not everyone can accept it. The monastic vows in the RB are not explicit about celibacy, focusing first on charity of heart as well as on stability in community and one's commitment to living the monastic life. The vow of celibacy (chap. 9–11) is neither a means to avoid intimacy or commitment nor a means to deny human sexuality and embodiment. Rather, it is a means by which a person makes oneself completely available to Christ and the world, unattached to any one person. Sexual energy and creativity is to be channeled into the nurturing of others in Christ.

The vow of obedience (chap. 12–14) is a means for active, rather than passive, response. It provides the means for detachment from and dying to individual preferences, for giving complete allegiance to the community and its rule, and for the common response of the community. Detachment from our own preferences encourages us to trust the wisdom of the community and enables us to respond promptly to the Lord's call in our lives (chap. 25).

Worship. Like the RB, the RSSJE gives significant attention to the worship and prayer life of the community. However, instead of giving detailed attention to the order and structure of the daily offices as well as to the use of psalmody in the office, the chapters on worship and prayer in the RSSJE give more attention to the theology supporting the community's liturgical practices. Eucharist is central because it intensifies union with Christ, draws the community together, and nourishes the community for the work of conversion and transformation (chap. 17,

p. 34). The daily offices enable persons and community "to enter more and more into the heart of Christ" and "to participate in his offering of love" (chap. 18, p. 36). Prayer, encompassing the whole of the Christian's life, is a means to participate in the divine life of the Trinity (chap. 21, p. 42). Scripture, encountered in preaching, study, and meditation, is to be received as "the living voice of God...continually active to convert, nourish, and transform us" (chap. 20, p. 40).

Mission and Service. All of the community's work grows out of the clear vision of its purpose. Its mission is fulfilled when the whole life of the community as expressed in prayer, worship, and the rhythms of daily life work together to "draw people into life in Christ" (chap. 31, p. 62). There are fewer chapters here than one might expect, given the detailed attention to the ordering of the community's life in other parts of the rule. But this reflects the community's understanding that in faithfulness to their purpose as a Christian community their work may change at the calling of the Holy Spirit. Even so, the SSJE understands its forms of service to church and world to include helping persons learn to pray and exercise discernment, serving as guides and confessors to those preparing for ordained ministry, assisting persons in the work of healing and reconciliation, and serving as active witnesses for peace and social justice (chap. 31). The community could be easily overwhelmed by many demands on its time and energy, so one chapter of the rule attends to the question of discernment, acknowledging the need to account for the resources of the community as well as its limitations as the brothers reflect on the particular needs presented to them (chap. 33).

Life in the Monastery. In the final section of the RSSJE, guidance is provided for reception, formation, and integration of new members into the community (chap. 36–39) and the need for continuing education and formation with the "riches of scripture and Christian tradition" (chap. 41). The community also recognized in creating the rule that, for a variety of reasons, monks occasionally leave the monastic life and that a monk's departure provides an opportunity for the community to learn some things about itself. Even though much has remained constant in monastic life over the centuries, some things, such as the need to deal with employees have changed. So RSSJE provides a chapter on employees, recognizing the dignity of all work, the need to treat all persons with respect, and the importance of employees respecting the privacy of the community (chap. 35). Where the RB seems to discourage friendships as disruptive to communal life, the RSSJE acknowledges the ways in which friendship may be a grace and a means of witnessing to persons "wounded by their quest for intimacy" even as it acknowledges the demands and limitations of friendship in a monastic context (chap. 42, p. 84). The final sequence of chapters addresses concerns for the need to maintain physical as well as spiritual health (44), the balance between work and rest and the need for recreation, even vacation (45), the challenges posed by illness and the reminders of human fragility it provides (46), as well as the particular gifts and challenges of old age (47), and a reminder that the Christian faces death in the faith that Christ's death and resurrection has forever transformed our encounter with death (48).

In its discussion of the theological foundations for its liturgical practices and its wise attention to contemporary issues, such as employer-employee relations, friendship, and the connections between bodily care and spiritual health, the RSSJE guides us to similar discernment. More evident here than in the RB, although no less true of Benedictine communities, the RSSJE provides an example of the ways in which rules, and similarly, curricula, are living documents. Both rules and curricula are developed in conversation with tradition and the particular circumstances of each community. A community undertakes revision never because of a rule's antiquity or curriculum's age, but because of the need for the community to remain true to its purposes and goals.

The General Rules of Methodism

"The people called Methodist" came to be so called because a life of intentional spiritual discipline lies at the heart of the movement's origins, first in the Holy Club at Oxford in which John and Charles Wesley participated and later in the organization of the "united societies"[26] as the Methodist movement expanded in and beyond London, Bristol, Kingswood, and Newcastle. Some critics, both inside and outside of the now United Methodist Church, have argued that what remains of this initial method is an institutional organizational structure separated from the life of spiritual discipline. D. Stephen Long and David Lowes Watson suggest that the purpose of Methodist discipline has "shifted from holiness of heart and life to being relevant to American culture"[27] in a context in which convenience has become "the norm of Christian discipleship"[28] and in which we have come to believe that our new-gained freedom in Christ "dispenses with the need for any basic guidelines."[29] Although the early Methodist movement was clearly not a monastic movement, it called Christian persons to renewal through practices of mutual accountability, service, and prayer that resonate with the ordered Christian life reflected in the RB and RSSJE.

In the preamble to "The Nature, Design, and General Rules of the United Societies," John Wesley describes how in 1739 a group of people "who appeared to be deeply convinced of sin, and earnestly groaning for redemption" came to him for counsel and direction, desiring that he would "spend some time with them in prayer, and advise them how to flee the wrath to come."[30] Wesley described the groups that grew out of this initial request as "a company of men [*sic*] 'having the form, and seeking the power of godliness', united in order to pray together, to receive the word of exhortation, and to watch over one another in love, that they may help each other to work out their salvation."[31] The first edition of these "General Rules" was published in 1743; and, although it appeared in some thirty-nine editions over the subsequent fifty years, the rules remained essentially the same.

Even though the General Rules are relatively unknown to contemporary Methodists, except perhaps as a historical document buried in *The United Methodist Book of Discipline*, originally they were integral to membership in the Methodist societies.[32] New members, admitted on a trial basis for three months, were given a copy of the General Rules at their first meeting.[33] The weekly class meeting under the leadership of a class leader provided a means of mutual accountability and obedience. Persons remained in membership "only if they continued to evince signs of their first desire" by their observance of the rules.[34] As Wesley makes clear, the only condition for admission into the societies was a desire for salvation, but continuation in the society meant that this desire would be manifest in its fruits and by continuing evidence of one's desire for salvation by keeping of the General Rules.[35]

Unlike the rules we have explored to this point, the General Rules of the Methodists are relatively brief. Those continuing in the societies were to "evidence their desire of salvation,…first, by doing no harm, by avoiding evil in every kind—especially that which is most generally practiced"; second, "by doing good, by being in every kind merciful after their power"; and third, by "attending upon all the ordinances of God." Doing no harm includes not taking the name of the Lord in vain or profaning the Lord's Day and refraining from drunkenness, fighting, usury, unprofitable conversation, wearing costly apparel, needless self-indulgence, and "doing to others what we would not they should do unto us." Doing good includes, first, care of the bodies of the hungry, naked, the sick, and the imprisoned and, second, the care of souls through instruction, reproof, and exhortation. Doing good also includes "diligence and frugality," denying oneself, and "submitting to the reproach of Christ." Attending on the ordinances of God, which Wesley often refers to as "the ordinary means of grace," includes "the public worship of God; the ministry of the Word, either read or expounded; the Supper of the Lord; family and private prayer; searching the scriptures; and fasting or abstinence."[36]

Although Wesley does refer to the societies or General Rules as a school as we find in the RB and RSSJE, central to the process is the weekly class meeting and the role of the class leader. Through the efforts of class and leader, guided by the General Rules, the Methodist societies were provided with a means for mutual accountability, for "watching over one another in love," and for building up consistent discipleship. The simplicity of the General Rules, rather than provide a "hopelessly dated precritical formulation,"[37] provides simple guidance available to all, regardless of class or education. In shaping these rules, Wesley holds together the often-separated active (doing no harm and doing good) and contemplative (attending on the ordinances) practices of the Christian life. He also emphasizes the communal nature of the Christian life. As Helmut Nausner observes: "holiness is certainly not the way of a pious eccentric or recluse; rather it is a way pursued in fellowship. Holiness is experienced and attained in community, in bearing one another's burdens and in watching over one another in helpfulness." Even in his attention to public worship, the Lord's Supper, and family prayer, Wesley is clear that our "meeting with God does not occur as an individual experience but rather in association with other believers."[38] "Ye are taught of God 'not to forsake the assembling of yourselves together, as the manner of some is;' but to instruct, admonish, exhort, reprove, comfort, confirm, and in every way 'build up one another'."[39]

Unlike Luther, who seemed to set works of faith over against the fullness of God's grace, Wesley sees a more integral relationship between faith and works. For Wesley, the Christian's

> one intention at all times and in all things is, not to please himself, but him whom his soul loveth…All that is in the soul is holiness to the Lord. There is not a motion in his heart but is according to his will. Every thought that arises points to him, and is in obedience to the law of Christ.
>
> All the commandments of God he accordingly keeps, and that with all his might. For his obedience is in proportion to his love, the source from whence it flows. And therefore, loving God with all his heart, he serves him with all his strength.[40]

Although the particular concerns about "works righteousness" expressed by the first generations of the Protestant reformation continue to play a role in the development of the Methodist movement, Wesley always seems clear on the priority of God's grace in the transformation of human life. Faith and works grow in response to the activity of God's grace in a person's life; the means of grace, as with the general rules, are practices with which a person responds to and cooperates with the working of God's grace.

As in narratives of the saints lives (e.g., *Life of Antony*), the general rules of Methodism emphasize the relationship between inward spiritual transformation and outward care for one's neighbors and the world. Living a full Christian life requires moving beyond a passive stance of doing no harm to an active engagement in doing good. As the other two rules, the General Rules are attentive not only to prayer, study, and piety, but also to the ways in which one lives in community. Attention to one without the other is insufficient.

Conclusion

The "school for the Lord's service" created by these rules of life, whether in the monastery or in the world, provides a "syllabus" that directs us in learning the way of Christ. The rules define the (narrow) path we are to follow, instruct us in the Christian life, and set before us an interwoven ensemble of practices by which we live this life. Although not speaking directly about rules of life but about a comprehensive life story, George Lindbeck provides a good summary of how the "school of the rule" teaches. A rule of life, as such a life story

> is not primarily a set of propositions to be believed, but is rather the medium in which one moves, a set of skills that one employs in living one's life...To become religious—no less than to become culturally or linguistically competent—is to interiorize a set of skills by practice and training. One learns how to feel, act, and think in conformity with a religious tradition that is, in its inner structure, far richer and more subtle than can be explicitly articulated. The primary knowledge is not *about* the religion, nor *that* the religion teaches such and such, but rather *how* to be religious in such and such ways.[41]

A rule of life, while not neglecting the work of doctrinal instruction, is a mode of formation that attends primarily to how to live the Christian life rather than to thinking about that life. While not ignoring what particular theological traditions teach, all three rules focus on helping persons and communities interiorize the Christian faith—making the Christian faith part of our bodies as well as our minds and hearts. Each rule emerges in the context of particular theological, ecclesial, and social structures and traditions as a means to help persons learn to be Christian in community. As Randy Maddox notes in a discussion of "disciple-making" in the Methodist traditions, the ruled or disciplined life is a practice or set of practices "that one engages in regularly in order to develop the capacity or 'freedom' for desired behaviors to flow forth naturally...Failure to practice means increased difficulty (and less reliability) in attaining one's desired goal."[42]

As we see especially in the RSSJE, but also implicitly in the RB and the General Rules, these rules are not adopted uncritically or forcibly. Persons carefully and willfully take on a rule only after individual and communal discernment. On the one hand, it is a moving experience for a nonmonastic to watch and listen a person petitioning to be received into a monastic community and to make the promise of stability, *conversatio*, and obedience. On the other hand, there is a different kind of "knowing" that a monastic might experience in the same context. For many of us, this knowledge might be reflected in what persons long-married know as they watch and listen to a young couple take the solemn vows of marriage promising their own modes of stability ("from this day forward…until we are parted by death"), *conversatio* ("for better, for worse, for richer, for poorer, in sickness and in health"), and obedience ("to love and to cherish"). Perhaps monastics have something to teach married nonmonastics about discernment and commitment in Christian community.

None of our discussion so far is intended to suggest that there are no tensions in the ruled life. Randy Maddox, in his discussion of "disciple-making," names three particular issues that warrant our attention. The first concerns the temptation to reduce the Christian life to an ungraceful legalism by which we either come to "despair at our failures or consume one another with judgmentalism."[43] So RSSJE, in its discussion of obedience, states that the "community is a school of reconciliation, conversion, and healing for sinners, in which we grow in our capacity to give ourselves to God" (chap. 25). And in the RB we find repeated injunctions against grumbling (or murmuring, see RB 5:14–19).

The second concern, more an issue in the seemingly unruled and ambivalent time in which we live than in the ruled life, is created by our misunderstanding of the costly nature of the gift of grace. Such misunderstanding leads to "an antinomian offer of forgiveness with any expectation…of change." The "generous strictness" of the RB is perhaps exemplified in the discipline and care the abbot is to exercise with those under his care, seeking out and carrying back to the flock the wayward or lost sheep (RB 27:5–9).

The third concern, introduced in some ways by Wesley's concern for Christian perfection, is the temptation "to get caught up in a false perfectionism that fails to recognize the continuing role of confession and growth in the Christian life."[44] Wesley's intent with the General Rules is that they become the means by which Christians continue to "evidence their desire of salvation." In the RSSJE, the chapter on life profession offers the reminder that, while life profession "brings to an end the period of probation, so it inaugurates a lifetime of developing response" (78).

Finally, in the listing of the tools for good works, the RB reminds us that we should not "aspire to be called holy before [we] really are, but [to] first be holy that [we] may more truly be called so" (RB 4:62). This, perhaps, is where a discussion of rules can end: They fulfill their purpose as a school for the Lord's service as they enable us to practice holy living and lead us to perfect love.

CHAPTER 8

The Way of Return
as Discipleship Method

The "real world" experience of living a Christian life and inviting others to learn how they might do the same offers frequent reminders of how far we can and do stray from our spiritual commitments and practices. We decide to rise half an hour early each morning to read a portion of scripture and then, a few days or weeks later, find ourselves hitting the snooze button on the alarm rather than rolling out of bed at the appointed time. We commit ourselves to love others as God loves us and then belittle the supermarket checker who is slow to ring up our purchases. We covenant to care for a partner through all that life brings and periodically feel resentment that his or her needs interfere with our plans. Our thoughts and actions do not always represent the person we would like to say we are or what we believe a Christian ought to be. The realities of sin and brokenness are ever evident in our lives.

The apostle Paul was fully aware of the difficulties we face in keeping our spiritual desires and our actions synchronized. "I do not understand my own actions," he wrote to the churches in Rome. "For I do not do what I want, but I do the very thing I hate...I can will what is right, but I cannot do it" (Rom. 7:15, 18b). He even went so far as to describe himself as a slave attempting to serve two masters: God, whom he acclaimed as sovereign in his mind, and sin, the vast collection of unhealthy and destructive temptations offered him daily in the guise of opportunities for self-fulfillment and social status. His metaphors for a life of faithfulness often contain the element of perseverance: we are to run the race set before us (Heb. 12:1), to put our hand to the plow with the expectation of eventual reward (1 Cor. 9:10), to endure suffering (Rom. 5:3; 12:12), and to become a living sacrifice awaiting transformation (Rom. 12:1–2). Being Christian is not an easy task in the view of this early church leader.

It seems to involve continual watchfulness, as one tries to stay true to God in the midst of myriad distractions.

The Jewish tradition upon which Paul built his understanding of discipleship also recognized the tensions inherent in human attempts to love and serve God. Over and over again, kings and prophets accused the people of Israel of going their own way rather than God's way. Hezekiah, ruler of Judah in the seventh century B.C.E., sent letters throughout Judah and Israel urging the people to repent of their sin. "O people of Israel, return to the LORD, the God of Abraham, Isaac, and Israel, so that he may turn again to the remnant of you who have escaped from the hand of the kings of Assyria" (2 Chr. 30:6). The prophet Isaiah, serving as God's mouthpiece, proclaims, "I have swept away your transgressions like a cloud, and your sins like mist; return to me, for I have redeemed you" (Isa. 44:22). Through the prophet Jeremiah comes the appeal, "Return, O faithless children, says the LORD, for I am your master" (Jer. 3:14a). The prophet Hosea exhorts, "Return, O Israel, to the LORD your God, for you have stumbled because of your iniquity" (Hos. 14:1). Similar words are repeated by the prophets Joel (2:13), Zechariah (1:3) and Malachi (3:7); and prophetic concern about the people's failure to return to God are refrains sounded by Amos (4:6–11) and Haggai (2:17). Even Job's friends were convinced that his difficulties arose because he had strayed from God's will. Eliphaz counsels Job, "Agree with God, and be at peace; in this way good will come to you. Receive instruction from his mouth, and lay up his words in your heart. If you return to the Almighty, you will be restored" (Job 22:21–23a). Eliphaz may have been wrong about why Job's afflictions began or what Job's loss of material, emotional, and physical well-being meant; but his assumption that persons need to align themselves with God for spiritual well-being is accurate. More often than not, our inability to find God in difficult circumstances stems from our need to see how we have distanced ourselves from what is holy and to return to our roots as persons created, loved, and commissioned by God.

To teach Christian spiritual formation, we must be prepared to acknowledge the human dilemma articulated by Paul and the need for returning to God proclaimed so readily by the Hebrew kings and prophets. This acknowledgement challenges conventional beliefs about human progress and achievement, as it suggests that spiritual formation depends upon nurturing our roots and pruning our branches for fullness rather than encouraging more runners to shoot forth or applying expedient gospels of success to our lives in hopes of acquiring acclaim for our extreme virtue and prosperity. Discipleship based on a way of return orients itself to looking back rather than looking forward: back to the creation, back to what God has done in the lives of God's people through the ages, back to the cross, and back to the promises made at our baptisms. It is the spiritual equivalent of coming back to one's senses after losing touch with reality in some way. Our guide for the way of return as a model for Christian discipleship is a female mystic from the medieval ages, Catherine of Siena.

Catherine of Siena

Born in Italy in 1347, Catherine was raised in a large, pious, and financially comfortable family. Stories about her childhood tell of early mystical experiences, such as angelic ministrations at age five and a first vision at age six. She would later identify this vision as her calling into a lifelong love affair with God.[1] At seventeen she became one of the Sisters of Penance of St. Dominic, a noncloistered order of women, and at twenty-three her visions led her to write numerous letters to influential church leaders challenging the purity of practice in her beloved church. She is credited with orchestrating the return of the papacy to Rome from its exile in Avignon, and she remained a powerfully influential figure in the Roman Church's life until her death in 1380 at the age of thirty-three. She left behind a mystical theology known as the *Dialogue* and almost four hundred letters that chronicle her theological reflections and ecclesial influence. Her canonization as Saint Catherine of Siena occurred in 1461, just eighty-one years after her death.[2]

Like other holy women of the Medieval period—Hildegard of Bingen, Julian of Norwich, and Mechthild of Magdeburg, for example—Catherine's social and political power arose primarily from her spiritual visions, which set her apart as a religious figure and contributed to her public and ecclesial acceptance as a Christian mystic and healer. She was no stranger to physical and spiritual suffering. Born during the scourge of the Black Death, she later was disfigured following a bout of smallpox just before her entry into monastic life. She experienced invisible stigmata, a mystical experience of the passion of Christ, and the physical sensation of being crushed during a vision of the church's sins resting on her shoulders.[3] She served those who were poor and sick in her community and eventually throughout much of Italy as an emissary of two popes, Gregory XI and Urban VI. As her public ministry grew, her monastic order assigned her a spiritual director, Brother Raymond, who encouraged her to write down her mystical visions in the *Dialogue* in 1378.

The Way of Return[4]

The *Dialogue* contains 167 chapters, sometimes divided by editors into four treatises (on Divine Providence, Discretion, Prayer, and Obedience) that Catherine dictated to others while caught up in ecstatic visions and then edited. In the first chapter (also called the prologue), her scribe reveals that the images and words Catherine was recounting were responses to four requests she made of God:

> So she addressed four petitions to the most high and eternal Father, holding up her desire for herself first of all—for she knew that she could be of no service to her neighbors in teaching or example or prayer without first doing herself the service of attaining and possessing virtue...The second was for the reform of holy Church. The third was for the whole world in general, and in particular for the peace of Christians who are rebelling against holy Church with great disrespect and persecution. In her fourth petition she asked divine providence to supply in general and in particular for a certain case which had arisen.[5]

The nature of the particular case mentioned as part of the fourth request remains unknown. The other three petitions are clearer; in each case, Catherine was calling for the reformation of persons or bodies who have strayed from God's intended way of being. She desired her own reformation so that God would grace her with visions for the good of the church and the church might receive the words borne of these visions with authority. She passionately sought the reformation of the church, which she believed had become highly politicized and tainted by corrupt priests and bishops. She feared for the salvation of the world in the face of schism in the church and argued fervently for Christian unity. She became a medieval prophet in the guise of the Hebrew prophets, calling Christians everywhere to return to their God.

Catherine identified the fall in the garden of Eden as the source of humanity's separation from God. In a vision, God told her the truth of why and how God brought persons into existence: "I had created them in my image and likeness so that they might have eternal life, sharing in my being and enjoying my supreme eternal tenderness and goodness."[6] Humanity, however, chose to challenge God's plan for the divine-human relationship, rebelling against God and one another and, in the process, disrupting the peaceful relationships among all created things that God intended. The vision portrays this lack of peace as "a stormy river that beats against [humanity] constantly with its waves, bringing weariness and troubles" to all those God intended to be under God's eternal care.[7] The only way out of the river is Christ, who is depicted in the vision as a bridge over the troubled waters linking earth and heaven. Catherine exhorted the church, its members and its leaders, as well as all humanity to return to God via the Christ Bridge before they were swept away by the river of sin.

The Christ Bridge is comprised of three steps, which Catherine imagined corresponding with three aspects of Christ's crucified body.

The first step is associated with Christ's feet and represents the necessity of choosing to walk the way of return. Just as Christ took on human flesh and walked the earthly path that led to Golgotha and the means of human salvation, Catherine contended that we must orient our hearts and minds to follow Christ, "for just as the feet carry the body, the affections carry the soul."[8] The second step brings us level with Christ's pierced side, through which we see the immense size of Christ's heart, become aware of God's great love for us, and feel stirring within us a corresponding and overwhelming love for God. Step three takes us to the level of Christ's mouth, where we receive the kiss of peace. Here the flood waters of earth's sinfulness can no longer touch us, for we have returned to the source from which we first drew breath and God has revived us, restoring the relationship with us that God intended. Characterizing the soul as a woman, Catherine summarized the movement of a Christian disciple in these terms: "At the first stair, lifting the feet of her affections from the earth, she stripped herself of sin. At the second she dressed herself in love for virtue. And at the third she tasted peace."[9]

Memory

Human beings possess within the soul three aspects of the divine image that enable persons to climb out of the tumultuous river and onto the Christ Bridge: memory, intellect, and will. The role of memory is the recollection of God's faithfulness in forgiving sin and providing blessings. Catherine joins the Hebrew prophets in pointing us toward our common salvation history as the impetus for seeking God's salvific grace once more. Memory is the tool that enables us to say with the psalmist, "O give thanks to the LORD, for God is good; for God's steadfast love endures forever" (Ps. 107:1). It enables us to see how the deliverance wrought by God in the past can become our deliverance as well, for we suffer similar difficulties in life. Sometimes we are faced with difficult transitions that leave us unsettled, hungry for the physical, emotional, and spiritual nurture of companions in life who, like us, thirst for both literal and living water to refresh our lives. The psalmist recalls God's faithfulness in the past when pilgrims on their way to Jerusalem suffered fear and anxiety as part of their journey: "Some wandered in desert wastes, finding no way to an inhabited town; hungry and thirsty, their soul fainted within them. Then they cried to the Lord in their trouble, and God delivered them from their distress; God led them by a straight way, until they reached an inhabited town" (Ps. 107:4–7). Psalm 107 offers similar reassurances for those in prison (10–16), sick (17–20), frightened by storms at sea (23–29), and impoverished and hungry (33–38). The authors of other psalms recall God's deliverance in the face of political adversaries (Ps. 18), personal calamity (Ps. 30), foreign enemies

(Ps. 44, 89), and physical infirmity (Ps. 103). While some of these problems manifest themselves differently in different eras, we are still confronted with the destructive power of disease, betrayal, hunger and famine, war, emotional and physical imprisonment, homelessness, fractured relationships, and myriad other timeless issues that trouble human society. We can allow these difficulties to overwhelm us, as the river in Catherine's vision buffets and eventually drowns those caught in it, or we can step onto the Christ Bridge by recalling the salvation history enacted by God through the ages and Christ's promise to return at the end of the age. The church ritualizes this recollection when it prays the Great Thanksgiving prayer in its eucharistic celebrations:

> We remember the covenant you made with your people Israel…

> We come in remembrance and celebration of the gift of Jesus Christ, whom you sent, in the fullness of time, to be the good news…

> We remember that on the night of betrayal and desertion, and on the eve of death, Jesus gathered the disciples for the feast of Passover. Jesus took bread, and after giving thanks to you, broke it, and gave it to the disciples, saying: "This is my body which is for you. Do this in remembrance of me." In the same way also the cup, after supper, saying: "This cup is the new covenant in my blood. Do this, as often as you drink it, in remembrance of me."[10]

This focal point of remembrance at Christ's table was central to Catherine's experience of the divine-human relationship; it can also be a means by which we encourage contemporary Christians to let memory direct them back to God. When we prepare a space for celebrating the eucharist, we create an opportunity for all who participate to experience again God's gracious forgiveness of sin and reformation of the soul. We encourage biblical literacy through the rehearsal of the stories chronicling interactions with God's people since the time of creation. We invite eyes to be opened to the truth of God's presence with us as we continue Jesus' acts of blessing and thanking God when breaking bread with his disciples. In the communal act of serving one another and being served, we remind ourselves that we are to share with one another the gifts of God just as God shared Godself with us. Catherine noted that "such remembrance makes the soul caring instead of indifferent, grateful instead of thankless."[11] We might also say that the kind of teaching we do when we draw people into liturgical table fellowship helps "the church imprint upon its people the memory of who and whose it is, the memory of a life with God in Jesus Christ, the memory of the One whose passion, death, and resurrection Christians claim for ourselves."[12]

Our task as teachers through the construction of liturgical learning spaces is not, however, to whip up nostalgic fervor for the "good ole days" when God was on our side. Instead, we invite persons to remember so that God's salvation is worked again in our lives through the acts of being broken and reformed as the body of Christ. Debra Murphy points to the significance of the Jewish Passover meal as the pattern for the Christian eucharist. Just as "remembrance [of Israel's deliverance from Egypt] was not simply nostalgia for the past but a proleptic, performative work that celebrated the great mystery of God's salvation in a ritual meal joining together past, present, and future,"[13] our recollection of Christ's death and resurrection points to the past, reconstitutes God's saving power in the present, and holds forth the promise on ongoing salvation in our future. Our liturgical teaching and the reflection we do with other Christians on our experiences of the eucharist must be attentive to how ritual transforms our present and future as well as recalls the past.

Another word of caution related to the cultivation of memory is appropriate given the historical and contemporary propensity of religious and social communities to use stories of past failures and indiscretions as means of unholy control through shaming persons or invoking guilt as an inducement for institutional service. The way of return has no place for a "deformed memory" that "wallows in its own misery and forgets that creation abounds with [God's] mercy."[14] Catherine clearly heard God proclaim that the spiritual power of memory lies in its attachment to the experience of God's grace rather than any catalog of human departures from God's will. While our sin may be the reason we need God's grace, it is God's action that is paramount, not ours. "The memory holds on to my blessings and my goodness to the soul," said God to Catherine.[15] In the recollection of grace we are equipped to take our first step back to God. If we teach a works righteousness type of spirituality focused on constantly atoning for our sins through our own dutiful actions, we miss the opportunity to cultivate through ritual and story a mindfulness of the many ways in which God already has and will continue to act on our behalf.

Intellect

The second aspect of the *imago dei* that can serve to guide our return to God is intellect. The human mind has the ability to contemplate what memory holds dear and to discern within the stories of the faith the way of life God would make known to us. Catherine instructed Christians of her time to seek the truth with the same eagerness a pilgrim in the desert gives to searching for water. Such passion for truth, she believed, flowed most easily from a memory oriented by its recollections of God's unfailing love, for memory sparks affection for God and God's ways, and affection then draws persons into a desire for union with God and the Christian life. She transcribed God's words to her on this topic:

> The soul cannot live without love. She always wants to love something because love is the stuff she is made of, and through love I created her. This is why I said that it is affection that moves the understanding, saying, as it were, "I want to love, because the food I feed on is love." And the understanding, feeling itself awakened by affection, gets up, as it were, and says, "If you want to love, I will give you something good that you can love." And at once it is aroused by the consideration of the soul's dignity and the indignity into which she has fallen through her own fault. In the dignity of her existence she tastes the immeasurable goodness and uncreated love with which I created her. And in the sight of her own wretchedness she discovers and tastes my mercy, for in mercy I have lent her time and drawn her out of darkness.[16]

Intellect, then, is like Abraham's servant Eliezer, returning to the old country in search of a worthy bride for Isaac (Gen. 24). Its challenge is to discern what constitutes a true object of affection, worthy of the soul's time and attention, and what does not. It must guard against other affections that compete with the memory of God's grace. Chief among these competitors, said Catherine, is sensual affection, which generates a selfish love characterized by possessiveness, impatience, and self-importance. The objects of sensual affection "glitter" with such brightness and beauty that they dazzle those who gaze on them, causing persons to be led astray by evil's disguise:

> Were it not for this glitter, people would never sin, for the soul by her very nature cannot desire anything but good. But vice is disguised as something good for her, and so the soul sins. Her eyes, though, cannot tell the difference because of her blindness, and she does not know the truth. So she wanders about searching for what is good and lovely where it is not to be found.[17]

What intellect needs is some sort of test to determine worthiness, just as Eliezer devised a test for the young women (prospective brides) who came to the well at Nahor. Catherine turned to the teachings of Jesus as the means by which we can discern whether we are holding in high esteem the goals to which right memory would recall us. The commandments and counsels of the one the gospel of John calls "the Word," conveyed in the words of scripture, function as signposts on the way of return, pointing out which paths lead to virtue and which to vice. Adverse spiritual conditions—contrary opinions, personal or communal adversity, and prosperity encouraging self-satisfaction or selfishness—can obscure what these signs would tell us, so we must persevere in our efforts to read and follow them. Catherine, drawing on the stories of the Samaritan woman at the well (Jn. 4:1–42) and Jesus' teaching during the Festival of the Booths (Jn. 7:37–38), considered a thirst for living water essential to the journey back to God, for "those who are not thirsty will never persevere in their journey. Either weariness or pleasure will make them stop. They cannot be bothered with carrying the vessel that would make it possible for them to draw the water."[18] The work of discernment takes effort, which only those committed to the task are willing to invest. The contemporary equivalent might be those who affiliate with a congregation because they want to satisfy some sort of spiritual longing, but limit their participation to attendance at worship when they have nothing "more important" to do. The glitter of other affections and the lack of a genuine thirst for God prevent their intellect from studying the scriptures with the single-mindedness of a parched pilgrim bent on discovering the next location of an oasis or well on the map provided for the journey. We must want to know the Word and be willing to engage in a lifelong study of the scriptures if the words are to make any real sense to us as means of grace.

The companionship of other wayfarers is necessary to the success of discernment as well. The familiar words of Matthew 18:20 inform Catherine's assertion of this requirement: "You must be thirsty, then, and you must gather together, as he said, either two or three or more" for "'[i]f two or three or more are gathered in my name, I shall be in their midst'."[19] The obvious interpretation of this requirement in a contemporary society that values democratic process and vigorous intellectual debate would be that multiple opinions are necessary if we are to discover what is true. However, Catherine emphasized a different purpose for companionship. She believed having other persons beside us on the way of return is both a reflection and cultivation of right affection and thus right understanding. Traveling alone suggests selfish motives, a desire to attain God's blessings for the building up of ourselves rather than the body of Christ. Memory focused on God's everlasting love for God's people generates an unselfish affection for the children of God. When we are oriented to love God and neighbor, we are "ready to be thirsty— thirsty for virtue and [God's] honor and the salvation of souls."[20] We cannot understand and persevere in the way of return without obeying the two greatest commandments: to love God and to love our neighbor as ourselves. Hence, intellect needs its vision focused and clarified by an active love of the neighbor, which can only be practiced in the neighbor's presence.

As teachers, we stand in a long line of spiritual leaders who have helped groups of Christians discern the scriptures through careful study and discussion. What does it mean, then, to engage in this traditional practice with the purpose of helping others return to God? One goal becomes the linkage of memory and intellect through the valuation of ritual knowledge as a tool that shapes, as well as is shaped by, our interpretation of the biblical text. The experience of praying the Great Thanksgiving in the eucharistic liturgy and the completion of that thanksgiving in receiving and consuming the sacramental elements establish in us an embodied religious anthropology (understanding of the self) and soteriology (understanding of salvation) that we bring to our study of the scriptures. Exploring these often unarticulated understandings helps those we teach test their religious affections to see if their attractive glitter is because they are the pure gold of love for God or iron pyrite, the fool's gold of our culture's illusory affections for self-improvement and social status.

A second goal is biblical literacy. If the teachings of Christ are the test by which we judge the worthiness of our affections, then we must know the Bible. Just this week I sat around a table with a pastor and three lay leaders in a congregation who fear that the church is severely handicapped in its attempts to be faithful because its members do not know the scriptures. Christian educators can lament the church's recent failings in this area and point fingers at parents for not enforcing church school attendance on their children, at adults for avoiding formal religious instruction, or at pastors for preaching sermons divorced from biblical texts. But our laments and attempts to lay blame elsewhere do not lessen our responsibility to provide multiple opportunities and means for persons of all ages to engage the stories of our faith tradition regularly. We need to ask ourselves: Do the curricula we choose encourage dialogue with the scriptures? Are Bibles and critical study resources (e.g., commentaries, dictionaries, concordances, atlases, etc.) readily available, and do we model their use in our own study and teaching? Do we tell Bible stories in our newsletter articles, reference them in our announcements, study them in teacher training events and education board meetings, proclaim them in intergenerational celebrations, and pray with them in our meditations? When and how are we granting the scriptures authority in our congregational decision making through our consideration of what they have to say to us about the practice of being the church? Teaching to encourage a return to God means teaching the stories of God's love and faithfulness passed down through the ages so that we might not forget who and whose we are.

The assembling of groups for spiritual companionship and accountability is a third goal. A primary characteristic of these groups becomes the hospitality members offer to one another in the name of love. However, this is not a superficial hospitality, in which anything members do is received and blessed for the sake of preserving a veneer of soft and cozy acceptability. Rather, this is a space in which we challenge members to a genuine love for one another, with the tough and tender elements that comprise true love. Parker Palmer suggests that the church needs to become "a place where people confront the stranger in each other and in themselves, and still know that they are members one of another."[21] In Catherine's terms, we might say that the strangers in ourselves are those affections counter to the soul's natural desire for the good. The stranger who is the other resides in the different ways in which we remember and express (or not) God's grace in our lives and the lives of all God's saints. And yet in the common memories of salvation claimed by the church in its liturgy, we are one, and thus can overcome our strangeness and estrangement through the reclamation of this memory.

Will

The will to act is the third aspect of humanity's participation in the divine image that combines with memory and intellect to rescue persons from the overwhelming of sin. As human beings, we are free to choose whether we will order our actions according to our love for God or to other, deformed, affections. Catherine focused on the choice between sensuality, which she also called self-love, and reason, which she believed reflected the innate sense of the good endowed in God's creation of the human mind. If will chooses to let self-love dominate, then reason is held captive to a warped perception of self-importance and cannot truly love God or neighbor. Choosing to love God, however, helps to pull all of life's actions into line with God's will. God revealed to Catherine "that when the soul decides to gather her powers with the hand of free choice in my name, all the actions that person does, whether spiritual or temporal, are gathered in. Free choice cuts itself off from sensuality and binds itself to reason. And then I dwell in their midst through grace."[22] The will to act in God's name orders our lives differently than the will to act by our own authority. The former draws us closer to God and to one another in peace because it enables us to imitate Christ; the latter sows disappointment, discord, and eventually death because it denies the importance of relationships as a means to truth. Catherine knew that God desires the former life for us because God wants us to escape the tumult of the raging river created by sin and to live secure in God's all-encompassing love. She wrote of God's hope for us: "When…the memory for holding and understanding for seeing and the will for loving are gathered together, you find that I am your companion, and I am your strength and your security. You discover the company of the virtues, and because I am in their midst you walk securely and are secure."[23]

Catherine's third guide on the way of return reminds us that discipleship extends beyond remembering God's love liturgically and understanding God's love as expressed in biblical stories to choosing a life of love on a daily basis. Any teaching method we might devise that does not include attention to all three of these aspects cannot facilitate a return to God, for, as Catherine wrote, "the one lends a hand to the other, for good or for evil, by free choice."[24] Each is essential if we are to persevere in the way while being buffeted by the gales of the storm of sin raging around us. Hence, we must teach the human will to choose to follow the two great commandments.

The early leaders of the Israelites approached this task directly. Moses presented the will's choices as two options in response to a divinely-authored covenant:

> I call heaven and earth witness against you today that I have set before you life and death, blessings and curses. Choose life so that you and your descendants may live, loving the Lord your God, obeying [God], and holding fast to [God]; for that means life to you and length of days, so that you may live in the land that the LORD swore to give to your ancestors, to Abraham, to Isaac, and to Jacob. (Deut. 30:19–20)

Joshua laid out a similar choice shortly before his death, telling the Israelites they must decide whether they would serve the God who brought them out of Egypt, the gods who had misled their ancestors, or the foreign gods of the surrounding nations (Josh. 24). Both leaders identified sets of divine laws and decrees the people must expect to live by if they chose to serve God, and both emphasized that a failure to keep these commandments is interpreted as evidence that the choice was not remembrance and love of God but allegiance to other gods. The consequence of such a misplaced will is the death of the nurturing and sustaining divine-human relationship essential to human peace and security.

This covenantal approach to aligning the will with memory and intellect may seem antithetical to the contemporary assumption that religious participation is and should be voluntary. However, the creation of covenant-based discipleship groups, which already operate in some denominational traditions, need not preclude free choice.[25] Persons can and should freely decide whether they will participate in such groups. What Catherine's way of return and the testimonies of Moses and Joshua call our attention to is the significant consequences attached to this choice. When we invite persons to join a covenant discipleship group, do we make plain the importance of cultivating the will in formative rather than deforming ways? Do we emphasize the life-or-death significance of memory, intellect, and will coming together in unified love of God and neighbor? Do we suggest to persons who plead a lack of time and energy that participation in the way of return will reorient their priorities such that they will no longer be overwhelmed by the storm of life but by the everlasting love of God? Teaching for spiritual formation requires us to become less hesitant about naming humanity's essential need to be in loving relationship with God and those around us if we are to know the true nature of life as God intended it. Persons cannot make a genuinely free choice if we collude in minimizing the consequences of their actions and thus permit them to substitute the fool's gold of personal prosperity for the real gold of divine blessing without pointing out the differences in their long-term value.

The call to clearly name the choice is not, however, permission to pass judgment on those who do not will to follow the way of return. Instead, we are to practice holy compassion toward those whose will is weak or misguided, even if a product of their poor choice is ill will toward us and our commitment to foster discipleship through the way of return. We are to love our enemies and pray for those who persecute us (Mt. 5:44), an act of will that keeps our memory and intellect firmly fixed on a godly love of neighbor rather than on personal hurt feelings and job security. Any other response renders our position on the Christ Bridge unsteady, because contempt for another distracts us from attending to God. Memory caught up in holding past slights cannot embrace fully the stories of God's grace, and intellect engaged in studying others' ill intentions cannot focus all its attention on discerning God's loving kindness toward humanity. God revealed to Catherine that only when our thoughts and actions remain aligned with what God asks of us will we experience real freedom from whoever or whatever appears to attack us:

> So if you would attain the purity you ask of me, there are three principal things you must do. You must be united with me in loving affection, bearing in your memory the blessings you have received from me. With the eye of your understanding you must see my affectionate charity, how unspeakably much I love you. And where the human will is concerned you must consider my will rather than people's evil intentions, for I am their judge— not you, but I. If you do this, all perfection will be yours.[26]

There is no promise, however, that this process will be easy, although Catherine received God's assurance that those who attempt this committed but nonjudgmental method of discipleship will be "happy because their longing is one with me, clothed in my gentle will" even as they also experience distress over the lack of absolute perfection in their neighbors and themselves.[27] Teaching the way of return requires keeping a vision of Christ crucified before us just as Catherine did, so we might remember that to lose one's life for the right reason—a God-given, reasonable commitment to love—is to save it. It requires "carrying your heart like a vessel emptied of every desire and every disordered earthly love,"[28] so that God's breath can animate us again as it did in the beginning, lifting us out of the muck and into a divine embrace. Catherine offers us a means to help ourselves, the church, and the world return to whom and what we were created to be: God's chosen and beloved people. Her four petitions can become our petitions as well; and like her, the work begins with our own movement toward the Christ Bridge, gathering others to accompany us as we go.

CHAPTER 9

The Cultivation of Spiritual Knowledge and Wisdom

Historical Background

The question of what constitutes spiritual knowledge, and hence religious literacy and wisdom, is an age-old concern. Augustine wrestled in the fourth century with what should be known and how Christians should seek such knowledge. *The Confessions* chronicles his early fascination with the works of Cicero and other philosophers, whose ideas he eventually rejected as seductive and deceitful. He struggled to see in scripture the same measure of logic and wisdom he initially perceived in his philosophical studies. "They seemed to me unworthy to be compared to the stateliness of Tully," he says in Book III.[1] However, his conversion experience reoriented his pursuits. His opening words in Book X ask of God, "Let me know Thee, O Lord, who knowest me: *let me know Thee, as I am known.*"[2] He claimed God as his teacher and exhorted God to open the meaning of the scriptures to him. Both reason and wisdom become the provinces of God, places in which Augustine believed he and the Christians to whom he wrote could and should dwell. He described them also as the actions of God, God's "eternal Reason," which shapes the laws of the Universe, and God's "Wisdom," which Augustine believed constituted the spiritual insight that "gleams through me, and strikes my heart without hurting it."[3] As Thomas Groome explains, Augustine's "purpose is a quest for practical spiritual wisdom, and his method is based on an experiential/relational way of knowing."[4]

In a similar manner, Pope Saint Gregory the Great described Saint Benedict in the second book of his *Dialogues* as one who "was truly wise, uneducated though he may have been."[5] Gregory lauded Benedict's decision to abandon the philosophical education intended by his parents, noting that the saint feared "that if he acquired any of [the world's] learning he would be drawn down with [the other students] to his eternal ruin."[6] Instead, Benedict chose the solitude of a cave in Subiaco as his way of learning. Here and through his lifelong practice of the spiritual disciplines and commitments that eventually shaped his Rule for monastic life, he came to know what God was thinking. Gregory explained to his literary dialogue partner, Peter, that holy persons like Benedict "understand [God's] judgments and can even pronounce them with their lips; for they keep their hearts united to God by dwelling continually on the words of Holy Scripture and on such private revelations as they may receive, until they grasp [God's] meaning."[7]

Much later, in the fourteenth century, Julian of Norwich explored the intersection of human reason, church teachings, and divine grace in the acquisition of knowledge of God and the Christian life. In one of the last chapters (chap. 80) of *Revelations of Divine Love* she argues:

> In this life [a person] is able to stand because of three things; by these same things God is worshipped, and we are helped, kept, and saved. The first is the use of [a person's] natural reason; the second, the everyday teaching of Holy Church; the third, the inner working of grace through the Holy Spirit. All three come from the one God. God is the source of our natural reason; God the basis of the teaching of Holy Church; and God is the Holy Spirit.[8]

Julian was less suspicious of human reason than Augustine, perhaps because she did not experience the same temptations of philosophical study that sorely plagued the fourth century saint. Yet she was acutely aware of the tensions that can develop when Christians critically reflect on the being and work of God in light of their personal experiences and religious truth claims and are unable to reconcile the two. Vexed herself by questions of election in the face of human sinfulness, her appeal to God for help, "Lord Jesus, King of bliss, how can I find the answer? Who will teach me and tell me what I need to know, if I cannot see it now in yourself?"[9] concretely reinforces her teaching of the primary role of grace within human understanding. Like the holy men about whom Gregory wrote, she dwelt with the revelations she received from God until God's meaning was made plain to her.

The struggle to identify and cultivate spiritual knowledge and wisdom continues in our time. Christian educators, whether in congregations or seminaries, are generally perceived by outsiders as persons responsible for facilitating student movement toward some established goal of orthodoxy and/or orthopraxy. Contemporary North American theological schools with mainstream Protestant ties have tended to link knowledge to the acquisition of information about particular subjects. While the so-called "banking" model of education, in which teachers deposit bits of truth into attentive students, is falling out of favor in many quarters, the legitimate desire to encourage transformation through an encounter with information about the histories, traditions, and psychosocial aspects of human and religious experience raises questions about the place of information in the cultivation of spiritual knowledge. Catholic seminaries (and some of their Protestant kin) have broadened the exploration of how information gathering might take place to include encounters with the sort of sensate knowledge gained through intentional faith formation. Still, curriculum revision conversations in seminaries and perennial curriculum selection debates in congregations suggest that contemporary Christian educators continue to wonder about the nature and form of spiritual knowledge and its cultivation.

Contemporary Definitions of Knowledge and Its Relationship to Religious Literacy

Parker Palmer suggests that there are three general historic understandings of knowledge with which contemporary teachers must contend. The first, born of curiosity, is "pure, speculative knowledge," in which knowing something is the goal itself.[10] The second, rooted in control, is "knowledge as a means to practical ends," or knowing something for utilitarian purposes. Palmer believes both these understandings are problematic because they tend to encourage amoral or corrupt passions. They promote the development of fact-based constructs, detached and objectified modes of theorizing, over-reliance on a concept of reality that prefers concrete objects and logic to intangibles such as mythology and the arts, and the dismissal of passion as a moral good.[11] They seek to separate the knower from what he or she knows rather than to recognize, as in the work of Michael Polanyi, the ways in which knowledge emerges from a complex psychological and biological interaction between the knower and the subject he or she desires to know, even in the generally objectified realm of *scientia*, or technical specialization knowledge.[12]

The better way, Palmer believes, is the third option he presents: "a knowledge arising from love," which has the goal of "the reunification and reconstruction of broken selves and worlds."[13] He finds this orientation toward knowledge represented in the writings of the fourth century desert fathers and mothers, who engaged in classical practices of prayer, contemplation, and solitude as the means by which they came to know that which exists "beyond the appearance of things."[14] This is closer to the classical category of *sapientia*, or contemplative wisdom. His discussion suggests that contemporary religious literacy comes through engagement in relationships and communities of learning that constitute themselves for the purpose of practicing faithful obedience to truth. The goal is to become experientially and personally engaged with

Christianity's stories, rituals, and practices in such an interdependent way that the God who is in and beyond these experiences is encountered and known.

Elliot Eisner's work on cognition elaborates on the historical and cultural definitions of knowledge as those have been influenced by analytic and positivist philosophy. He notes that conventional philosophical categories restrict use of the term *knowledge* to a "warranted assertion" that is either "analytic" or "synthetic." The former "are propositions that are true by definition"; the latter "are assertions about empirical conditions that can be falsified through specific operations that a community of competent inquirers can employ."[15] However, this conventional perspective fails to account for the sensory quality of much of the data and experiences scientists and philosophers use in making assertions.

> [T]o restrict the term *knowledge* and, by implication, *knowing* to what propositions about qualities can reveal is to exclude from the arena of knowledge all that propositions as a form of representation cannot embody...Shakespeare's rendering of jealousy in *Othello*, Picasso's revelations of the horror of Guernica, Schiller's "Ode to Joy" cannot be reduced to propositions.[16]

Eisner underscores the inescapable importance of both direct engagement and imagination in knowing. He objects to the separation of cognitive awareness from affective experience, arguing that "concepts initiate in the forms of experience that the senses make possible."[17] Furthermore, he observes that persons interact with the sensate world in multiple ways, rooted in personal preferences and past experiences, that affect what they know. One can easily transpose this argument to suggest that God and the spiritual life are also experienced through the senses and interpreted in different ways by different persons. Hence the development of religious literacy may depend in part on the "ability to experience the multiplicity of environmental qualities" constituting religious experience.[18]

Transformational learning theorists, such as Jack Mezirow, Robert Kegan, Mary Belenky, and Ann Stanton work primarily with epistemologies (ways of knowing) and may comment only indirectly on the nature of knowledge itself. However, their adoption of a constructive developmental approach to meaning making suggests a bias toward objective (or controlled) knowledge as the goal of maturation. Kegan notes that all ways of knowing involve negotiating the relationship between "the subject and the object in one's knowing." He writes:

> That which is "object" we can look at, take responsibility for, reflect upon, exercise control over, integrate with some other

way of knowing. That which is "subject" we are run by, identified with, fused with, at the effect of. We cannot be responsible for that to which we are subject. What is "object" in our knowing describes the thoughts and feelings we say we have; what is "subject" describes the thinking and feeling that has us.[19]

The goal of transformational learning, say Kegan and his colleagues, is to move what is "subject" toward what is "object" in such a way that one is no longer captive to one's way of knowing, but has control of one's knowing. On the one hand, this epistemology may encourage the reunion of the broken self Palmer ascribes to compassion-generated knowledge, as it reintegrates thinking and feeling. On the other hand, the knowledge such an epistemology is likely to produce might also resemble the utilitarian form of knowledge Palmer identified with a desire for control. The lingering danger associated with knowledge forged in an educational process that constructively emphasizes "contextual understanding, critical reflection on assumptions, and validating meaning by assessing reasons"[20] is that it may not be formed with a full appreciation for the subjectivity (Palmer's "truth") of knowledge itself. Nor, in the case of spiritual knowledge and religious literacy, may it appreciate the fundamentally unequal relationship between God and the one who seeks to know and be known by God.

Mary Belenky and Ann Stanton's work attempts to moderate some of the potential dangers of transformational learning theory by exploring the various structures of women's ways of knowing in relation to the idealized epistemology offered by Mezirow. Belenky identifies five categories (one of which is split into two subcategories) of female knowers and their knowledge.[21] "The Silenced" have no sense that they have knowledge or are competent to seek or receive knowledge. They actually do acquire knowledge through concrete experience, but such knowledge is virtually invisible to them and they would not expect religious literacy. "Received Knowers" possess knowledge that has been, in their view, passed on to them by others who received it before them. Knowledge, then, consists of self-evident truths that go from one who has already been taught to one who requires teaching. A simplistic view of "passing on the faith" patterned primarily on the uncritical transference of religious data (creedal statements or spiritual practices) for literacy could fit this category. "Subjective Knowers" define knowledge in terms of their own opinions, intuitions, and insights. Religious literacy could consist of the formulation of ideas about topics of personal interest in theology and religious practice.

"Separate Knowers" are one half of the category "Procedural Knowers." They dissect the knowledge of others, adopting for themselves either the ideas that survive their piercing scrutiny or an opposite proposition. For them, religious literacy might consist of a commitment to a reduced canon of acceptable narratives and practices that have met their tests for usefulness and defensibility. Their twin sisters, "Connected Knowers," on the other hand, attempt to immerse themselves in the other's epistemology so that they can know what the other knows in the way the other knows it. Although they may legitimize multiple and competing knowledge claims, they may also tend toward a harmonizing approach to religious literacy, in which all ideas will eventually come together in (or under) one unified truth. "Constructed Knowers" intentionally embrace processes of constructing knowledge that draw on multiple forms of engagement with the subject to be known. As described by Belenky and Stanton: "They stand back, question, take apart, and criticize points of view they see as partial, unfair, and/or destructive. They also move inward, see the whole, listen, understand, integrate, build up, and create."[22] They might consider religious literacy an ever-evolving and lifelong process of dialogue with established and emerging spiritual knowledge.

Transformational learning theory helpfully underscores the social nature of knowledge, both as experienced in the communal discourse that shapes the construction of knowledge and in the interaction between knower and what is known. However, as Peter Hodgson points out, several questions pertinent to the cultivation of spiritual knowledge and wisdom are left unanswered:

> When knowers enter into union with what is to be known through a construction of it, what actually *is* known? Where and what is truth in this process?…Is the process of constructing meaning in an interactive, intersubjective nexus in some way a mirror, or speculum, of an ultimate relationality that pervades all that is, including God? Is truth to be measured more in its pragmatic effects than in its disclosure of the being of things?[23]

Hodgson seeks the help of Bernard Meland in suggesting an approach to knowing that respects the commitments of developmental constructivism while addressing the theological and religious education concerns embedded in these questions. Meland characterizes religious knowledge as truth emerging from a process of religious thinking that involves a level of "imaginative interpretation" combined with and extending beyond analytic and constructive thinking to help persons in religious meaning making. (In his invoking of the imagination, he echoes Eisner's concern for moving beyond epistemologies that presume a purely representative concept of propositional knowledge.) Such imaginative interpretation "has an aesthetic quality"[24] Hodgson finds critical to the "insightful seeing or envisioning of what shows or presents itself" that he calls "Wisdom."[25]

Letting Past and Present Critically Shape One Another

How then, do we navigate among the many issues raised historically and currently about knowledge, epistemology, spiritual knowledge, and wisdom in a constructive and theologically coherent way that contributes to the formation of contemporary people in Christian faith? Perhaps we can invite a historical guide, Saint Diadochos of Photiki, to direct us on the journey. This spiritual director can lead us into a discussion of what might be essential elements of contemporary Christian epistemologies and teaching models, whether in the congregational or theological school setting.

Diadochos, a fifth-century Greek bishop, approached the question of spiritual knowledge with at least two assumptions: that such knowledge is necessary for human salvation and sanctification and that mystical experience (particularly through the practices of prayer and contemplation) is essential to faithful perception of religious truth. His short treatise, *On Spiritual Knowledge and Discrimination: One Hundred Texts*, provides guidance for exploring the relationships among divine inspiration, knowledge and wisdom, and intellectual perception and mystical experience, and for considering the ways in which our understandings of these relationships shape our teaching.

In the customary manner of the time, the full title of Diadochos's treatise describes the work's theological perspective and educational purpose:

> On Spiritual Knowledge and Discrimination, Explaining what kind of spiritual knowledge we need in order to reach, under the Lord's guidance, the perfection which He has revealed, so that each of us may apply to himself the parable of deliverance and bring to fruition the seed which is the Logos: One Hundred Texts[26]

This statement sets up a progression from spiritual knowledge to divinely-assisted perfection. The parable referenced (identified by the editors as Mt. 13:3–8) is that of the sower whose seed falls on various types of soil with predictably different results. Diadochos's title, then, suggests that spiritual knowledge is analogous to "good soil" in which the Word of God can grow easily and abundantly.

Diadochos quickly established a link between spiritual knowledge and free will, defining the latter as the ability to choose to what end the soul will direct itself and then identifying "true knowledge" with "the power to discriminate without error between good and evil."[27] His treatise clearly states that this knowledge is not self-generated; rather, it is God's gift. "Nothing," he wrote, "is so destitute as a mind philosophizing about God when it is without Him."[28] At the same time, he understood that the human mind could be rightly engaged and satisfied by theological reflection if God inspired a person's intellectual perceptions. He advised his readers to make themselves "a dwelling-place for the Holy Spirit. Then we shall have the lamp of spiritual knowledge burning always within us."[29]

Diadochos, then, guides us initially into an exploration of spiritual knowledge that reinforces Palmer's third option. The constructive role he assigns spiritual knowledge in the process of sanctification can coexist with Palmer's emphasis on spiritual knowledge as a means for redressing human brokenness. His attention to right moral discernment as a mark of spiritual knowledge is also compatible with Palmer's claim about practicing obedience to truth. These early texts thus can easily be read as supporting an epistemology focused on the development of *sapientia* in line with the kind of knowledge Palmer identifies as rooted in compassion. But Diadochos carries his epistemology further.

Spiritual knowledge is also connected to wisdom, both in their shared origin in God and in the latter's role as an outward expression and augmentation of the former. Diadochos believed some receive spiritual knowledge, which illuminates the inner life, and a few receive spiritual knowledge and wisdom, which gives one the ability to interpret to others the "energy of love" experienced in one's life. His use of the term *wisdom* is associated with persons who teach or "speak about God" as he is doing.[30] In the latter sections of the treatise, he also refers to "the gift of theology" (also characterized as a "gift of contemplative vision"), which is the movement in internal spiritual knowledge to complete and inseparable communion with God.[31] We might term this a form of wisdom in which the self interprets its experience to itself rather than the external world.

Implicit in Diadochos's gifts of wisdom and theology is a kind of negotiation between what we can and cannot say about what we know that is also at stake in the epistemologies developed by Mezirow and his associates. But whereas transformational learning theorists imagine a progression from subjectivity to greater objectivity, Diadochos guides us to consider the possibility that what we can say about what we know is dependent on how thoroughly the subject of our knowing, God, has us. Within Diadochos's system, we are no longer responsible for gaining control of our thinking and feeling, but for practicing an obedience to God that leaves us subject to God's all encompassing love.

For this fifth century saint, the divine gift of spiritual knowledge comes to those who sit with God in prayer. Only in silencing the noisiness of external and internal demands on one's time and energy can persons encounter the fullness of God's love that unites the human soul with the divine:

> Those pursuing the spiritual way must always keep the mind
> free from agitation in order that the intellect, as it discriminates

among the thoughts that pass through the mind, may store in the treasuries of its memory those thoughts which are good and have been sent by God, while casting out those which are evil and come from the devil.[32]

This work, assisted by the Spirit, creates space for a "faith energized by love" and opens up the possibility that God might also give one the gift of wisdom if the soil is right. Hence, the lifelong work of Christians is to prepare the fields of their lives through prayer and study, for "spiritual knowledge comes through prayer, deep stillness and complete detachment, while wisdom comes through humble meditation on Holy Scripture and, above all, through grace given by God."[33]

Diadochos warned, however, that the mind may prefer study over prayer because of the human interest in philosophical speculation and the perceived rewards of public acclaim and personal satisfaction associated with knowledge acquired through study. His counsel is simple: pray more, study less.

> We should spend most of our time in prayer, in singing psalms and reading the Holy Scriptures, yet without neglecting the speculations of wise men whose faith has been revealed in their writings. In this way we shall prevent the intellect from confusing its own utterances with the utterances of grace, and stop it from being led astray by self-esteem and dispersed through over-elation and loquacity.[34]

Once again, the emphasis in the latter sections of the treatise is not on a separation of intellectual perception from mystical experience but on the union of heart and mind through divinely-inspired insights.

Here Diadochos directs us to attend to the importance of Eisner's claim that genuine knowledge involves direct and imaginative engagement with a subject as well as rational analysis. He also encourages us to appreciate Eisner's emphasis on the multisensory quality of seemingly empirical data and its interpretations. For Diadochos, God reveals Godself through devotional reading of the scriptures and through critical theological analyses of the same texts read in tandem. He warns against overdependence on the latter for much the same reason that Eisner challenges the epistemologies of analytic and positivist philosophy: the danger of over-reliance on human objectivity and disinterestedness in a world in which our environment and experiences unavoidably shape our perceptions.

Given his assumption of the need to balance prayerful and critical engagement with the divine and his belief in the relative rarity of wisdom, Diadochos recognized the need for spiritual teachers to speak from, but not out of, their experiences of mystical union with God and cautioned those among the unilluminated who might be tempted to teach that their attempts would fail out of ignorance. He noted that in the former case, speech is not possible, for everything else falls away when the soul is caught up in the love of God; and in the latter case, the emptiness of the teacher's experience provides nothing to interpret. Instead, we teach from a middle place between our experiences of what we do not know and our experiences of the joyous embrace of God and the spiritual knowledge given in those times. "This balance confers a certain harmony on our words glorifying God; as we speak and teach, our faith is nourished by the richness of the illumination and so, because of our love, we are the first to taste the fruits of knowledge."[35]

Diadochos also recognized the ease with which the lifelong work of prayer and study could be disrupted by interpersonal discord, addiction, depression, and the other psychosocial ills of fifth century (and contemporary) cultures. He wrote, "When the soul is disturbed by anger, confused by drunkenness, or sunk in deep depression, the intellect cannot hold fast to the remembrance of God no matter how hard we try to force it."[36] He noted that Christians are similar to young children, novices in prayer who struggle with distractibility and require divine redirection. He pointed out that the activity of spiritual knowledge within us can work to reorient our relationships by bidding us to view all persons "with an overflowing of compassion in our soul."[37] He also believed that some emotions, such as anger over injustice, are signs of spiritual progress toward a higher level of theological understanding. To deal with the disruptiveness of these emotions, we must turn our anger into a lament over "the insensitivity of the unjust,...since when hatred is present in the soul spiritual knowledge is paralyzed."[38]

On this point Diadochos directs us to the useful aspects of Belenky and Stanton's work. Persons in the epistemological categories of The Silenced, Received Knowers, and Subjective Knowers can be interpreted as individuals whose life circumstances deprive them of sufficient opportunities for the remembrance of God. The Silenced and Received Knowers do not recognize themselves as persons capable of a responsible relationship with God in a freely chosen obedience. While God's illuminating love may shine on them, they do not experience the energy and warmth of God's presence. Subjective Knowers suffer from an addiction to their own perspective, and God's light of illumination may recede from them because they do not make room in their hearts or minds for divine inspiration.[39]

Procedural Knowers, on the other hand, are more aware of God's illuminative presence, but they may suffer from the imbalance between critical study and contemplative prayer of which Diadochos warned. They may become caught up in theological speculation about the nature and will of God without the necessary corrective of an intimate relationship with the divine. When this happens, it is difficult for the grace of God "to paint the divine likeness over the divine image in us,"[40] for we do not spend sufficient time in the artist's studio for the work to be completed.

Diadochos underscores for us the possibilities for cultivating spiritual knowledge and preparing the soil for the gifts of wisdom and theology among those Belenky and Stanton call Constructed Knowers. But even with this group he reminds us that the passions that can flare in response to injustice can obscure the remembrance of God. And the confidence of Constructed Knowers in their ability to negotiate among the various streams of data they admit for consideration may hinder their ability to rely on the grace of God as the orienting and unifying energy at work in their discernment process.

Thus, Diadochos bids us seriously consider the questions posed by Hodgson and the partial answer Hodgson finds in the work of Meland. While the fifth-century saint would have us value religious imagination as a form of divine inspiration (he even celebrates the potential for our dreams to reveal God and fill our souls "with spiritual gladness"[41]), he is also adamant that we recognize the limitations of even our God-given creativity. His own work characterizes the danger of the religious imagination in terms of demonic activity and the susceptibility of the human intellect to suggestion, as well as the way in which "as a result of the primal deception the remembrance of evil has become as it were a habit."[42] Belenky and Stanton's description of the Subjective Knower, whose knowledge exists in his or her own opinions without regard for the merit of those ideas in relation to some process of accountability, may be a more palatable explanation for why the imagination remains suspect in the twenty-first century. Nonetheless, the conundrum continues to exist: religious imagination is essential to the cultivation of spiritual knowledge and is itself insufficient to guarantee an encounter with God and the development of spiritual wisdom.

What, then, does Diadochos offer us that these other epistemologies and their definitions of knowledge do not? He invites us to consider an epistemology that recognizes God and union with God as our primary way of spiritual knowing, a third way even more radical than that proposed by Palmer, because it moves beyond both *scientia* (technical knowledge) and *sapientia* (practical wisdom) to what we might call *contemplatia*,[43] a mystical knowledge that must be experienced and cannot be taught in the usual sense of the word. This is the kind of knowledge the anonymous author of the fourteenth century *The Cloud of Unknowing* had in mind when he designed his exercise of forgetting all else and gazing on God so that we might "leave [God] to act alone."[44] Diadochos wants us to understand that "our power of perception shows us that we are being formed into the divine likeness; *but the perfecting of this likeness we shall know only by the light of grace*."[45] Hence, "we should try always to face towards the life-creating and purifying wind of the Holy Spirit"[46] so that we are hospitable to the divine gift of mystical knowledge.

The implications of this emphasis on *contemplatia* for our teaching for spiritual knowledge and wisdom are at least twofold. First, as teachers, our spiritual knowledge comes from our personal experiences of God and God's self-revelation. Recall that Diadochos positions the teacher's speech at a midpoint between the blissful experience of divine illumination (where words are impossible) and the void of ignorance that tempts us to make unholy speculations. The safeguard that prevents our teaching from slipping into the void is an ongoing contemplative relationship with God that continues to invite new experiences of illumination. While we do not control God's actions in this relationship, we create a contemplative space in our lives (through various spiritual practices of prayer, worship, solitude, and study) where God may chose to enter and draw us into communion.

Second, our role as teachers of an unteachable yet learnable form of knowledge is to guide others into the spiritual exercises (disciplines, practices) that render their lives hospitable to God's self-revelation as well. This includes modeling the balance between contemplation and critical readings of the scriptures and their theological commentators and providing opportunities for our students to practice this balance as well. We will need to keep in mind the descriptions of various knowers provided by Belenky and Stanton and develop teaching strategies that provide students with the skills to become Constructive Knowers without obscuring their need also to become Mystical Knowers who simply gaze on God and wait for God to illuminate their understanding. This may mean, for instance, that we must prod Received Knowers to question the authority of texts and Subjective Knowers to submit their interpretations to the scrutiny of their peers. We may need to insist that Separate Knowers reckon with the scriptural canon as a whole rather than a collection of discrete parts to be accepted or rejected on individual merit and that Connected Knowers acknowledge and struggle with the paradoxical nature of Christian theology. And we may need to prompt the voices of The Silenced into speech even as we encourage them to experience a different kind of silence more freely chosen. In every case, we need to challenge our students to experience theological (Christian) education as a spiritual practice that points beyond itself to our need for divine illumination if we are to know God and not simply know about God.

If we permit Diadochos to guide us, the cultivation of spiritual knowledge and wisdom becomes a personal and professional spiritual concern for Christian teachers. We cannot teach mystical knowledge if we do not continually "taste the fruits of knowledge"[47] ourselves through spiritual illumination and the exercise of the divinely given gifts of theology and wisdom. And we cannot rely on our own intellect or our gifts of wisdom and theological acumen to develop spiritual knowledge or wisdom in our students, for that is God's work. We are limited to the work of spiritual midwifery, sharing the divine gifts we cultivate under God's guidance and encouraging our students to welcome the same action of God in their own lives.

PART IV

Evaluation of Teaching

CHAPTER 10

Examination of Conscience as Evaluative Practice

Good teaching requires ongoing critical evaluation of the educational process. But what does that evaluation look like? What is the purpose of ongoing evaluation? If we say "this worked" or "these tasks met my objectives," what do we mean by these claims? Over time, many educators and spiritual leaders have tried to answer these questions. The growing library of resources on educational evaluation demonstrates both the complexity of these questions as well as shifting understandings of the tasks of evaluation in the educational process.[1] But when we add to these questions concerns about the processes of spiritual formation, far fewer resources are available to us.

Our goal in this chapter, therefore, is not to survey the literature on educational evaluation. Rather we want to continue our conversation with the resources of the Christian spiritual traditions, drawing on one particular practice, the Ignatian practice of examen or examination of conscience, as a means of reflecting on one's teaching and on oneself as a teacher.

Ignatius of Loyola and the *Spiritual Exercises*

There are many accounts of the life of Ignatius of Loyola, as might be expected for the person who founded the Society of Jesus, commonly known as the Jesuits, and whom the church has designated a saint.[2] Briefly, Ignatius was born into a noble family in Spain in 1491, trained for court life as a young man, and, although not a professional soldier, "sought to distinguish himself in military glory"[3] as a soldier in the Navarran army until he was seriously wounded in the French siege of Pamplona in 1521. During his recovery from that wound, he began reading. Although he sought novels of courtly chivalry, he was given the lives of the saints and a life of Christ. As his reading and meditation continued, his desire to imitate the saints and to give himself in service to Christ grew. This growing desire led to an intense year of prayer and self-examination; his *Spiritual Exercises* began to emerge from the notes Ignatius made during this time. His service to Christ led next to a yearlong pilgrimage to Jerusalem and, finally, to an extended period of study in Alcalá and Paris. During his years in Paris, he began to give his exercises to several of his fellow students, who soon became a small community committed to the imitation of Christ and the spiritual welfare of their neighbors. By the time he left Paris in 1535, the basic structure of the *Exercises* was set.[4] The small company gathered in Venice in 1537 with the hope of continuing in pilgrimage to Jerusalem. During this year, they were all ordained. Prevented from finding passage due to war with the Turks, they turned toward Rome to offer their services to the Pope. In 1540, Paul III approved the foundation of the Society of Jesus, an apostolic order "directed to the spiritual welfare of individuals (by conversations and the *Exercises*), and of relatively small groups (by preaching or catechizing)."[5] In 1541, Ignatius was elected superior general of the order, a position he held until his death in 1556.

The *Spiritual Exercises* were not written as devotional literature, much less as a form of a "spiritual classic." That is, they were not written as something primarily to be read. They were written for a person directing or giving a spiritual retreat for another person who is "making" the *Exercises*. They are, like Augustine's *First Catechetical Instruction*, a tool to be used by those teaching or leading others into the practices and ways of Christian living. Yet, unlike Augustine's work, the *Exercises* are not a manual about what should be taught the new Christian. Rather, as Elisabeth Tetlow suggests in the following, they are something to be lived through:

> The *Spiritual Exercises* was designed to be a school of love. The work was intended, not to be read through, but to be lived through. When a person spends a portion of his or her life in the school of the *Exercises*, he or she learns to grow as a Christian, that is, to grow in the freedom to be able to love. Through making the *Spiritual Exercises*, one can learn to love God and other persons more totally through a process whereby one grows in ever greater freedom and wholeness.[6]

The *Exercises* emerged as a kind of concretization of Ignatius's own conversion experience during and after his recovery, "a sort of objectified recording of his own religious journey for the help of others."[7] They are intended, Ignatius wrote, "to overcome oneself, and to order one's life without reaching a decision through some disordered affection."[8] Others have described the *Exercises* as intending "to assist an individual in seeking and finding God's will and to serve as a channel for God's grace that will enable a person to put God's will, once discerned, into actual practice in life."[9] Above all, they are intended to form a person into patterns of discernment and action that serve only one end: the greater glory of God (*ad majorem Dei gloriam*).

The *Spiritual Exercises* are structured in a sequence of four parts or weeks, reflecting Ignatius's expectation that the process of the *Exercises* be completed in about a month. This remains the standard time frame for Jesuit novices. The first week invites consideration and contemplation of sin; the second, reflection on the life of Christ up to Palm Sunday; the third, the passion of Christ; and the fourth, Christ's resurrection and ascension (*Exercises*, 4).[10] Ganss suggests that the weeks of the *Exercises* follow the traditional contemplative path from purgation (first week: confession of sin) to illumination (second week: contemplation of the life and teachings of Christ) to union (third and fourth weeks: joining oneself to Christ's passion and resurrection).[11] Yet even with this structure, Ignatius encourages the director to adapt the *Exercises* "to the condition of the persons who seek to make them…to their age, education and ability" and to give persons "those exercises which would be most helpful and profitable according to his or her willingness of disposition" (*Exercises*, 8).

The Structure and Practice of Examen

The examen, or more specifically the "daily particular examination of conscience" and the "general examination of conscience," forms the opening practice of the *Spiritual Exercises*. They build on and are in service of the foundational goal of the *Exercises*, "to desire and elect only the thing which is more conducive to the end for which I was created," which is "to praise, reverence, and serve God our Lord" (*Exercises*, 23). In the subsequent Ignatian/Jesuit tradition, especially in its renewal in the wake of Vatican II's mandate that religious orders recover the vitality of their original charisms, the practice of examination of conscience has been referred to with several related and seemingly interchangeable words or phrases: examen, examination of conscience, and examination of consciousness. The first, examen, is the Latin and French form. It refers to a process of testing as well as to a part of a scale, thus directing us to a sense of something being weighed or measured. Examen also provides a kind of shorthand, which we will take advantage of, for speaking about examination of conscience or of consciousness. These latter two phrases reflect a tension in the Ignatian practice of examen. The first of these, examination of conscience, focuses on moral assessment, a kind of cataloging of misbehavior and sin. The second, examination of consciousness, seems to invite us to shift away from such cataloging and to turn to an assessment of spiritual awareness. Exploring this tension further may help us clarify the attitude with which we want to approach evaluation.

Historian Joseph Tetlow suggests that examination of conscience has long reflected a form of the "purgative" way that moves from the naming of our sinfulness to an act of confession, a kind of balancing of accounts with God the "divine bookkeeper and stern judge." He calls this form the "accountant's examen." Tetlow argues that this understanding of examen has two problematic consequences. First, it seems to suggest that "our sin moves God to act," that our broken unfaithful lives are what move God to act for our redemption.[12] Second, an account-keeping approach to our sins leads to an understanding of sin as extrinsic rather than intrinsic, "more like bad manners than a character flaw."[13] Deborah Smith Douglas suggests that this approach leads, on the one hand, to a "single-minded, grim-hearted quest for sin" and, on the other hand, leaves us "blind to everything that was not dented or torn or incomplete."[14] As Tetlow notes, this form of examen is difficult to sustain, even for those living the vowed religious life.[15]

Tetlow then describes a shift in Jesuit teachings from purgative to unitive understandings of examen accompanied by a shift in interpreting sin as lawlessness to sin as sickness. This twentieth century change was based, in part, on a renewed emphasis on a personal relationship with Jesus, by a shift in Catholic sacramental terminology from confession to reconciliation, as well as by developments in the psychological sciences. This view no longer sees persons as the accused "standing before a strict judge," but rather as those hurting and "accepting the care of a loving Savior."[16] The consequences of this change in perspective for our understanding and practice of examen were most clearly described in a brief but seminal article by George Aschenbrenner in 1972 and are reflected in the use of the phrase "examination of consciousness."[17] No longer is examen focused on moral conscience, on sin and guilt; rather, examen is to be focused on our consciousness of our relationship with God and our consequent availability to God and the world.[18] Aschenbrenner describes examen as "daily intensive exercise of discernment in one's life" concerned with "how the Lord is affecting and moving us…deep in our own affective consciousness."[19] "The operative questions are: what has been happening in us, how has the Lord been working in us, and what has He been asking of us."[20] Rather than focusing on good and bad actions (although these are part of the work of discerning and electing those things more conducive to the ends for which we were created), "our concern is with specific details and incidents as they reveal patterns and bring some clarity and insight."[21] Noticing and atoning for our faults becomes only a minor part of cultivating greater spiritual awareness.

The Particular Examen

The daily particular examination of conscience has three parts: on rising each morning, resolve to be on guard against particular sins or faults we are seeking to correct; after the noon meal, review the day to that point, recalling and accounting for occurrences of the fault we are seeking to correct and renewing our resolve to do better; and, after the evening meal, a similar review of the second half of the day (*Exercises*, 24–26). With the midday and evening examination, Ignatius asks us to keep a record of the number of times we have committed the particular fault during the period under review. This provides a concrete record by which to compare the two periods as well as by which to track our progress each day throughout the week (*Exercises*, 29–31). Ignatius also directs us to "touch one's hand to one's breast in sorrow for having fallen" each time we commit a particular sin or fault (*Exercises*, 27), providing a physical response to our mental consciousness of sin and fault.

The process of making a mark for each occurrence of a particular fault or sin does seem to be a "bookkeeping" mode of self-examination. Yet when we pay close attention to what Ignatius is asking of us, and to the context in which he is asking, we begin to see that the primary purpose of this action is not to list or count our faults, but to strengthen our resolve, to seek improvement, and to choose rightly. Think, for example, of the story of the prodigal son. The parable begins with the younger son asking, receiving, and then squandering his inheritance. In Ignatian terms, we might say that the son desired and elected something other than that which serves the end for which he was created. The eventual consequences of this disordered desire, poverty and hunger, led him to examine his choices and desires. As a result of this examination, "he came to himself" (Lk. 15:17). In doing so, we see him reordering his desire, choosing rightly, returning to his father, and repenting of his sin. As Jacque Pasquier writes, "This return to oneself which the examen is designed to effect makes a person face up to his everyday experience; he stands alongside himself—takes stock of himself and his inner motivations."[22] Pasquier follows this statement with the observation that "examen prepares us for response, leaves us wholly open to that grace which alone can transform us completely."[23] As the prodigal comes to himself, returns home, and acknowledges his sin, he is greeted with open arms and a feast. This welcome is not the action of a stern account-keeping God but of the Triune One whose nature is to be merciful and loving.

The General Examination

The general examination of conscience (*Exercises* 32–43) is intended to prepare a person "to make a better confession." Here Ignatius invites us to examine our thoughts (33–37), our words (38–41), and our deeds (42). The structure reminds us of the beginning of the general confession as found in the *Book of Common Prayer* and other liturgical books: "Most merciful God, we confess that we have sinned against you in thought, word, and deed, by what we have done, and by what we have left undone." And as with Ignatius's principle and foundation, the purpose of this confession is not realized in our seeking and receiving forgiveness but, in the end, what such forgiveness makes possible: "that we may delight in [God's] will and walk in [God's] ways."

Although in Ignatius's day persons were under obligation to make a general confession only annually, and although Ignatius suggests that this confession occur at the end of the first week of the *Exercises* (44), the five points or steps in the examen suggest a closer tie to the daily particular examen. And when the method of the examen is discussed in spiritual formation literature, these five steps are usually referenced (43):

1. Give thanks to God for the gifts we have received.
2. Ask God for the grace to know our sins and to rid us of them.
3. As in the particular examen, give an account of our souls in regard to thoughts, words, and deeds for the period of time being reviewed.
4. Ask God for pardon.
5. Resolve, with God's grace, to amend our ways.

This examen does not begin with our sins or even with us. It begins with God, with who God is and what God has done. This starting point reinforces a sense of the appropriateness of the shift from examination of conscience to examination of consciousness. In the examen we are trying to name the ways in which God has been present within the period of time under review.[24] The attention we give to our sins and faults, both in our acknowledgment of them as well as in our seeking to amend them, occurs only in the context of our attention to and consciousness of God's presence with us. We do not begin without God's grace, nor do we end without that grace.

Of course, just as we can easily avoid these practices of self-examination, we can also easily misuse these practices. We can become so focused on identifying good and bad actions that we fail to attend to the desires and choices that lie behind these actions. By focusing only on the actions and not the underlying desires and choices, we risk keeping the process of examen external to our daily lives. Or, by giving constant attention to our sins and faults, we may "simply reinforce a sense of habitual failure."[25] This last focus may also place us at risk of turning the examen into such an intellectual or mental exercise that we become obsessed with our moral actions (an obsessive scrupulosity) and with ourselves—a kind of "morbid narcissism."[26]

If these are the risks of regular practice of examen, what are the benefits? There are several.[27] First, a regular practice of examen invites us to reflect on our various experiences in ministry and service, regardless of the place or mode of service. If God is to be found in action as well as in contemplation, examen invites us to attend to God's presence in all of our life and work. Second, as examen leads us to better know ourselves, it gives us a better knowledge of the ways in which our desires and choices have shaped our actions with ourselves, with others, and with God and frees us from any sense of determinism or fatalism. We become aware of our responsibility in shaping our past and our coresponsibility with God for shaping our future. Third, if we avoid the risks of scrupulosity and narcissism, we discover through examen increasing awareness of, awe and wonder in, and thanksgiving for God's love and mercy in our lives and in our world. Fourth, rather than tying us to our past failures, regular practice of examen invites us to look to the future with specific decisions and choices to be made, with resolutions that embody new attitudes and purified choices.[28] Katherine Dyckman and her colleagues provide the following summary: "The practice of examen can evolve from exterior norms to interior movements, from individualistic assessment to communal and social responsibility, from a specific list of daily practices to a discerning way of life, from externally imposed norms to a sense of personal co-responsibility with God."[29]

Implications for Evaluation: Teachers and Teaching

On the surface, the practices of particular and general examen tell us little about what a student learns, how a classroom functions, or whether a particular learning goal has been met; and thus they seem less than helpful as evaluation tools. However, these practices lead to self-awareness, which promotes greater availability to ourselves, the resources we have within us, and those with whom we learn. This availability cultivates a more discerning readiness for action in response to God's grace. As we explore the ways in which these themes converse with several discussions of educational practice, we will see several implications arise from these conversations.

The Ignatian practice of examen invites us, above all else, to grow in self-awareness, to attend to the desires and assumptions that influence the choices we make as teachers, and to discern more carefully and critically the actions we continue to take as teachers. As Stephen Brookfield writes in his work on teaching: "critically reflective teaching happens when we identify and scrutinize the assumptions that undergird how we work."[30] Examen not only invites us to attend to who we are as teachers but also who we are as persons graced by God. Another way of saying this is that the practice of examen enables the development of what Howard Gardner, in his work on multiple intelligences, calls *intrapersonal intelligence*, which Gardner defines as the core capacity for *"access to one's own feeling life*—one's range of affects or emotions."[31] But this capacity is not just the capacity for awareness of what we are feeling;

it is also, in Gardner's words, "the capacity instantly to effect discriminations among these feelings and, eventually, to label them, to enmesh them in symbolic codes, to draw upon them as a means of understanding and guiding one's behavior."[32] Such self-knowledge, serves three purposes. The first is freedom, where, through self-knowledge, we prevent ourselves from falling prey to or being held captive by our internal and emotional lives. (Such insight is often the work of psychotherapy.) Second is wisdom, by which, through self-knowledge, we make the internal part of our lives available as a resource upon which we can draw in the classroom and in the world.[33] As Gardner notes, such wisdom is what, in addition to their specialized training, psychotherapists and spiritual directors bring to their work. This well-developed critical knowledge of one's self that makes the self a resource to others is also what we usually find in those we consider to be "wise elders" in our communities. Finally, there is hope, where, through self-knowledge, we are able to choose and act on new ways of being, thereby creating a different future for those with whom we are in relationship and for ourselves.

Of course, as therapists and spiritual directors know, and as Ignatius's instructions for the examen make clear, the practice of examen is neither a one-time event nor even only an annual event. The practice of examen is intended to be daily or at least frequent. The point is to have the ability to be consistently and constantly discerning the presence and direction of God in our lives. Through continued and consistent practice we learn to recognize the patterns within our lives, to see the "devises and desires" that lead us away from or toward God, and to attend to the ways in which we make ourselves available, open, and vulnerable to God and others each day.[34]

A number of similarities exist between the practice of examen and the tools for critically reflective teaching developed in the work of Stephen Brookfield. For Brookfield, part of the work of critical self-reflection is to be able to name the assumptions we make about our selves and our work. He names three kinds of assumptions: paradigmatic, prescriptive, and causal.[35]

Paradigmatic assumptions are those "basic structuring axioms" we use in life and work. These tend to be the things we resist exploring because they are "just the way things are" (or so we have come to think). We might think, for example, of how and why we believe in God, what we believe about God's work in creation, or even what lies behind "bad things that happen to good people." Think, too, of when you have challenged these assumptions or had them challenged by others.

Prescriptive assumptions are those things we believe about "what ought to be happening." We should behave a certain way or a classroom should function in a certain way. The emphasis here, obviously, is on those assumptions we have that always seem to begin with "what we *should* do."

Causal assumptions are those assumptions we have about how things work together or influence one another. These assumptions fall into "if…then" patterns. If I structure my lesson plan this way, if I pray this way, if…then my class will, or God will, or… We often depend upon these assumptions as stepping stones from one point in a lesson to another.

Because the Ignatian process of examen is concerned with self-knowledge that leads to discerning action, part of our examen must include a testing or exploring of the assumptions we have about our selves and our work. In the context of the particular examen, we can resolve each morning to attend to a particular assumption we make (to attend to more than one at a time is likely to be overwhelming). We can pause midday to explore how we have lived out that assumption and the consequences of doing so, and then resolve to continue to attend to this assumption. At the end of the day, we can again note what has happened with us and to us in light of this assumption. In obedience to Ignatius's method, we would continue working with this one assumption throughout a week, or even weeks, until we have come to some kind of resolution or new understanding of it. By doing so, Brookfield argues, we increase "the probability that we will take informed actions" and will come to embed "not only our actions but also our sense of who we are as teachers in an examined reality."[36] For Brookfield, as with Ignatius, the process of examen provides both intrapersonal and interpersonal knowledge; it both grounds us emotionally and alerts us "to the effects we are having on students."[37]

Brookfield provides several tools that, when used consistently, facilitate self-awareness. The first, which he calls critical incident reports, can function as a kind of particular examen at the end of a class session or at the end of a week of sessions. Like Ignatius, he encourages us to keep a log of these reports as a way to help track patterns in our work. He suggests that in our self-reports we note when we are most engaged or unengaged, connected or disconnected, anxious or surprised. Brookfield is also aware of our need to explore these questions with others as we might explore similar questions with a retreat leader, spiritual director, or spiritual companion. Perhaps monthly we can meet with a colleague who can act as a mirror for us, spotting "patterns in our behavior or assumptions about our practice that are too close to our experience to be clearly visible to us."[38]

A second tool Brookfield describes is the annual teaching audit. It, like the general examen, invites us to reflect more comprehensively on our life and work and, combined with the cumulative record of our critical incident reports, helps us get "into the habit of thinking of [oneself] as a learner about teaching,...become aware of how much learning [we] are undertaking already in an informal and incidental way," and gain a "more accurate sense of how [we] change and learn as a teacher." So we ask ourselves what we know about ourselves and our teaching, what we are better able to do, what or how we can better teach, and what assumptions have been confirmed or overturned this year in comparison with the same time last year.[39]

Note that in all of these processes, as in both the particular and general examen, the focus is not (or not necessarily) on our failures. Failure is not exempt from attention, but it is not the primary focus of our attention. Rather, we are concerned with bringing our desires and habits to consciousness, where we can attend to them, examine them, and change them. As Michael Connelly and Jean Clandenin argue:

> If in our lives we are constantly constituting, reporting, and revising various narrative unities [individually, that "continuum within a person's experience which renders life experiences meaningful through the unity they achieve for the person"], then education should somehow draw on, develop, remake, and introduce such narratives. Education cannot...occur unless it calls up and makes use of some aspect of each student's dominant narrative unities.[40]

What Connelly and Clandenin underscore for us is that the work of learning about teaching is often hidden from us, especially if we allow it to remain unconscious. Bringing this work to consciousness through examen reveals what we are learning about ourselves and our teaching, enables us to learn more intentionally, and provides us with more ready access to the wisdom developing within us.

Examen is not the end of the process, but the beginning; examen makes us available to ourselves and prepares us for response. The prodigal's work was not completed when he "came to himself" but when he returned home and rejoined his family. Perhaps the imagery of another portion of the parables of the lost can help us here. In the parable of the woman and the lost coin (Lk. 15:8–10), the woman sweeps her house until she finds the coin. Notice, the coin is still somewhere in the house (in our unconscious?). Notice too that once she has found the coin she summons her friends and neighbors to celebrate with her. Examen is at times like the process of sweeping one's house until what is precious again becomes visible. Examen unclutters our minds, sorts through our desires, and opens our hearts to the love already working in us. What has been invisible to us again becomes visible, what was inaccessible (freedom, wisdom, and hope) becomes accessible. And once these things become visible and accessible to us, we complete the work as we bring these gifts to the community. As Dyckman and her colleagues remind us, the *Spiritual Exercises* culminate in the Contemplation to Attain Love in which we call to mind all of the gifts God has given us, how God dwells in all creatures and in us, how God labors on our behalf, and how even our limited power comes from "the Supreme and Infinite Power above" (*Exercises* 234–37). This final contemplation "invites seekers to discover new meanings in current reality, for God will transform and empower them to be with God and to act with God in the midst of the world...love becomes the basis of all a seeker does and is, love expressed not only in words but also in deeds."[41]

These comments bring us full circle in the *Exercises*. The first week of the *Exercises*, in the practice of the particular and general examen of conscience/consciousness, called us to begin with an act of recollection, noting what God has already given us, how God's grace enables us to attend to our faults and failures, and finally, how God's grace gives us the strength to change and the willingness to make ourselves available to God in examination and retreat. The model of the examen invites us to frame the work of evaluating our teaching in the same way, beginning and ending with God's grace. The final week of the *Exercises* leads us to a consideration of all God has given us, done for us, and continues to labor for with us. Ignatius included the following prayer in this final contemplation:

> Take, Lord, and receive all my liberty, my memory, my understanding, and all my will—all that I Have and possess. You, Lord, have given all that to me. I now give back to you, O Lord. All of it is yours. Dispose of it according to your will. Give me your love and your grace, for that is enough for me. (*Exercises*, 234)[42]

The *Spiritual Exercises* and, therefore, the examen is intended to form patterns of discernment and action that serve only one end: the greater glory of God. We must also remember that the Ignatian tradition is not focused on creating contemplatives but contemplatives in action. Our knowledge of ourselves and of God is intended to lead us into God's service with others. In what ways, then, does this work of becoming more available to God also make us more available to those we teach or serve? Ignatius does not explicitly answer this question for us. We will only know the answer by persisting in and living with the questions his practice of the examen asks of us.

CHAPTER 11

Overcoming Obstacles to Teaching Well

Contemporary culture and the contemporary church offer us competing messages about our purpose as teachers, messages that may become more apparent to us through the regular practice of examen. Henri Nouwen suggests that what we hear from the world around and in the church is a trio of interrelated temptations that obstruct good teaching: calls to relevance, powerfulness, and successfulness.[1] Under the guise of relevance, we are encouraged to focus on all the things we are able to contribute that society values: well-constructed arguments to support our perspectives, creative lesson plans that meet every learner's needs, nurturing relationships that inspire young people, and insightful commentary delivered with an expert's certainty of the truth. We are also invited—in this age of narrowly defined social cohorts who want their needs met to the exclusion of other groups—to dwell entirely in the language, issues, and practices of an age or life-cycle defined group in order to have our teaching accepted as relevant by that group. One of the watchwords of the current debate over worship styles is *relevance*. Curriculum publishers survey congregations to find out what faith issues are considered relevant by prospective buyers of their products. Practices and topics not in vogue get set aside or relegated to "traditional" worship services and classrooms, while the "cutting edge" crowds seek out more relevant resources and leaders.

To be relevant, then, is to acquire power, and it becomes easy to see this power as an essential tool for ministry rather than as an obstructing temptation. Nouwen writes, "We keep hearing from others, as well as saying to ourselves, that having power—provided it is used in the service of God and your fellow beings—is a good thing."[2] Yet as Nouwen and other scholars remind us, church history is littered with examples of power run amuck: the Crusades, the enslavement of indigenous peoples, clergy sex scandals, the Holocaust. The magnitude of these atrocities, however, sometimes blinds us to more minor abuses of power and their consequences. When we use our reputations as experts to deposit bits of faith knowledge in person's minds without inviting them to explore ideas for themselves, we use our power as authority figures in an attempt to control their thinking. If we eschew the use of traditional theological terms or historic practices because we fear accusations of irrelevance, we exert power over the future riches of the church in much the same way the servant who buried the talent given by his master chose to forgo possible gains for the kingdom of God for fear that he or his reputation might suffer if what was entrusted were put at risk.[3] The lure of power is seductive, and Nouwen contends this is because being powerful is easier than practicing sacrificial love:

> What makes the temptation of power so seemingly irresistible? Maybe it is that power offers an easy substitute for the hard task of love. It seems easier to be God than to love God, easier to control people than to love people, easier to own life than to love life. Jesus asks, "Do you love me?" We ask, "Can we sit at your right hand and your left hand in your Kingdom?" (Mt. 20:21). Ever since the snake said, "the day you eat of this tree your eyes will be open and you will be like gods, knowing good from evil" (Gen. 3:5), we have been tempted to replace love with power.[4]

Power also appeals to us because we believe we need it to answer the third call of society: to be successful. We and others imagine ourselves to have value when we acquire the trappings indicative of social status, or some Christians would say, of God's blessings on our life. The American myth of the self-made man (or woman) is held before us as a model for our individual strivings, and when we ask the age-old question of theodicy (why do bad things happen to good people?), we ask in part because we equate goodness with success, not with adversity and failure. The church often equates pastoral success with numeric growth or public influence; the quiet ministries of pastors and teachers in small, struggling congregations go unnoticed and undervalued. "Stardom and individual heroism, which are such obvious aspects of our competitive society, are not at all alien to the Church," comments Nouwen. "There too the dominant image is that of the self-made man or woman who can do it all alone."[5]

How do we resist this dominant cultural and ecclesial pull to be a self-sufficient Christian leader, with its attendant temptations to seek relevance and popularity? Nouwen suggests we need to turn to three long-practiced spiritual disciplines to assist us. These practices will school us in a different image, that of the servant leader revealed to us in the stories of Jesus' postbaptism temptations (Mt. 4:1–11) and his post-resurrection conversation with Peter after breakfast on the beach (Jn. 21:15–19).

Contemplative Prayer: Resisting Relevance

The first practice, which Nouwen earmarks as an antidote to the temptation to relevance, is contemplative prayer. He notes:

> Christian leaders cannot simply be persons who have well-informed opinions about the burning issues of our time. Their leadership must be rooted in the permanent, intimate relationship with the incarnate Word, Jesus, and they need to find there the source for their words, advice, and guidance. Through the discipline of contemplative prayer, Christian leaders have to learn to listen again and again to the voice of love and to find there the wisdom and courage to address whatever issue presents itself to them.[6]

Contemplative prayer, then, orients us to what is truly relevant: the radical knowledge that God is present in the world as a force for unconditional love and justice. It redirects our attention from questions of whether we are taken seriously by others or have socially recognizable results to prove we are accomplished teachers to a different question: Do we teach out of our knowledge of the heart of God?[7] Like Peter in John 21, we need to spend time pondering the question, "Do you love me?" in the presence of God and permit God to show us how to love so thoroughly what God desires for us and the world that we are no longer fooled by the false claims made by harbingers of social relevance.

Confession and Forgiveness: Resisting Successfulness

Alongside the spiritual discipline of contemplative prayer that helps us to resist the temptation to be relevant, Nouwen invites us to practice the discipline of confession and forgiveness as an antidote to the "temptation of individual heroism"[8] inherent in our illusions of autonomy and successfulness. Here he echoes the sentiment of all those through the ages (like Ignatius) who have advocated for the regular examination of conscience, but with a twist: he accents the communal practice of confessing our sins and forgiving one another rather than the more individual form of examen. His focus is on what the community needs to be remade as God's realm; and within that context, we who teach can model an appropriate vulnerability with our students that is essential to the well-being of all God's people. Nouwen observes,

"Confession and forgiveness are the concrete forms in which we sinful people love one another."[9] Without teachers who offer their real lives to their students, the church cannot become a community of true love because the persons who comprise the community are not wholly in relationship with one another. We teach for the coming of God's realm most effectively when we are full members of our communities, "accountable to them" and cognizant of our need for their "affection and support," when we bring to our ministries all that we are, including our brokenness.[10]

French philosopher Simone Weil also points us toward this practice when she describes the benefits of contemplating "our stupidity" in order to fix in ourselves "a sense of our mediocrity" based upon "irresistible evidence."[11] Her approach seems to contradict that of Ignatius, whose practice of examen discourages undue dwelling on our failures. But the purpose of this exercise for Weil is to emphasize our dependence on the correctives offered by others for our spiritual progress. We do not grow closer to God by ignoring and denying our faults. Our mistakes and shortcomings need our sustained attention so that we can "get down to the origin of each fault"[12] and begin to change our ways with the help of the One who pointed out our error.

As teachers, then, we need to invite others to observe and comment critically on our work so that we can discover areas in need of improvement or re-visioning. The most obvious group of critics we can consult is our students, who participate in the learning processes we construct and facilitate. Such consultation, however, must move beyond the customer satisfaction surveys popular in congregational study groups and academic classrooms, for such surveys most often measure likes and dislikes rather than vision and faithfulness. Religious educator Michael Warren urges us to be mindful of our enculturation into an overly-simplistic system of judging experiences based on personal preferences:

> Margaret Miles is right in warning that we live in an entertainment culture, bent on assigning us roles as spectators or passive voyeurs, whose role in the end is to say either "I liked it" or "I didn't like it" and whose own core of judgment has been slowly but surely eroded.[13]

What we need from students instead is their willingness to explore with us what is and is not happening in their own quest to encounter and serve the living God and how their experiences are shaped by and ought to shape our teaching. We also need to guide students in reflection on their own engagements with and resistances to learning. These explorations then lead the teacher and students to a place of confession to one another and God for the ways in which both our faults interfere with this quest, followed by mutual forgiveness and recommitment to faithfulness in our shared journey of teaching and learning.

Another group of persons we might invite to reflect with us on our teaching are other teachers. We can accomplish this both by opening our teaching sessions to colleagues as observers and by observing our colleagues at work in their own settings. Through the former practice, our colleagues act as mirrors and magnifiers, reflecting back to us what occurred and scrutinizing with us aspects of our teaching that seemed less effective in furthering the coming of God's realm. In the latter, our encounters with different teaching strategies provide images and ideas against which we can contrast our own practices and make comparative judgments. A collegial practice of confession and forgiveness within such a system of observational exchanges helps keep us mindful of whom we seek to please; the goal is not to win the approval of our colleagues, but to realign ourselves continually with God's desires.

Authors of books on teaching are a third group we might consult. This might seem an odd group to include as observers, but only if we limit the concept of observation to physical presence and sight. What authors offer to us is insight, often based on years of experience and reflection, which, when considered alongside our recollections of our own teaching practices, provides another version of the mirroring and magnifying process we might experience with a local colleague. Using our imagination to invite these distant colleagues into our teaching sessions can broaden the perspectives to which we have access, allowing us to engage in dialogue with methods and experiences outside our immediate environment or community without a hefty continuing education travel budget. It also permits us to engage in dialogue with historic voices from the church's past, whose wisdom and experience might otherwise be lost to us. Our encounters with these ancient and contemporary observers may prompt us to confess the parochialism of our practices and our failure to look beyond our immediate setting in the quest for an ever-expanding view of what is possible and desirable in God's realm.

Permitting the scriptures to talk with us about our teaching is another crucial evaluative practice. The *New Revised Standard Version* contains 366 specific references to teachers, teachings, or the act of teaching. It has an additional one hundred references to learning or having learned.[14] In the letters to Timothy ascribed to Paul, the apostle contends, "All scripture is inspired by God and is useful for teaching, for reproof, for correction, and for training in righteousness, so that everyone who belongs to God may be proficient, equipped for every good work" (2 Tim. 3:16–17). Studying the teaching goals and practices of the law and prophets, gospel writers and apostles, and other leaders raised up by

God through the biblical ages, as well as the teaching ministry of Jesus, can help us measure spiritual coherence between our practices and those of the teachers who have gone before us. Praying with these biblical texts about teaching and learning, particularly using a method of *Lectio Divina*, can open us to the Spirit's commentary on our own teaching through the biblical witness. Through this process, we may experience the reproof of what Simone Weil so inelegantly labeled "our stupidity," corrective advice or images that reframe our vision, and training in a more righteous approach to our ministry that better equips us to endure in the struggle to resist successfulness. As we are convicted by the Spirit, we can repent of our mistakes, confess our misguidedness, and move forward with the assurance that God forgives us as part of the process of equipping us for more proficient work.

While some of our evaluative practice of confession and forgiveness may take place in the secret reflections of our personal prayers, both Henri Nouwen's reminder of our need to be truthful with our students about our human failings and the inherently communal nature of Christian teaching and learning press us toward regular corporate rituals of confession and absolution. (Such prayers have been part of the church's liturgies throughout the centuries.) Our effectiveness as teachers is linked with our students' efforts as learners; our students' ability to actively participate in the learning process is entwined with our teaching methodologies.

The writer of the Letter to the Hebrews expressed some frustration with this symbiotic relationship. As a teacher whose students seemed unwilling to learn despite sustained efforts to convey the gospel in a compelling way, the writer confronted them with the problem: "For though by this time you ought to be teachers, you need someone to teach you again the basic elements of the oracles of God" (Heb. 5:12a). The problem is that the students have become sluggish rather than "imitators of those who through faith and patience inherit the promises" (Heb. 6:12). Our gift of teaching cannot be judged solely on the responsiveness of our students and their ability to grasp and embody the ideas and practices we have introduced. Sometimes the disconnection is on their side, characterized by a reluctance to set aside other commitments, ideas, and activities for a wholehearted engagement in Christian discipleship.

However, the temptation to assume that our efforts are ineffectual solely because of some failure on the part of our students must be checked by our willingness to hear the students' side of the story. What might the recipients of the Letter to the Hebrews say about their difficulties in grasping the foundational principles of the faith their teacher claims to have made so plain? Would they offer a different explanation for their inability to progress from beginning students to teachers of the faith themselves? When we establish communal space in which to confess teacher and student faults and ask forgiveness of one another, we allow for a joint exploration of the teaching and learning process that is more likely to uncover a variety of flawed intentions and actions among all participants. Such space also has the potential to generate more creative ideas about how to improve the teaching and learning process necessary for God's people to be "heirs of the promise" (Heb. 6:17) of a new heaven and a new earth.

Theological Reflection: Resisting Powerfulness

The third discipline, which completes Nouwen's spiritual resistance kit, is the practice of "strenuous theological reflection" that "will allow us to discern critically where we are being led" rather than to focus on where we and others think we need to lead the church.[15] Nouwen points to Jesus' powerful yet cryptic words to Peter in John 21:18 about being led to his own crucifixion experience as a reordering of our assumptions about human and spiritual maturity. We grow up believing every year brings us closer to the time when we are rightfully in charge of our own destinies, but the exchange between Jesus and Peter suggests that, in the realm of God, the "willingness to be led where [we] would rather not go" makes us fully over into God's image.[16] Only deliberate and ongoing theological reflection can help us discern the myriad ways in which God wants to turn upside down our assumptions, stereotypes, and prejudices about the way the world does and should work. We are called to put on the mind of Christ, so that we will "be able to discern from moment to moment how God acts in human history and how the personal, communal, national and international events that occur during our lives can make us more and more sensitive to the ways in which we are led to the cross and through the cross to the resurrection."[17]

This practice of theological reflection needs further explanation, particularly in relation to the companion practice of contemplative prayer. Perhaps the place to begin is the indissoluble unity of the two spiritual disciplines. Karl Barth observed, "Prayer without study would be empty. Study without prayer would be blind."[18] He described prayer as representing the vertical axis of the cross, pointing to the movement of humanity toward God and God toward humanity, with study being one aspect of the horizontal axis that draws humanity into thoughtful relationship and activity on earth. Prayer instills in us the mind of Christ. Study engages us in the process of discerning from a Christlike perspective the ways of God in the world and the world's response to God. Our study then leads us back to prayer, as we check our interpretations and offer ourselves as returning students in God's school of prayer.

We often think of study as the effort we expend in order to acquire knowledge about something or to prepare us for a particular task or job. From this perspective, theological reflection could be interpreted as the acquisition of knowledge about God and preparation for Christian life. But such a definition does not sufficiently describe the shape or purpose of theological reflection. We study primarily to cultivate in ourselves a habit of attentiveness.

Weil emphatically claimed that the practice of study was far more important than the actual products of intellectual reflection:

> When we set out to do a piece of work, it is necessary to wish to do it correctly, because such a wish is indispensable in any true effort. Underlying this immediate objective, however, our deep purpose should aim solely at increasing the power of attention with a view to prayer.[19]

Weil describes the way in which students often come to their studies with an attitude of long-suffering resignation, applying themselves to the task because of some external pressure to achieve certain academic standards in order to be rewarded with grades or coveted work prospects. This operative mode of study requires the exertion of willpower and physical concentration, which, says Weil, have little place in genuine theological reflection. Instead, she contends that "intelligence can only be led by desire," which grows out of "pleasure and joy in the work."[20] A lack of desire for learning leads to a lack of attentiveness. The mind, eager to apply itself and be done with the odious task of figuring out the problem before it, seizes upon its first impression as the answer rather than paying careful and sustained attention to the issue at hand and waiting for the truth to emerge.

Weil's understanding of studious attention bears an intentional resemblance to the practice of self-emptying forms of contemplative prayer. True attention "consists of suspending our thought, leaving it detached, empty, and ready" to receive the self-communication of the object under study.[21] All of the data we have gathered through observation, experience, and previous reflection remains "within reach of this thought, but on a lower level and not in contact with it," so we are less likely to rush to judgment before we have truly attended to that about which we are wondering.[22] Weil reminds us that we often make mistakes when we study (we need only recall the red marks penned by countless teachers on school papers to know this is true) and we must approach theological reflection with the humility such errors should, in her judgment, evoke.[23]

This approach may seem to promote a decontextualized encounter with truth, but what Weil is attempting to fashion is similar to what Parker Palmer advocates when he defines teaching as creating "a space in which obedience to truth is practiced."[24] Authentic study occurs in spaces where we permit the object of our study to become a subject actively communicating its own truth to us while we actively attempt to set aside our personal prejudices about the topic.[25] This radical hospitality to initially uncensored ideas increases the odds that we will learn something new and meaningful as we bring these ideas into conversation with what God has already revealed to us and to the faith community in previous study.

However, this form of radical openness is hard to sustain because the effort to keep our cultural assumptions and prejudgments at bay can tire us to the point where sustained attention is difficult. Weil advises: "It is better to stop working altogether, to seek some relaxation, and then a little later to return to the task; we have to press on and loosen up alternately, just as we breathe in and out."[26] The antidote to inattention is Sabbath rest, a rhythm of study and relaxation that mirrors the breath of life given by God in our creation.

Weil's focus on attention as a means to prayer and her advocacy of a Sabbath rhythm may seem far removed from the topic of resisting successfulness via theological reflection. But the very title of her essay, "Reflections on the Right Use of School Studies with a View to the Love of God," demonstrates the connection between the two. How we study has consequences not only for our love of God but also for our ability to be taught by God.

Weil's emphasis on study as a means of cultivating attention raises a basic question about our regular engagement in theological reflection as a spiritual discipline necessary for truthful teaching. Are we spending time in study, or are we simply implementing someone else's lesson plan, replete with unexamined ideas and the expectation that our students will accept uncritically whatever we put before them as the truth because it comes from reputable sources? The temptation, when we have what we judge to be authoritative materials at hand, is to rely on another's thinking rather than to make time for our own careful exploration of the subject. Personal study may not lead to disagreement with our curricular materials, but the quality of our attention to the subject and to God's incarnation in the world will be improved.

Weil's concept of attention confronts us with another question about our classroom practices. Do we study together with the goal of improving the quality of our relationship with God, or with some other agenda in mind? Being able to say that our students have read the Bible through in a year, passed the confirmation class exam, or agreed to join the congregation does not necessarily mean they have learned something new about how to love God with their whole heart, mind, and strength. Group (or individual) study can be a mental exercise powered by willpower rather than the cultivation of attention fueled by the joy of learning. What means have we used in our teaching to generate a love of learning and attentiveness to the things of God? How is our own joy in learning evident to our students? What are the stated and implicit goals of our classes?

The focus of Weil's essay on nonreligious schooling as a context for spiritual nurture offers a third possible connection for us to explore. How are we paying attention to God's world outside the institutional church as a setting for God's activity? Our temptation to successfulness may restrict our attention to matters within congregational life or the moral declarations of our tradition. Weil models a different approach: careful attention to a public arena—schools—and their potential to serve as incubators for prayer. She identifies some of the barriers to spirituality that participation in school studies may also erect. When do we reflect theologically on the formative power of social systems and practices with an ear to what those arenas might teach us as well as challenge us to change? What degree of humility do we bring to these reflections, especially as they relate to complicated and sometimes intractable conflicts within the human community? How do they "make us better able to give someone in affliction exactly the help required to save him [or her], at the supreme moment of his [or her] need"?[27]

The way we discover the answers to these diverse questions is through regular theological reflection on our practice of theological reflection. By paying close attention to how and why we and our students study and the effects study has on our living as Christians in the public realm, we learn what ideas elicit our resistance, what prejudicial assumptions cloud our vision, and what new subjects may need our attention if God's realm is to be fully realized.

Teaching Well in the Sight of God

None of us are immune to the temptations of relevance, successfulness, and powerfulness. We may spend too much time counting and seeking acclamation for our successes. We may feel insecure or hurt when no one praises our teaching methodology or comes to us after class with an affirming story of an important "aha" experience generated by our presentation. We may crave moments of recognition for our dedication and efforts even as we demure when actually acknowledged publicly. Despite our sincere belief that humility is a Christian virtue, we may also think that a little pride in what we do is only human and, if kept in check, a sign of a healthy sense of identity. After all, we want to be *good* teachers, and we need some indications from our students and other leaders that we are teaching well.

We ought to teach well, but remembering the ultimate goal of our efforts must serve as a general corrective to hold our tendency toward self-congratulation in check. We do not teach so we can feel good about our abilities or so others can point to us and say, "There goes a great teacher." We teach to further the coming of the realm of God. The Revelation to John calls our attention to God's work throughout time to create "a new heaven and a new earth" in which "death will be no more;

mourning and crying and pain will be no more, for the first things have passed away" (21:1, 4). Our teaching is meant to function as one aspect of God's creation of this new reality; and the central feature of this new heaven and new earth is God's promise to be our God and to hold us close to Godself as God's children, not our recognition as great teachers of the faith.

As "already" heirs but "not yet" occupiers of this new creation, we enjoy the goodwill of a God who anticipates we will do our best and provides all we need to be faithful teachers for the further realization of the divine realm on earth. Our daily challenge is to resist the culturally condoned temptations of relevance, popularity, and powerfulness through the spiritual disciplines of contemplation, confession and forgiveness, and theological reflection. Regular personal and communal evaluation of our teaching practices assists us in our resistance and invites our students to help us overcome the various barriers humanity unintentionally erects to obstruct and undermine the work of God in the world. This evaluation belongs in a context of mutual commitment to Christian discipleship by all participants, as well as mutual acknowledgement that the only worthy judge of our teaching or learning is God.

When we seek to discover what we are doing well and where we are going wrong, we do so as teachers and students whose ultimate and shared teacher is the God who created, redeemed, and sustains us. This God wills that eventually the need for human intermediaries in the teaching of the gospel will cease because, says God, "I will put my law within them, and I will write it on their hearts; and I will be their God, and they shall be my people. No longer shall they teach one another, or say to each other, 'Know the LORD,' for they shall all know me, from the least of them to the greatest" (Jer. 31:33–34a). They will be *theodidaktoi*, taught by God. To teach well in the sight of God, then, we must hold fast to the idea that God chooses to use us for a time as facilitators of an educational process in which God is the Great Teacher and we are God's assistants. To be worthy assistants, we must continually receive direction from the master teacher. We must carefully and regularly check our plans and activities against the overarching goals of the divine curriculum. And we must assess with our students the outcomes of our and their efforts to be taught by God in the formal and informal learning environments we create and cultivate. Only then may we discover that we have taught ourselves out of a job, as the gospel takes root in the hearts of our students and they become teachers too, until eventually, the world has no more need of human teachers and the realm of God is fully realized.

POSTSCRIPT

Something New, Something Old

We began this book with the observation that Christian teachers, like our cultural peers, are caught in a tension between the old and the new, the traditional and the contemporary. Our argument throughout this book has been that the Christian spiritual traditions we have received through the ages continue to be gifts to us as teachers and learners, providing us with well-tested yet still life-giving resources for our work as Christian spiritual leaders. Implicitly, we have tried to demonstrate that these traditions are not primarily concerned with the fixed and decisive passing on of truths nor are they concerned with the standardization of moral values. At the same time, we have presented voices cautious about "up-to-dateness" and "relevance." These warnings are not to deny the role that truth and morality have played and continue to play in Christian tradition, nor are they to deny the importance of the "Protestant principle," the church always reforming. They are, however, to realize that for Christians, as David Power argues, "tradition is first and foremost the transmission of life in Christ and the Spirit, down through time and across cultures."[1] When we are confronted by new issues and new questions, as the church has been throughout its history, faithfulness to this tradition will always call us back to the Christ event and the evangelical tradition recorded in scripture. Who will know this tradition and call us to faithfulness as we teach and learn together?

Such faithfulness to the tradition does not mean that in the face of new situations we turn our gaze to past. Rather, it is about our present life in Christ, just as our practice of eucharist is not a fond looking back on what Jesus said and did but is a means by which we continue to know Christ present with us and moving ahead of us. Faithfulness to this tradition is, Power writes, "a constant process of interpretation, a process of retrieving the past as we redress the present. Indeed, there is a sense in which the present is always in the very act of passing, since what brings people into the future is the core concern of a tradition."[2] Power argues, "when the conditions of an age in the life of the Church and of those to whom the Gospel is addressed bring forth new issues and new questions," then practices that serve this tradition will be questioned, scrutinized, and reinterpreted.[3] Who will know this tradition and help us question, scrutinize, and reinterpret it as we teach and learn together?

There are several ideas about what tradition is and is not that we have kept in mind as we wrote and that we commend to all Christian teachers: First, tradition is not primarily about the past. It is the past reaching through the present to shape a future in which all may have life (Jn. 3:16). Edward Shils talks about this as the ways in which institutions, beliefs, and practices of earlier times "live forward into the present," creating "a consensus between the living and the dead" that, from the beginning, has exercised processes of selection, adaptation, and interpretation.[4] Tradition is about knowing and teaching how to live today, not about how others lived long ago. How will we teach the Christian tradition so that it will shape our future?

Second, tradition continues to develop as it is lived and interpreted. Part of the church's task is to "figure out what is unchangeable, as well as give attention to how modification of a part may affect the whole."[5] Yet "the maintenance of the constant element in the tradition is supported by religious practices."[6] We have continually emphasized the role of spiritual practices in the education and formation of people of faith because through these practices tradition is and will continue to be authentically developed. How will we support this ongoing practice of discernment and development?

Third, "the authority of tradition dies when we proceed on the assumption of...efficiency, rationality, expediency, 'up-to-dateness', or progressivism" as means of judging contemporary relevance.[7] We might easily have dismissed most of the spiritual teachers cited in this book on the grounds that some of what they taught and wrote appears at first glance to be antiquated and out of touch with contemporary life. But to ignore the enduring spiritual questions and concerns embodied in these texts because they come dressed in the clothes of a different historical era would prevent us from remembering, receiving, and living with the precious gifts entrusted to us. How can we see, despite the period clothing, the lives of those taught by God that would also teach us and through whom God might also teach us?

Finally, the practices (or traditions) that serve the tradition have been and will continue to be questioned, scrutinized, and reinterpreted as the "conditions of an age in the life of the Church and of those to whom the Gospel is addressed bring forth new issues and new questions."[8] Tradition and the practices that continue the tradition will change over time. Some of what we hear from church members disenchanted with conventional church school classes and publishers trying to sell congregations curriculum does address new issues and questions; some of it will help us better enact the gospel in our world. But some of it simply represents a different or opposing tradition, and some of it confuses market share or new product consumption with signs of the gospel. How will we know the difference?

We are not left with any easy answers to these questions. We are provided, however, with many new and old ways to look, to imagine, and to listen for how God continues to seek us, to love us, and to teach us. "For whatever was written in former days was written for our instruction, so that by steadfastness and by the encouragement of the scriptures we might have hope" (Rom. 15:4).

Notes

Introduction: Something Old, Something New

[1]Clark M. Williamson and Ronald J. Allen, *The Teaching Minister* (Louisville: Westminster/John Knox Press, 1991), 22.

Chapter 1: The Spiritual Leader as Christian Teacher

[1]Benedicta Ward, S.L.G., trans, *The Sayings of the Desert Fathers* (Kalamazoo: Cistercian Publications, 1975), 233.

[2]Parker J. Palmer, *The Active Life* (San Francisco: HarperSanFrancisco, 1990). At the same time, Palmer offers the reminder that "as we act, we not only express what is in us and help give shape to the world; we also receive what is outside us, and we reshape our inner selves" (p. 17).

[3]Mariana Caplan, "Questioning Authority," *Parabola* 25, no. 3 (Fall 2000): 100.

[4]*Sayings of the Desert Fathers*, 83.

[5]Athanasius, *The Life of St. Antony*, (Mawhaw, N.J.: Paulist Press, 1978), 79. Ysabel de Andia elaborates on this, summarizing the wisdom of Antony as specifically Trinitarian in its formation. Antony was led by a "voice from heaven," instructed by the "teachings of Christ," and inspired by the "gift [charisma] of the Spirit," giving him the ability to discern the spirits, know the will of God, and search out the intentions of all people. "Antoine le Grand, Theodidaktos," in *Actes de IV Congres Copte (1988)*, vol. 2 (Louvain: Peters, 1992), 39.

[6]George E. Ganss, S.J., ed., *Ignatius of Loyola: Spiritual Exercises and Selected Works* (New York: Paulist Press, 1991), 79.

[7]Martin Luther, *Luther's Works*, vol. 31, *Career of the Reformer*, ed. Harold J. Grimm, trans. W. A. Lambert (Philadelphia: Muhlenberg Press, 1957), 376.

[8]Calvin Roetzel, "*Theodidaktoi* and hand-work in Philo and 1 Thessalonians" in *L'Apotre Paul*, ed. Albert Vanhoye (Leuven: Uitgeverij Peeters, 1986), 324.

[9]John Oswalt, *The Book of Isaiah: 40–66* (Grand Rapids: Eerdmans, 1998), 428.

[10]John KcKenzie, *Second Isaiah* (Garden City, N.Y.: Doubleday, 1968), 140.

[11]Duncan Derrett, "Mt. 23.8–10: a Midrash on Is. 54.13 and Jer. 31.31–34," *Biblica* 62, no. 3 (1981): 373, 374.

[12]For a summary of this discussion, see Roetzel, "*Theodidaktoi* and hand-work in Philo and 1 Thessalonians" and John Kloppenberg, "*Philadelphia, Theodidaktos,* and the Dioscuri: Rhetorical Engagement in 1 Thessalonians 4:9–12," *New Testament Studies* 39 (April 1993): 265–89.

[13]Derrett, "Mt. 23.8–10: a Midrash on Is. 54.13 and Jer. 31.31–34," 377.

[14]Extended discussions are provided in Martinus Menken, "The Old Testament quotation in John 6.45: source and redaction," *Ephemerides theologicae Lovanienses* 64 no. 1 (1988): 164–72, and chapter 4 of Bruce G. Suchard's *Scripture within Scripture* (Atlanta: Scholars Press, 1992), 47–57.

[15]Rudolf Schnackenberg, *The Gospel According to John* (New York: Seabury Press, 1980), 52.

[16]Francis J. Maloney, *The Gospel of John* (Collegeville, Minn.: Michael Glazier/Liturgical Press, 1998), 218.

[17]Schnackenberg, *The Gospel According to John*, 51.

[18]Rodney A. Whitacre, *John* (Downers Grove, Ill.: InterVarsity, 1999), 164.

[19]Roger Gryson, "The Authority of the Teacher in the Ancient and Medieval Church," *Journal of Ecumenical Studies* 19, no. 2 (Spring 1982), 176.

[20]Charles R. Foster, *Teaching in the Community of Faith* (Nashville: Abingdon Press, 1982), 119.

[21]*Sayings of the Desert Fathers*, 175.

[22]Saint Gregory of Sinai, "On commandments and doctrines, warnings and promises," in *The Philokalia*, vol. 4, trans. and ed. G. E. H. Palmer, Philip Sherrad, Kallistos Ware (London: Faber and Faber, 1995), 232.

²³Parker Palmer, *The Courage to Teach* (San Francisco: Jossey-Bass, 1998), 29.

²⁴Ibid., 31.

²⁵Ibid.

²⁶Ibid., 33.

²⁷*The Methodist Hymnal* (Nashville: The Methodist Publishing House, 1966), 315.

²⁸Mary Frohlich, "Spiritual Discipline, Discipline of Spirituality: Revisiting Questions of Definition and Method," in *Minding the Spirit: The Study of Christian Spirituality,* ed. Elizabeth A. Dreyer and Mark S. Burrows (Baltimore: Johns Hopkins University Press, 2005), 75. Frohlich credits Jean-Luc Marion, *God without Being* (Chicago: University of Chicago Press, 1991) for this distinction.

²⁹*Sayings of the Desert Fathers*, xxi.

³⁰Douglas Burton-Christie, *The Word in the Desert* (New York: Oxford University Press, 1993), 145.

³¹Ibid., 153.

³²Ibid., 154.

³³*The Sayings of the Desert Fathers*, 224.

³⁴Foster, *Teaching in the Community of Faith*, 122.

³⁵Frohlich, "Spiritual Discipline, Discipline of Spirituality," 76.

³⁶Maximus the Confessor, "Various Texts on Theology, the Divine Economy, and Virtue and Vice," in *The Philokalia*, vol. 2, trans. and ed. G. E. H. Palmer, Philip Sherrad, Kallistos Ware (London: Faber and Faber, 1981), 261.

³⁷*The Sayings of the Desert Fathers*, 185.

Chapter 2: Teaching from a Life of Prayer

¹Sara Little, *To Set One's Heart: Belief and Teaching in the Church* (Atlanta: John Knox Press, 1983), 1.

²Parker Palmer, *The Courage to Teach* (San Francisco: Jossey-Bass, 1998), 1–2.

³Elizabeth Stopp, "Francois de Sales," in *The Study of Spirituality,* ed. Cheslyn Jones, Geoffrey Wainwright, and Edward Yarnold (New York: Oxford University Press, 1986), 380; John K. Ryan, Translator's Introduction to Francis de Sales, *Introduction to the Devout Life* (New York: Image Books, 1989), 1. Subsequent references to de Sales's *Introduction* are to Ryan's edition.

⁴Jordan Aumann, "St. Francis de Sales: Theologian for the Laity," *Listening* 26 (Fall 1991): 246.

⁵Stopp, "Francois de Sales," 380.

⁶André Ravier, *Francis de Sales: Sage and Saint*, trans. Joseph D. Bowler (San Francisco: Ignatius Press, 1988), 177.

⁷Stopp, "Francois de Sales," 382.

⁸Ibid.

⁹Aumann, "St. Francis de Sales," 253.

¹⁰Ryan, Translator's Introduction, 17.

¹¹Michael J. Buckley, "Seventeenth Century French Spirituality: Three Figures," in *Christian Spirituality: Post-Reformation and Modern,* ed. Louis Dupré and Don Saliers (New York: Crossroad, 1991), 37. In this sense, to *introduce* is similar to but moves in the opposite direction of *educare*, which means to "draw out."

¹²Ryan, Translator's Introduction, 14.

¹³De Sales, *Introduction to the Devout Life*, 33, 43.

¹⁴Ibid., 35.

¹⁵Ibid.

¹⁶Ibid., 40, 45.

¹⁷Ibid., 77, 78.

¹⁸Ibid., 84–85.

¹⁹Ibid., 56–57.

²⁰Ibid., 88.

²¹Ibid., 97.

²²Pierre Hegy, "Metaphorical Shift: From Chivalrous Obedience to Soulful Healing," in *Feminist Voices in Spirituality,* ed. Pierre Hegy (New York: Edwin Mellon, 1996), 14.

²³De Sales, *Introduction to the Devout Life*, 81.

²⁴Ibid., 119.

[25]Ibid., 96.

[26]Ibid., 122.

[27]Ibid., 184.

[28]Ibid., 215.

[29]Ibid., 218, 229.

[30]Ibid., 256.

[31]Ibid., 271.

[32]Ibid., 280.

[33]The translation and edition used here, *Purity of Heart Is to Will One Thing*, trans. Douglas Steere (New York: Harper and Row, 1948), had been the standard English translation until it was included in the critical edition of Kierkegaard's work. See *Upbuilding Discourses in Various Spirits*, ed. and trans. Howard V. Hong and Edna H. Hong (Princeton: Princeton University Press, 1993).

[34]Albert Outler, "Pietism and Enlightenment," in Dupré and Saliers, *Christian Spirituality: Post-Reformation and Modern*, 250.

[35]*Purity of Heart*, 18.

[36]Gordon Marino, "About Soren Kierkegaard: Biography and Significance," *www.stolaf.edu/collections/kierkegaard/aboutkierkegaard.html*, accessed March 2006.

[37]Ibid.

[38]Jeremy D. B. Walker, *To Will One Thing: Reflections on Kierkegaard's 'Purity of Heart'* (Montreal: McGill-Queen's University Press, 1972), 4. Throughout *Purity of Heart*, Kierkegaard refers to our seeking or willing the Good. By "the Good" he does not mean "the good life" or any temporal form of what we think of as "good behavior," although seeking "the Good" cannot be separated from the moral life. As becomes at least implicit late in the work is that "the Good" refers to an absolute good, an absolute that is present only in God. Therefore, in seeking to will one thing and in that one thing being "the Good," we are seeking and willing the one thing that is God.

[39]*Purity of Heart*, 178.

[40]Ibid., 27. The "solitary individual" in Kierkegaard refers to the truly Christian person who turns to God personally, as a single person," not to the autonomous individualism of our day. The "individual" is the person who is "at one with oneself" before God. Vernard Eller, *Kierkegaard and Radical Discipleship* (Princeton; Princeton University Press, 1968), 105, 114.

[41]*Purity of Heart*, 31, 39.

[42]Ibid., 135.

[43]Ibid., 182.

[44]Ibid., 197, 198.

[45]Ibid., 199, 205, 210.

[46]Ibid., 57.

[47]Ibid., 68, 69, 79, 89, 100, 105, respectively.

[48]Ibid., 145.

[49]Michael Plekon, "Protest and Affirmation: The Late Kierkegaard on Christ, the Church, and Society, *Quarterly Review* 2 (Fall 1982), 48.

[50]*Purity of Heart*, 189, 197.

[51]Ibid., 203.

[52]Ibid., 210.

Chapter 3: Life Together as Teacher and Learner

[1]Parker Palmer, *To Know As We Are Known* (San Francisco: HarperSanFrancisco, 1993), 37.

[2]Ibid., 36.

[3]Ibid., 39.

[4]Dietrich Bonhoeffer, *Life Together* (New York: Harper & Row, 1954), 23.

[5]Ibid., 28.

[6]Palmer, *To Know As We Are Known*, 42–43.

[7]Ibid., 43.

[8]Margaret Guenther, *Holy Listening: The Art of Spiritual Direction* (Boston: Cowley Publications, 1992), 44.

⁹This refrain is picked up six more times in the gospel stories of Jesus; see Mt. 13:9, 43; Mk. 4:9, 23; Lk. 8:8, 14:35.

¹⁰This teaching and modification of the text found in Isa. 6:9–10 is also attributed to Jesus in Mt. 13:15 and Jn. 12:40. It has been used by Christians to castigate Jews for their unwillingness to accept Jesus as their Messiah; my inclusion of the text here has the altogether different purpose of suggesting the importance of a teacher listening attentively to the insights and experiences of students with the goal of mutual discernment of God's word for the student and the teacher.

¹¹Guenther, *Holy Listening,* 44 (referencing 2 Kings 5:11).

¹²Henri Nouwen, *Reaching Out: The Three Movements of the Spiritual Life* (New York: Doubleday, 1975), 70.

¹³Ibid., 72.

¹⁴Ibid., 74–75.

¹⁵Palmer, *To Know As We Are Known,* 54.

¹⁶Julian of Norwich, *Revelations of Divine Love,* trans. Clifton Wolters (New York: Penguin Books, 1966), 68.

¹⁷John Eusden and John Westerhoff, *Sensing Beauty: Aesthetics, the Human Spirit, and the Church* (Cleveland: United Church Press, 1998), 83.

¹⁸C. I. Scofield, ed., *The New Scofield Reference Bible* (New York: Oxford University Press, 1967), 693.

¹⁹Maria Harris, *Teaching & Religious Imagination* (New York: HarperSanFrancisco, 1987), 3.

²⁰Ibid., 20–22.

²¹Ibid., 60, 76.

²²Julian of Norwich, *Revelations,* 191.

²³Ibid., 76.

²⁴Ibid., 74.

²⁵Ibid., 77.

²⁶Ibid., 85.

²⁷Ibid., 103.

²⁸Ibid., 96.

²⁹Ibid., 182.

³⁰Ibid., 77.

³¹Ibid., 86.

³²Ibid., 87.

³³Eugene Peterson, *Subversive Spirituality* (Grand Rapids, Mich.: Eerdmans, 1997), 252. First published in *TSF Bulletin* (March-April 1984).

Chapter 4: The Contemporary Search for Spirituality

¹Douglas Burton-Christie, *The Word in the Desert* (New York: Oxford University Press, 1993), 215.

²Ibid.

³John Bunyan, *The Pilgrim's Progress,* ed. Roger Sharrock (New York: Viking Penguin, 1987), 65–67, 83–84. Bunyan's work will be discussed further in chapter 6.

⁴Ibid., 54.

⁵Walter Rauschenbusch, *Dare We Be Christians?* The William Bradford Collection ed. (Cleveland: Pilgrim Press, 1993), 33.

⁶Walter Rauschenbusch, *A Theology for the Social Gospel* (Nashville: Abingdon Press, 1981), 69.

⁷H. Richard Niebuhr, *Christ and Culture* (New York: Harper & Row, 1951), 32.

⁸Ibid., 40–43.

⁹Ibid., 238.

¹⁰Ibid., 256.

¹¹Robert Wuthnow, *After Heaven: Spirituality in America Since the 1950s* (Berkeley: University of California Press, 1998), 3.

¹²See C. Kirk Hadaway & David Roozen, *Rerouting the Protestant Mainstream* (Nashville: Abingdon Press, 1995) for statistical documentation of this decline beginning in the 1960s.

¹³Wuthnow, *After Heaven,* 7.

[14]Ibid., 8–10.

[15]Ibid., 33.

[16]Ibid., 39.

[17]Ibid., 57.

[18]Ibid., 67. Wuthnow notes that the length of time between an adolescent's confirmation in a faith community and his or her movement into parenthood doubled (from seven to fifteen years) between the mid-1950s and the late 1960s as a result of mass marketed contraceptives, allowing young people more socially acceptable time to "drop out" of church communities before they were expected to bring their children (and themselves) into the congregational fold. Many chose not to return.

[19]Ibid., 93.

[20]Ibid., 95.

[21]Ibid., 101.

[22]Ibid., 106

[23]Ibid., 129.

[24]Ibid., 160.

[25]Ibid., 158.

[26]See Eiesland and Warner, "Ecology: Seeing the Congregation in Context" in Nancy Ammerman et al., *Studying Congregations: A New Handbook* (Nashville: Abingdon Press, 1998), 40–77.

[27]Rowan Williams, *Lost Icons: Reflections on Cultural Bereavement* (New York: T & T Clark, 2000), 1.

[28]Ibid., 137–38.

[29]Michael Warren, *At This Time in This Place: The Spirit Embodied in the Local Assembly* (Harrisburg, Pa.: Trinity Press International, 1999), 9.

[30]Ibid., 105.

[31]Ibid., 74–75.

[32]Ibid., 18, emphasis in original.

[33]Miroslav Volf, "Theology for a Way of Life" in *Practicing Theology*, ed. Miroslav Volf and Dorothy Bass (Grand Rapids, Mich.: Eerdmans, 2002), 257–58, emphasis in original.

[34]Parker Palmer, *To Know As We Are Known* (San Francisco: HarperSanFrancisco, 1993), 65.

[35]Wuthnow, *After Heaven*, 196.

[36]Ibid., 197.

[37]Palmer, *To Know As We Are Known*, 71.

[38]Ibid., 72.

[39]Ibid., 80.

[40]Ibid., 82.

[41]Ibid., 84–85.

Chapter 5: Modes of Teaching the Spiritual Life

[1]Brett Webb-Mitchell, *Christly Gestures: Learning to be Members of the Body of Christ* (Grand Rapids: Eerdmans, 2003), 1–2.

[2]Ibid., 19.

[3]Ibid., 206.

[4]Ibid., 209.

[5]Ibid., 210.

[6]Columba Stewart, *Cassian the Monk* (New York: Oxford University Press, 1998), 38. Stewart provides the most comprehensive study of the life and theology of Cassian currently available.

[7]Ibid., 30.

[8]Ibid., 29.

[9]Those in the Methodist families will know this as the process of government within which the Methodist churches function. Those who know their Methodist history, however, will recall that the first conferences convened and led by John Wesley attended less to organizational questions than seems to be the case today. As Wesley records in his minutes from the first conference in 1744, his concern was with "what to teach, how to teach, and

what to do, that is, how to regulate our doctrine, discipline, and practice." *The Works of John Wesley*, ed. Thomas Jackson, 8 (Grand Rapids: Zondervan, 1958), 275.

[10]Boniface Ramsey, Translators Introduction to *John Cassian: The Conferences*, trans. and annot. Boniface Ramsey, O.P. (New York: Paulist Press, 1997), 14.

[11]Ibid., 16. In Conference 18, with Abba Pianum speaking on the kinds of monks, Pianum says "follow with great humility whatever you see our elders do or teach"; do not "be moved or diverted or held back from imitating them even if the reason or the cause for a particular thing or deed is not clear to you at the time, because knowledge of everything is attained by those who think well and with simplicity about all matters and who *strive to imitate* faithfully *rather than to discuss* everything that they see being taught and done by the elders" [emphasis added]. *Conference* 18.3.1, 636.

[12]Ibid., 501.

[13]Stewart, *Cassian the Monk*, 37.

[14]Ramsey, Introduction in *John Cassian: The Conferences*, 10. References to the texts of the *Conferences* will be to this edition, noted by conference, chapter, paragraph, and page number.

[15]Stewart, *Cassian the Monk*, 39.

[16]Ibid., 86, 92.

[17]*St. Francis de Sales: Selected Letters*, trans. and intro. Elisabeth Stopp (London: Faber and Faber, 1960), 19.

[18]Calvin Roetzel, *Paul: The Man and the Myth* (Minneapolis: Fortress Press, 1999), 69.

[19]Ibid.

[20]Ibid., 70, 77.

[21]E. Glenn Hinson, "Letters for Spiritual Guidance" in *Spirituality in Ecumenical Perspective*, ed. E. Glenn Hinson (Louisville: Westminster John Knox Press, 1993), 161–62.

[22]Ibid., 168.

[23]*Francis de Sales, Jane de Chantal: Letters of Spiritual Direction*, trans. Péronne Marie Thibert, intro. Wendy M. Wright and Joseph F. Powers (New York: Paulist Press, 1988), 87.

[24]Wendy M. Wright, "'That is what it is made for': The image of the heart in the spirituality of Francis de Sales and Jane de Chantal," in *Spiritualities of the Heart*, ed. Annice Callahan (Mahwah, N.J.: Paulist Press, 1990), 152. For more extended treatments of the relationship between de Chantal and de Sales, see Wendy Wright, "Spiritual Friendship and Spiritual Direction in the Salesian World," *Studia Mystica* 12 (Spring 1989): 46–63, and her book *Bond of Perfection* (Mahwah, N.J.: Paulist Press, 1985). We also see some hints of their changing relationship in the forms of address de Sales uses in his letters to de Chantal. The earliest, from 1604, are the most formal in style and tone, addressed to "Madame" or "the Baronne de Chantal." Within the year, de Sales addresses de Chantal as sister and, more consistently as "dear daughter." Once the Visitation is founded in 1610, the exchange becomes more clearly an exchange between equals—"dear Father" and "dear Mother"— and the tone is increasingly personal.

[25]*Francis de Sales, Jane de Chantal*, 30.

[26]Ibid., 11.

[27]Stopp, *Francis de Sales: Selected Letters*, 35.

[28]Ibid., 33.

[29]*Francis de Sales, Jane de Chantal*, 38.

[30]Ibid., 45.

[31]Ibid., 30.

[32]Ibid., 77.

[33]Stopp, *Francis de Sales: Selected Letters*, 135.

[34]Ibid., 136.

[35]*Francis de Sales, Jane de Chantal*, 262.

[36]Wendy Wright provides an extended treatment as well as full English translations of this exchange in her book *Bond of Perfection*, 162–73. As might be expected, the excerpts do not do justice to the intensity and emotion of the letters.

[37]Wright, *Bond of Perfection*, 163.

[38]Ibid., 164.

[39]Ibid., 171.

[40]Ibid., 165.

[41]Ibid., 166.
[42]Ibid., 167.
[43]Ibid.
[44]Ibid., 168.
[45]Ibid., 169.
[46]Ibid., 170.
[47]James Fowler, *Becoming Adult, Becoming Christian* (San Francisco: Harper and Row, 1984), 140.
[48]L. Gregory Jones, "For All the Saints: Autobiography in Christian Theology," *Asbury Theological Journal* 47, no.1 (Spring 1992): 35.
[49]Ibid.
[50]Jones, "For All the Saints," 31.
[51]Robert Louis Wilken, *The Spirit of Early Christian Thought* (New Haven, Conn.: Yale University Press, 2003), 263.
[52]Gerard Loughlin, *Telling God's Story: Bible, Church and Narrative Theology* (Cambridge: Cambridge University Press, 1996), 139.
[53]Ibid., 218.
[54]Edith Wyschogrod, *Saints and Postmodernism: Revisioning Moral Philosophy* (Chicago: University of Chicago Press, 1990), xxiii.
[55]Ibid., 3.
[56]Ibid., 10.
[57]Ibid., 13.
[58]Frances Young, *From Nicaea to Chalcedon* (London: SCM Press, 1983), 70–72.
[59]Ibid., 82.
[60]Athanasius, *The Life of Antony and the Letter to Marcellinus*, trans. Robert C. Gregg (New York: Paulist Press, 1980), 29.
[61]This paragraph summarizes Athanasius, *The Life of Antony*, 30–32.
[62]Ibid., 45.
[63]Ibid., 67–68.
[64]Ibid., 89.
[65]Ibid., 97.
[66]Ibid., 87.

Chapter 6: Images of the Christian Spiritual Life

[1]Alistair McGrath discusses some of these images in *Christian Spirituality* (Malden, Mass.: Blackwell, 1999), 88–109.

[2]In his discussion of metaphor theory, Edward Slingerland explores as an example the metaphor of "purposeful life as a journey." He highlights the ways in which this single metaphor penetrates our consciousness and comes to expression in related images. If life is a journey, then we begin to think and talk about reaching a destination, getting sidetracked or bogged down, being led astray, and needing to backtrack. As we will see, all of these images come into play in *Pilgrim's Progress*. Edward Slingerland, "Conceptual Metaphor Theory as Methodology for Comparative Religion," *Journal of the American Academy of Religion* 72, no. 1 (March 2004): 12–13.

[3]Gordon Mursell, *English Spirituality: From Earliest Times to 1700* (Louisville: Westminster John Knox Press, 2001), 400.

[4]Gordon Wakefield, *Bunyan the Christian* (London: HarperCollins, 1992), 31.

[5]John Bunyan, *The Pilgrim's Progress*, ed. and intro. Roger Sharrock (New York: Penguin, 1987), 3.

[6]The following quotes are from the Sharrock edition of *The Pilgrim's Progress*, here pp. 8–9.

[7]Ibid., 11–12.
[8]Ibid., 17.
[9]Ibid., 35.
[10]Ibid., 36.
[11]Ibid., 42.
[12]Ibid., 58.
[13]Ibid., 60.

[14]Ibid., 71.

[15]Ibid., 73.

[16]Ibid., 74.

[17]Ibid., 120–24.

[18]Ibid., 139.

[19]Monica Furlong, *Puritan's Progress* (London: Hodden and Stoughton, 1975), 107.

[20]Wakefield, *Bunyan the Christian*, 86.

[21]Bunyan, *The Pilgrim's Progress*, 38.

[22]Mursell, *English Spirituality*, 402.

[23]Bunyan, *The Pilgrim's Progress*, ix, xi.

[24]Wakefield, *Bunyan the Christian*, 81.

[25]Furlong, *Puritan's Progress*, 107.

[26]Kallistos Ware, Introduction to *John Climacus: The Ladder of Divine Ascent*, trans. Colm Lubheid and Norman Russell (Mahwah, N.J.: Paulist Press, 1982), 1, 5.

[27]Kallistos Ware, "The Origins of the Jesus Prayer: Diadochus, Gaza, Sinai" in *The Study of Spirituality*, ed. Cheslyn Jones, Geoffrey Wainwright, and Edward Yarnold (New York: Oxford, 1986), 181.

[28]Ware, Introduction, 11.

[29]Climacus, *The Ladder of Divine Ascent*, 291.

[30]As of April 10, 2006, images of this icon can be found at the following links: http://www.abcgallery.com/I/icons/icons39.html; http://www.monachos.net/patristics/klimakos_repentance.shtml; http://www.comeandseeicons.com/pds07.htm; and http://www.goarch.org/en/resources/clipart/john_ladder.asp.

[31]Richard T. Lawrence, "The Three-fold Structure of the Ladder of Divine Ascent," *St. Vladimir's Theological Quarterly* 32.2 (1988): 115–16.

[32]Lawrence, "Three-fold Structure," 117.

[33]Ware, Introduction, 15.

[34]Climacus, *The Ladder of Divine Ascent*, 83.

[35]Ibid., 218. Here one might compare the opening paragraphs of Step 25, On Humility, in *The Ladder* with the conversation between Christian, Faithful, and Talkative in *Pilgrim's Progress*.

[36]Ibid., 229.

[37]Ibid., 242.

[38]William Creasy, Introduction to Thomas à Kempis, *The Imitation of Christ*, trans. and intro. William Creasy (Notre Dame: Ave Maria Press, 1989), 14, 24. Quotations from *The Imitation of Christ* all come from Creasy's translation.

[39]Mark S. Burrows, "Devotio Moderna: Reforming Piety in the Later Middle Ages," in *Spiritual Traditions for the Contemporary Church*, ed. Robin Maas and Gabriel O'Donnell (Nashville: Abingdon Press, 1990), 111.

[40]*The Imitation of Christ*, 31, 33.

[41]Burrows, "Devotio Moderna," 124.

[42]Margaret Miles, *Practicing Christianity* (New York: Crossroad, 1988), 23.

[43]*The Imitation of Christ*, 60.

[44]Ibid., 65.

[45]Ibid., 78.

[46]Ibid., 86, 115.

[47]Ibid., 156.

[48]Ibid., 166.

[49]Ibid., 166, 172.

[50]Ibid., 69.

[51]Ibid., 81.

[52]Joyce Salisbury's *Perpetua's Passion: The Death and Memory of a Young Roman Woman* (New York: Routledge, 1997) is perhaps the most comprehensive study of the political and religious contexts of Perpetua's story.

[53]*The Martyrdom of Perpetua*, intro. and commentary Sara Maitland, trans. W. H. Shewring [(translation: Sheed and Ward, 1931) Evesham: Arthur James, 1996], 12.

[54]Lisa M. Sullivan, "'I responded, I will not…': Christianity as Catalyst for Resistance in the Passio Perpetuae et Felicitatis," *Semeia* 79 (1997): 68, 73.

[55]*The Martyrdom of Perpetua*, 26–27.

[56]In Athanasius's *Life of Antony*, Antony yearns to offer himself as a martyr in Alexandria but is unwilling to hand himself over. He is not martyred and must accept the way of "bloodless" martyrdom, the martyrdom of his conscience as a solitary in the desert. See Athanasius, *The Life of Antony* (Mahwah, N.J.: Paulist Press, 1980), 65–66.

[57]*The Martyrdom of Perpetua*, 35.

[58]Kate Cooper, "The Voice of the Victim: Gender, Representation, and Early Christian Martyrdom," *Bulletin of the John Rylands University Library of Manchester*, 80 (Autumn 1988): 148, 152.

Chapter 7: The Rule as Teacher

[1]Prologue 45–49, *RB 1980: The Rule of Benedict*, ed. Timothy Fry, O.S.B. (Collegeville, Minn.: The Liturgical Press, 1981), 165. Hereafter, citations from the Rule of Benedict will be given as RB followed by chapter and verse. All citations come from *RB 1980*. Adalbert de Vogüé provides an extended discussion about the monastery as the school of the Lord's service in *The Rule of Saint Benedict: A Doctrinal and Spiritual Commentary*, trans. John Baptist Hasbrouck (Kalamazoo: Cistercian Publications, 1983), 13–38.

[2]*The Rule of the Society of Saint John the Evangelist: North American Congregation* (Boston: Cowley Publications, 1997), 25, hereafter referred to as RSSJE.

[3]Martin Smith, Introduction to ibid., xii.

[4]Terence Kardong, *Benedict's Rule: A Translation and Commentary* (Collegeville, Minn.: Liturgical Press, 1996), 20.

[5]Esther de Waal, *A Life-Giving Way* (Collegeville, Minn.: Liturgical Press, 1995), 12.

[6]Ibid., 13.

[7]A number of helpful references and links can be found at http://www.osb.org/gen/bendct.html, including links to full texts of the RB, the *Dialogues* of Gregory the Great, and images of Benedict.

[8]*RB 1980*, 75. An English translation of Book II of Gregory's *Dialogues*, providing *The Life of Benedict*, is available at http://www.osb.org/gen/greg/.

[9]*RB 1980*, 76.

[10]Ibid., 84.

[11]Columba Stewart, *Prayer and Community: The Benedictine Tradition* (Maryknoll, N.Y.: Orbis, 1998), 15.

[12]Ibid., 20.

[13]Ibid.

[14]Ibid., 89.

[15]Ibid., 21.

[16]*RB 1980*, 86.

[17]Brian C. Taylor, *Spirituality for Everyday Living* (Collegeville, Minn.: Liturgical Press, 1989), 63.

[18]Mark Gibbard, "R. M. Benson: The Founder of SSJE," *Theology* 69 (May 1966): 194–95.

[19]Ibid., 195.

[20]Smith, Introduction, x–xi. An overview of the community's life and work can be found at its Web site: http://www.ssje.org/. Smith was the superior of the community when the RSSJE was published in 1997.

[21]Smith, Introduction, xiii–xiv.

[22]Ibid., xv.

[23]RSSJE, 7.

[24]Ibid., 118.

[25]The Protestant reformers critiqued this distinction, suggesting it created a kind of Christian elite of those who lived beyond the "evangelical precepts" of love of God and neighbor. So, for example, Martin Luther, in "The Judgment of Martin Luther on Monastic Vows" [*Luther's Works*, vol. 44: *The Christian in Society*, ed. James Atkinson (Philadelphia: Fortress Press, 1966)], argues that the division of the gospel into counsels and precepts, one for monastics, the other for ordinary men, is contrary to the gospel, a sign of unbelief (256), and contrary to Christian freedom (297). Yet even as he makes this argument, Luther is not arguing against the practices of poverty, chastity, and obedience; rather, he is arguing against characterizing these as vows other than or more than what the Christian vows in

baptism (356). Finally, Luther argues that "whatever is not against love is a matter of free choice, permissible and sanctioned,…nothing that is contrary to love, and nothing more than love, is or can be binding" (393).

[26]Rupert Davies, in his Introduction to *The Works of John Wesley*, vol. 9, *The Methodist Societies*, ed. Rupert Davies (Nashville: Abingdon Press, 1989), develops a distinction between church, sect, and society. Where "church" claims the "width and depth of catholic tradition," "sect" cuts itself off from the church with the claim of "embodying the only authentic form of Christian discipleship." A "society" acknowledges the truth claims of the church and does not separate from it, "but claims to cultivate, by means of sacrament and fellowship, the type of inward holiness, which too great an objectivity can easily neglect and of which the church needs constantly to be reminded." A society, Davies argues, "calls its own members within the larger church to a special personal commitment which respects the commitments of others" (3). Rather surprisingly, Davies suggests that the Moravians and Methodists are the most notable examples in church history, excluding any discussion of the monastic orders within the Roman Catholic Church. Perhaps, as we have already noted in the development of the SSJE, which calls itself a society, the four-hundred–year absence of monasticism in England prevents him from seeing the ways in which his description of society fits most monastic and religious orders today.

[27]D. Stephen Long, *Living the Discipline: United Methodist Theological Reflection on War, Civilization, and Holiness* (Grand Rapids: Eerdmans, 1992), 3.

[28]David Lowes Watson, "Aldersgate Street and the General Rules: The Form and the Power of Methodist Discipleship," in *Aldersgate Reconsidered*, ed. Randy Maddox (Nashville: Kingswood, 1990), 34.

[29]David Lowes Watson, *Christian Formation through Mutual Accountability* (Nashville: Discipleship Resources, 1991), 80.

[30]John Wesley, "The Nature, Design, and General Rules of the United Societies," in *The Works of John Wesley*, vol. 9, 69. Because they were neither church nor sect, the Methodist societies were not denominationally restricted in membership.

[31]Ibid.

[32]Among the larger Methodist family, the General Rules function (or do not function) in a similar way. In *The Book of Discipline of the Christian Methodist Episcopal Church* (Memphis: CME Publishing House, 1998), they appear under "Basic Principles" but are not included in discussion of the process or requirements for church membership. In *The Book of Discipline of the African Methodist Episcopal Church* (Nashville: AMEC Publishing House, 1988) they appear as part of the Doctrinal Statements, immediately following the "Cathechism on Faith." Although new church members are initially on probation and under the supervision of a class leader, the General Rules are not related to membership. *The Book of Discipline of the African Methodist Episcopal Zion Church* (Charlotte: AMEZ Publishing House, 1996) makes the most explicit use the General Rules. Although like the other Methodist churches, they appear in the *Book of Discipline* as part of the doctrinal standards, the requirements for church membership include the following statement: "Let every Pastor and Class Leader see that all persons on probation be instructed in the Rules and Doctrines of the AMEZ Church before they are admitted to Full Membership" (p. 27). Finally, within 1999 *The Book of Discipline of the Free Methodist Church* (http://www.freemethodistchurch.org), the General Rules are incorporated into an historical appendix; but the intent of the Rules has been incorporated into the membership covenant of the church (¶ A/157–158, pp. 21–22).

[33]Watson, "Aldersgate Street," 41.

[34]Davies, Introduction to *The Works of John Wesley*, 11.

[35]Wesley, "General Rules," 70.

[36]Ibid., 71–73.

[37]Christopher P. Momany, "Wesley's General Rules: Paradigm for Postmodern Ethics," *Wesleyan Theological Journal* 28 (Spring-Fall 1993): 9.

[38]Helmut Nausner, "The Meaning of Wesley's General Rules: An Interpretation," trans. J. Steven O'Malley, *Asbury Theological Journal* 44 (Fall 1989): 46, 56.

[39]John Wesley, Preface to *Hymns and Sacred Poems* (1739) in *The Works of John Wesley*, vol. 14, ed. Thomas Jackson (Grand Rapids: Zondervan, 1958–1959), 322.

[40]John Wesley, "The Character of a Methodist," in *The Works of John Wesley*, vol. 9, 38–39.

[41]George Lindbeck, *The Nature of Doctrine* (Philadelphia: Westminster Press, 1984), 35.

[42]Ibid.

[43]Randy Maddox, "Wesley's Prescriptions for Making Disciples of Jesus Christ: Insights for the 21st Century Church," www.pulpitandpew.duke.edu/otherpub.html (downloaded June 21, 2004), 12.

[44]Ibid., 6. Maddox sets these up in relation to Wesley's emphasis on "forming our Christian lives in keeping with the balance of…'Christ in all his offices'." He suggests the following parallels between the three offices and the tensions/temptations described here: prophet-legalism, priest-antinomianism, king-perfectionism.

Chapter 8: The Way of Return as Discipleship Method

[1]Algar Thorold, trans., *The Dialogue of Catherine of Siena* (Rockford, Ill.: Tan Books and Publishers, 1974), 11–14.

[2]Alois Maria Haas, "Schools of Late Medieval Mysticism," in *Christian Spirituality: High Middle Ages and Reformation*, ed. Jill Raitt (New York: Crossroad, 1987), 167.

[3]Elizabeth Petroff, "The Spirituality of Mediaeval Holy Women" in *Vox Benedictina* 6:1 (1989): 28–29.

[4]I am indebted to the work of Susan Muto for the identification of a "way of return" theology in the *Dialogue*, which sparked my interest in the connections between Catherine's writings and the Hebrew prophets. Susan Muto, "Foundations of Christian Formation in the *Dialogue* of St. Catherine of Siena" in John Nichols and Lillian Shank, *Peace Weavers: Medieval Religious Women*, vol. 2 (Kalamazoo, Mich.: Cistercian Publications, 1987): 275–87.

[5]Suzanne Noffke, O.P., trans., *Catherine of Siena: The Dialogue* (New York: Paulist Press, 1980), 26.

[6]Ibid., 58.

[7]Ibid.

[8]Ibid., 64.

[9]Ibid., 65.

[10]*Book of Worship* (New York: United Church of Christ Office for Church Life and Leadership, 1986), 45–47.

[11]Noffke, *Catherine of Siena*, 103.

[12]E. Byron Anderson, *Worship and Christian Identity: Practicing Ourselves* (Collegeville, Minn.: Liturgical Press, 2003), 59.

[13]Debra Dean Murphy, *Teaching That Transforms: Worship as the Heart of Christian Education* (Grand Rapids: Brazos Press, 2004), 194. The whole of chapter 7 explores the relationship of the eucharist and spiritual formation.

[14]Muto, "Foundations of Christian Formation," 279.

[15]Noffke, *Catherine of Siena*, 108.

[16]Ibid., 103–4.

[17]Ibid., 104.

[18]Ibid., 107.

[19]Ibid.

[20]Ibid., 108.

[21]Parker Palmer, *The Company of Strangers: Christians and the Renewal of America's Public Life* (New York: Crossroad, 1981), 125.

[22]Noffke, *Catherine of Siena*, 105.

[23]Ibid., 108–9.

[24]Ibid., 104.

[25]For instance, the United Methodist Church has developed its Disciple Bible Study series on this model. Group members agree to participate in weekly sessions for approximately nine months, as well as be accountable to one another for preparatory study, prayer, and outreach activities. Parishioners decide whether they are willing to meet these requirements, but participation in a covenant group is not necessary for church membership.

[26]Noffke, *Catherine of Siena*, 191–92.

[27]Ibid., 193.

[28]Ibid., 109.

Chapter 9: The Cultivation of Spiritual Knowledge and Wisdom

[1]Francis Gemme, trans., *The Confessions of Saint Augustine* (New York: Airmont Publishing, 1969), 34.

[2]Ibid., 170.

[3]Ibid., 214–15.

[4]Thomas Groome, *Christian Religious Education: Sharing Our Story and Vision* (San Francisco: Harper & Row, 1980), 159.

[5]Odo Zimmermann and Benedict Avery, trans., *Life and Miracles of St. Benedict (Book Two of the Dialogues) by Pope St. Gregory the Great* (Collegeville, Minn.: The Liturgical Press), 2.

[6]Ibid., 1–2.

[7]Ibid., 42.

[8]Julian of Norwich, *Revelations of Divine Love,* trans. Clifton Wolters (New York: Penguin Books, 1966), 204.

[9]Ibid., 140.

[10]All three understandings are identified and initially summarized in Parker Palmer, *To Know As We Are Known* (San Francisco: HarperSanFrancisco, 1993), 7–8.

[11]Ibid., 22–24.

[12]Ibid., 28–29.

[13]Ibid., 8.

[14]Ibid., 19.

[15]Elliot W. Eisner, *Cognition and Curriculum Reconsidered*, 2d ed. (New York: Teachers College Press, 1994), 31–32.

[16]Ibid.

[17]Ibid., 33–34.

[18]Ibid., 35.

[19]Robert Kegan, "What 'Form' Transforms? A Constructive-Developmental Approach to Transformative Learning" in Jack Mezirow & Associates, *Learning as Transformation: Critical Perspectives on a Theory in Progress* (San Francisco: Jossey-Bass, 2000), 53.

[20]Jack Mezirow, "Learning to Think Like an Adult: Core Concepts of Transformation Theory" in Mezirow & Associates, *Learning as Transformation*, 3.

[21]The following discussion is derived from Mary Belenky's continued reflections on the categories she and others first identified in *Women's Ways of Knowing*, which is included as a section of her and Ann Stanton's essay, "Inequality, Development, and Connected Knowing" in Mezirow & Associates, *Learning as Transformation*, 80–91. The comments on the implications of these categories for religious literacy are my own.

[22]Belenky and Stanton, "Inequality, Development, and Connected Knowing," 90.

[23]Peter Hodgson, *God's Wisdom: Toward a Theology of Education* (Louisville: Westminster John Knox Press, 1999), 68–69.

[24]Quoted in ibid., 69.

[25]Ibid., 7.

[26]G. E. H. Palmer, Philip Sherrard, and Kallistos Ware, eds., *The Philokalia: The Complete Text compiled by St. Nikodimos of the Holy Mountain and St. Makarios of Corinth*, vol. 1 (London: Faber and Faber, 1979), 253.

[27]To facilitate conversation across different edited volumes, we will identify ideas and quotations from the treatise by the numbers assigned to the statements. This quotation comes from Text 6.

[28]Text 7.

[29]Text 28.

[30]Texts 7, 9.

[31]Text 67.

[32]Text 26.

[33]Text 9.

[34]Text 68.

[35]Text 8.

[36]Text 61.

[37]Text 92.

[38]Text 70.

[39]Text 86.

[40]Text 89.

[41]Text 37.

[42]Text 83.

[43]Throughout the history of Christian spirituality, this mystical union has been named as *theoria* or *gnostike*, terms that now carry problematic connotations. The English translation of *theoria* to "theory" evokes the separation of theory from practice in many educational models, and *gnostike* references a secret knowledge available only to an initiated few.

[44]James Walsh, S.J., ed., *The Cloud of Unknowing* (New York: Paulist Press, 1981), 119.

[45]Text 89, emphasis mine.

[46]Text 75.

[47]Text 8.

Chapter 10: Examination of Conscience as Evaluative Practice

[1]A quick review of recent issues of the journal *Assessment & Evaluation in Higher Education* provides an entry point into some of this literature.

[2]Among the more recent works, see George E. Ganss, ed., *Ignatius of Loyola: Spiritual Exercises and Selected Works* (New York: Paulist Press, 1991), which includes Ignatius's autobiography; J. Ignacio Tellechea Idígoras, *Ignatius of Loyola: The Pilgrim Saint*, trans. Cornelius Michael Buckley (Chicago: Loyola University Press, 1994); and *A Pilgrim's Journey: The Autobiography of Ignatius of Loyola*, trans. Joseph N. Tylenda (Wilmington, Del.: Michael Glazier, 1985). I am drawing on Ganss's introduction for this biographical summary.

[3]Ganss, *Ignatius of Loyola*, 14.

[4]Ibid., 37.

[5]Ibid., 46.

[6]Elizabeth Meier Tetlow, Preface to *The Spiritual Exercises of St. Ignatius Loyola*, trans. Tetlow (Lanham, Md.: University Press of America, 1987), xiv.

[7]John O'Malley, "Early Jesuit Spirituality: Spain and Italy" in *Christian Spirituality Post-Reformation and Modern*, ed. Louis Dupré and Don Saliers (New York: Crossroad, 1991), 3.

[8]*Spiritual Exercises*, 21.

[9]Barbara Bedolla and Dominic Totaro, S.J. "Ignatian Spirituality," in *Spiritual Traditions for the Contemporary Church*, ed. Robin Maas and Gabriel O'Donnell (Nashville: Abingdon Press, 1990), 174.

[10]Particular sections of the *Spiritual Exercises* are referenced throughout our discussion by number. This permits comparison among the various translations.

[11]Ganss, *Ignatius of Loyola*, 51–53.

[12]Joseph A. Tetlow, "The Most Postmodern Prayer: American Jesuit Identity and the Examen of Conscience, 1920–1990," *Studies in the Spirituality of Jesuits* 26, no. 1 (January 1994): 10.

[13]Ibid., 14. Of course, we need only turn to Ignatius's younger contemporary John Calvin for a clear naming of this flaw and a process of confession that grows from it. Calvin was more oriented to the greatness of our sin, our total depravity, and our standing before God's judgment: "In order that we may rightly examine ourselves, our consciences must necessarily be called before God's judgment seat. For there is need to strip entirely bare in its light the secret places of our depravity, which otherwise are too deeply hidden" [*Institutes of the Christian Religion*, ed. John T. McNeill (Philadelphia: Westminster, 1960), I: 759 (3.12.5).] See David Foxgrover's "Self-Examination in John Calvin and William Ames," in *Later Calvinism*, ed. W. Fred Graham (Kirksville, Mo.: Sixteenth Century Journal Publications, 1994), 451–70.

[14]Deborah Smith Douglas, "The Examen Re-examined," *Weavings* 10 (March-April 1995): 35, 34.

[15]Tetlow, "The Most Postmodern Prayer," 8.

[16]Ibid., 22–23.

[17]George A. Aschenbrenner, "Consciousness Examen," *Review for Religious* 31, no. 1 (1972): 14–21.

[18]Tetlow, "The Most Postmodern Prayer," 43. Tetlow names this change the "Aschenbrenner shift."

[19]Aschenbrenner, "Consciousness Examen," 14.

[20]Ibid., 18.

[21]Ibid.

[22]Jacque Pasquier, "Examination of Conscience and *Revision de Vie*," *The Way* 11 (1971): 306.

[23]Pasquier, "Examination of Conscience," 307.

[24]The priority of God's grace and love in the Ignatian examen becomes even more evident when compared to the steps for self-examination Calvin provides in his commentary on Psalm 51: (1) "confession of the greatness of one's offense," (2) "a sense of the complete depravity of our nature," (3) direct [one's] thoughts to the strict judgment of God," (4) "turn to the 'peculiarity of [our] own case'," and (5) let his recall of one sin be the occasion to recall others "until 'we are brought before God in deep self-abasement'" (Foxgrover, "Self-Examination in John Calvin," 456).

[25]Katherine Dyckman, Mary Garvin, and Elizabeth Liebert, *The Spiritual Exercises Reclaimed* (Mahwah, N.J.: Paulist Press, 2001), 115. Dyckman, Garvin, and Liebert provide a careful and constructive reading of the "problems and possibilities" offered in the *Exercises* in regard to the particular questions they raise with and for women.

[26]Pasquier, "Examination of Conscience," 311.

[27]In this list of benefits, I am drawing on Donald St. Louis, "The Ignatian Examen" in *The Way of Ignatius Loyola: Contemporary Approaches to the Spiritual Exercises*, ed. Philip Sheldrake (London: SPCK, 1991), 157–60.

[28]St. Louis, "The Ignatian Examen," 162.

[29]Dyckman, et al., *The Spiritual Exercises Reclaimed*, 126.

[30]Stephen Brookfield, *Becoming a Critically Reflective Teacher* (San Francisco: Jossey-Bass, 1995), xii.

[31]Howard Gardner, *Frames of Mind: The Theory of Multiple Intelligences* (New York: Basic Books, 1985), 239.

[32]Ibid.

[33]Ibid., 254.

[34]Dwayne Huebner explores the themes of availability, openness, and vulnerability in his essay "Spirituality and Knowing" in *Learning and Teaching the Ways of Knowing*, ed. Elliot Eisner (Chicago: National Society for the Study of Education, 1985), 159–73. He notes, "every mode of knowing is a mode of being open, vulnerable, and available to the internal *and* [our emphasis] external world" (170).

[35]Brookfield, *Becoming a Critically Reflective Teacher*, 2–3.

[36]Ibid., 22, 23.

[37]Ibid., 24, 26.

[38]Ibid., 75.

[39]Ibid., 76.

[40]F. Michael Connelly and D. Jean Clandenin, "Personal Practical Knowledge and the Modes of Knowing," in Eisner, *Learning and Teaching the Ways of Knowing*, 191 and 198 n11.

[41]Dyckman, et al., *The Spiritual Exercises Reclaimed*, 241.

[42]Some readers will hear in this prayer echoes of the Wesleyan covenant prayer: "I am no longer my own, but thine. Put to me what thou wilt…I freely and heartily yield all things to thy pleasure and disposal." See *The United Methodist Hymnal* (Nashville: United Methodist Publishing House, 1989), 607, for a brief version of this and *The United Methodist Book of Worship* (Nashville: United Methodist Publishing House, 1992), 288ff, for a more extended version.

Chapter 11: Overcoming Obstacles to Teaching Well

[1]Henri Nouwen, *In the Name of Jesus* (New York: Crossroad, 1989).

[2]Ibid., 58.

[3]See Mt. 25:14–30 or Lk. 19:12–27.

[4]Nouwen, *In the Name of Jesus*, 59–60.

[5]Ibid., 39.

[6]Ibid., 31.

[7]Ibid., 24–25.

[8]Ibid., 45.

[9]Ibid., 46.

[10]Ibid., 50.

[11]Simone Weil, "Reflections on the Right Use of School Studies with a View to the Love of God" in *Waiting for God* (New York: HarperCollins, 2001), 60.

[12]Ibid., 60.

[13]Michael Warren, *At This Time in This Place: The Spirit Embodied in the Local Assembly* (Harrisburg, Pa.: Trinity Press, 1999), 6.

[14]According to Bruce M. Metzger, ed., *NRSV Exhaustive Concordance* (Nashville: Thomas Nelson Publishers, 1991), 1259–1261, 737–738.

[15]Nouwen, *In the Name of Jesus*, 65.

[16]Ibid., 62.

[17]Ibid., 66–67.

[18]Karl Barth, *Evangelical Theology* (New York: Holt, Rinehart and Winston, 1963), 171.

[19]Weil, "Reflections on the Right Use of School Studies," 59.

[20]Ibid., 61.

[21]Ibid., 62.

[22]Ibid.

[23]Ibid., 60.

[24]Parker Palmer, *To Know as We are Known* (San Francisco: HarperSanFrancisco, 1993), xii.

[25]Ibid., 62.

[26]Weil, "Reflections on the Right Use of School Studies," 61.

[27]Ibid., 65.

Postscript: Something New, Something Old

[1]David N. Power, *Sacrament: The Language of God's Giving* (New York: Herder and Herder, 1989), 39.

[2]Ibid.

[3]Ibid.

[4]Edward Shils, *Tradition* (Chicago: University of Chicago Press, 1981), 168.

[5]Power, *Sacrament*, 22.

[6]Shils, *Tradition*, 95.

[7]Ibid., 1.

[8]Power, *Sacrament*, 39.

Index